THE ICONOCLAST
AS REFORMER

Jerome Frank's Impact on American Law

Robert Jerome Glennon

Cornell University Press

ITHACA AND LONDON

First published 1985 by Cornell University Press.
Published in the United Kingdom by
Cornell University Press Ltd., London.

International Standard Book Number 0-8014-1565-9
Library of Congress Catalog Card Number 84-17504
Printed in the United States of America
Librarians: Library of Congress cataloging information
appears on the last page of the book.

The paper in this book is acid-free and meets the guidelines
for permanence and durability of the Committee on Production
Guidelines for Book Longevity of the Council on Library Resources.

To the memory of my father

CONTENTS

PREFACE

Being married to Jerome is like being tied to the tail of a comet.
—Florence Kiper Frank

Jerome Frank brought tremendous energy, enthusiasm, and creativity to his work as a corporate lawyer, New Dealer, federal appeals judge, and legal philosopher. One is amazed not only by Frank's broad impact but also by the degree to which his career personifies the central themes in twentieth-century American law. He contributed to the pervasive role played by law in American society by his significant participation in the rise of the regulatory state. Jerome Frank's career, particularly in his effort to make law humane without disturbing its essential structure, provides a case study of the strengths and weaknesses of American liberalism.

During the twenty years in which Frank practiced law in Chicago and New York, he was concerned mainly with the complex legal and financial problems surrounding corporate reorganizations. With the election of Franklin D. Roosevelt in 1932, however, he became a significant figure in the New Deal, serving as an adviser to FDR, general counsel to the Agricultural Adjustment Administration, and chairman of the Securities and Exchange Commission. Frank also provided the legal impetus behind the creation of the Federal Surplus Relief Corporation, the country's first food program for the needy, and was a principal founder of the National Lawyers Guild. Between 1941 and his death in 1957, he served on the U.S. Court of Appeals for the Second Circuit. He produced some of the country's most important civil rights and civil liberties decisions—decisions that significantly influenced the U.S. Supreme Court. Judge Frank was quick to protest "third degree" police interrogations and the arbitrary deportation of aliens, yet he was slow to criticize the treason convictions of Julius and Ethel Rosenberg and the jail sentences meted out to lawyers who defended Communists in the early 1950s. He sprinkled his unorthodox judicial opinions with quotations from such disparate thinkers as Aristotle and Jonathan Swift in an effort to demonstrate how music, art, philosophy, and politics shaped the law.

Frank elaborated his philosophy of legal realism in six books and countless articles. His writing was lively and provocative, challenging to professional philosophers yet accessible to general readers. Frank melded Freudian psychology with legal analysis to produce a skeptical, reform-oriented philosophy that minimized the role of precedent in the legal system by arguing that judges have all but unfettered discretion in deciding the cases before them. His cynicism led him to begin one book by cautioning readers: "What follows consists of a series of guesses most of which are based on highly doubtful evidence—so doubtful that the reader is warned to take little of this book very seriously."

As one explores Frank's judicial career, the portrait that emerges is that of a creative, witty, and brilliant man, but one deeply troubled, conflicted, and ultimately insecure. Initially I had envisioned a traditional biography—an exhaustive chronological life story—but eventually decided that I would find it more interesting, as would readers, to focus on his significance and on key questions posed by his career. What were the nature and impact of Frank's legal realism? What does one learn from the Roosevelt administration's decision to purge Frank from the Agricultural Adjustment Administration for urging protection for consumers, sharecroppers, and tenant farmers? How could the skeptical legal realist don judicial robes and take legal doctrine seriously? How could the judge who passionately protested against injustice remain silent in the face of the Cold War hysteria of the 1950s? How does an intermediate appeals judge influence the U.S. Supreme Court? These are among the questions that this book explores.

It is a pleasure to acknowledge the help I have received along the way, for I am fortunate to have had suggestions from many good friends. I received helpful comments on drafts of individual chapters from Martin Adelman, Jerold Auerbach, Henry Bourguignon, Anthony Chase, James Fraser, Jane Friedman, Barry Goldman, Kermit Hall, Maurice Kelman, William McGovern, Annina Mitchell, Dennis Nolan, Todd Rapp, Stephen Schulman, David Sfair, Zoë Smialek, Vincent Wellman, Stephen Whitfield, Lawrence Zacharias, and Robert Zieger. Janet Poppendieck planted the original idea for this project. Edward Wise, a Renaissance man if there ever was one, read most of an early version and kept me from some glaring substantive errors and innumerable syntactical infelicities. Elizabeth Mason called my attention to a number of typographical errors. Peter Irons, drawing on his knowledge of New Deal lawyers, offered some excellent comments on a presentation I made to a legal history session of the Association of American Law Schools.

Several friends encouraged me to make significant changes. Morton Keller taught me to appreciate complexity, although I sometimes fail to recognize it. From Marvin Meyers I gained respect for subtlety and nuance, and to Morton Horwitz I owe an understanding of the link between political ideology and legal thought. Their intellectual integrity and patience provided a model of humane scholarship. Steven Fraser, Stephen Presser, and John Schlegel offered detailed criticisms. Robert Ames, Mark Krysinski, and Deborah Nelson subjected later versions to careful editing. Cornell University Press's Lawrence Malley bolstered my weak moments with his uncommon enthusiasm and Barbara Salazar did a splendid job of editing the final manuscript. Stanley Katz has my special gratitude for his unflinching encouragement and remarkable generosity. An influential scholar, critical editor, supportive mentor, and compassionate colleague, Stan Katz epitomizes the noblest ideals of the profession.

My life has been made more pleasant and less financially worrisome by an Irving and Rose Crown Fellowship from Brandeis University, a Wayne State University Faculty Research Award, an American Bar Foundation Fellowship in Legal History, a National Endowment for the Humanities Summer Stipend, and faculty research support from former dean Donald Gordon of Wayne State University Law School. John Roberts, current Wayne State dean, has helped me with summer research grants and enthusiastic encouragement. An office at the University of Michigan Law School one summer and housing at Yale Law School during a trip to New Haven, thanks to Charles Black, provided the proper ambience for serious work. Librarians at a number of institutions have aided me, but I am particularly indebted to Patti Bodak, Susan Grigg, Judith Shiff, and Linda Wrigley of Yale University's Manuscripts and Archives Division of Sterling Memorial Library. I am very grateful to Mary Eilers, Cynthia Kiser, Robynn Rhodes, Denise Saukko, and Bernice Zaccardelli, who expertly typed the numerous drafts.

ROBERT JEROME GLENNON

Detroit, Michigan

THE ICONOCLAST
AS REFORMER

Chapter One

"A Charmingly
Disporting Gazelle"

Dear Professor,
   I guess you know the bad news by now, I have read last week in Times Magazine. One of the Great Judges of the Federal Judge's for the poor man and for a man's constitutional rights, Hon. Judge Jerome N. Frank has died. He was our friend and one of the Judges in the appeal that granted me the appeal. He died in Conn. State, 67 years old. He put out some big opinions in all cases. That is one Judge I can speak for best. The good always died, the old saying goes. . . . Judge Frank has all my blessing. I cannot say no more. It really shocks me when I read it. He will be greatly miss by all. He really knew law and was a Liberal Judge. Without him I would never had a chance. . . .
   —Stormville, N.Y., prison inmate to his counsel

I

   The grandson of German Jews who immigrated to the United States around 1850, Jerome New Frank was born in New York City on September 10, 1889.[1] He moved with his parents, Herman and Clara New Frank, to Chicago at the age of seven. Herman, an exceptionally clever man with a quick mind and a delightful sense of humor, was a moderately prosperous lawyer who represented, among other clients, the Shubert brothers' theater interests.[2] Clara was talented, attractive, kind, gentle, and an accomplished musician with concert potential, who raised Jerome on music, including regular attendance at Friday concerts. Although he had two older sisters, Jerome was raised as though he were an adored only child.

His family sheltered him to the extent of denying him a bicycle as a child—a precaution thought unnecessary for his sisters.[3]

A precocious child, Jerome challenged his kindergarten teacher on such esoteric subjects as Greek mythology.[4] He attended Chicago public schools, graduated from Hyde Park High School at the age of sixteen, and then enrolled at the University of Chicago. He had wanted to attend the University of Michigan and, foreshadowing his future legal career, wrote a "brief" to his father comparing the relative merits of the two schools and arguing that he should be permitted to go to Ann Arbor. Frank lost his first case when his parents decided that he should stay closer to home. At the University of Chicago, Frank studied literature, philosophy, and social sciences, but under Charles Merriam's influence concentrated on political science. A nationally prominent political scientist, Merriam ultimately sought to develop a scientific approach to the study of politics by using empirical methods and the insights of psychology.[5] At the time Frank studied with him, however, it was Frank, not Merriam, that found psychology intriguing.[6] By attending summer terms, Frank graduated in three years, receiving his Ph.B. in 1909.

That fall Frank entered law school at the University of Chicago, but dropped out to work as secretary to Merriam, who, as a reformist alderman, had just been elected to the Chicago City Council. Although Merriam helped to build the Progressive party in Illinois, he mistrusted such mechanical reforms as the initiative, referendum, and recall. Merriam's belief that these reforms could not operate automatically, but depended on unreliable human beings for their administration, deeply affected Frank.[7] Jerome returned to law school in 1910, and by taking summer courses graduated in 1912 with the highest grades ever achieved at the University of Chicago Law School. With characteristic humility, he shunned interview-seeking reporters.[8] He became a member of the Illinois bar and in 1914 joined the law firm of Levinson, Becker, Cleveland & Schwartz, which specialized in corporate finance and reorganizations.[9]

In 1914 he married Florence Kiper, whom he had met during his last year of college, five years earlier, at a wedding of family friends. They became engaged six weeks later but postponed marriage until Jerome could support them. His family opposed his early engagement, believing that he should finish his schooling and establish himself before contemplating marriage. Florence, three years Jerome's senior, came from a very similar family background. A well-known poet and writer in Chicago literary circles, she contributed to such journals as *The Forum* and *Poetry*. As a member of the elite Book and Plate Club, she introduced Jerome to her literary coterie, including Albert Loeb and Julius Rosenwald, president of Sears, Roebuck. The club met once a month at the home of a member, and invited highly respected and professional lecturers, such as Edna St. Vincent Millay and Louis Mumford, to address the group at black-tie affairs. Although Frank served for a time as president of the club, he shunned the customary dinner jacket and wore a business suit instead. At such meetings he occasionally displayed a somewhat impish streak. At one meeting of this all-Jewish club to which three Gentile couples had been invited, Frank embarrassed everyone by introducing the speaker: "I will now throw the lion to the Christians, and to the rest of us."[10]

Jerome also belonged to a literary group that met informally for lunch on Saturdays at Scholgel's Restaurant. The group's membership included Carl Sandburg, Sherwood Anderson, Harry Hansen, Ben Hecht, John Gunther, and Henry Justin Smith. Frank eagerly sought out such activities as a respite from his law practice, which brought him little satisfaction. Although he had become a lawyer at his father's insistence, he still dreamed of writing fiction. He even began a novel, "Show Me an Angel," which he never finished and later remembered as "a neurotic effort."[11]

Shortly after they were married, Jerome and Florence moved to the village of Winnetka, north of Chicago, where Jerome served as a trustee—the only elective position he ever held. With Alderman Ulysses S. Schwartz, Frank also worked on an effort to improve Chicago's transportation system by converting it from a private street railway to a municipally owned system.[12] That work brought him in contact with William E. Dever, the reform mayor of Chicago, who sought Jerome's advice and counsel. As part of Dever's "kitchen" cabinet, Frank volunteered his nights and holidays to solve transportation and other problems. Jerome worked with boundless energy, mastering enormous detail, and impressing fellow workers with his remarkable ability to do an enormous amount of work without losing his composure or cheery disposition.[13] Despite years of work, the plan for a municipally owned transportation network went down to defeat in a 1925 referendum at the hands of Dever's political enemies. Ironically, Chicago ultimately adopted the same plan in the 1950s.[14] During World War I, Frank also helped Joseph P. Cotton, the administrator of Chicago's stockyards under Herbert Hoover's Food Administration. Cotton handled the purchase of meat for the Allies and Frank provided legal counsel. Concurrently with his duties as counsel for the Food Administration, his efforts with Mayor Dever, his responsibilities as trustee of Winnetka, and his literary interests, Frank also managed to practice law full time.

Though Levinson, Becker, Cleveland & Schwartz was not a large firm, its clients included major banks, railroads, and industrial concerns.[15] Its partners held an impressive list of civic and private posts. Salmon O. Levinson was a joint author of the Kellogg-Briand Pact to outlaw war; Benjamin Becker was one of Chicago's outstanding corporate lawyers; and Otis F. Glenn, a later partner, subsequently became United States senator from Illinois.[16] In 1919 Frank became a partner of the firm, renamed Levinson, Becker, Schwartz & Frank, and he practiced until the firm's dissolution in 1929, after Frank had moved to New York City.[17] The firm handled a range of corporate law problems but Frank concentrated on corporate finance and reorganizations, gaining experience later ignored by those who opposed his appointment to the Securities and Exchange Commission.

This practice suited Frank's personality and intellectual orientation. Before amendments to the Bankruptcy Act in the 1930s provided a statutory framework that permitted financially troubled corporations to reorganize and continue operations, federal equity receivership constituted the principal method for reorganizing corporations.[18] This procedure, a product of judicial creativity, served the public interest of preventing creditors from dismembering potentially economically viable concerns facing current cash-flow problems. The equity proceeding preserved the corporation's assets by readjusting its debts and allowing the business to continue

functioning. Corporate reorganizations required the harmoniza-
tion of the competing economic interests of bondholders, various
classes of stockholders, and secured and unsecured creditors, all of
whom had to be persuaded that the reorganization plan would best
protect their individual interests. Development of a reorganization
plan required limitless patience, mastery of an immense quantity of
facts and figures, and a knack for communication and persuasiveness. Ultimately the plan required a federal judge's approval. Jerome Frank's remarkable memory, his dogged persistence, his boundless energy, his facile research abilities, his even
disposition, and his sense of humor equipped him nicely to handle
corporate reorganizations. He quickly came to be recognized as
one of the nation's leading corporate reorganization lawyers. His
practice frequently took him to New York City, where he developed
a close friendship with Randolph Paul, founding partner of New
York's prestigious firm of Paul, Weiss.

Frank's probing and creative legal mind intimidated younger
associates in the law firm.[19] Colleagues marveled at his ability to
dissect a legal problem, unraveling subtle aspects and identifying
countless problems and details that required attention. His partners appreciated his knack for managing the most complicated
reorganizations. Frank possessed an extraordinary ability to draft
complicated legal documents. He could quickly recast elaborate
provisions and thus answer objections without changing the meaning of the original draft.[20] Associates also admired his disposition,
as not even the longest, most demanding negotiations ruffled
Frank's even temperament or caused him to lose his wry humor. As
Frank became more firmly established and was named a partner, he
remained friendly with younger associates. Unlike other partners,
he socialized with them and encouraged them in their work.[21] His
enthusiasm and didactic style pervaded all aspects of his life.

Although a great legal mind, Frank was not a businessman and
not mercenary. Money merely served to provide a comfortable
life.[22] His lack of acquisitiveness led his hungrier partners to take
advantage of him. On the dissolution of the firm in 1929, Frank
received a paltry settlement because his partners gave him no
credit for accounts receivable.[23] He also lacked the entrepreneurial

ability to attract affluent clients. When he left the firm, he took with him only a single client. Frank paid little attention to practical affairs. He had the absent-minded professor's habit of forgetting even basic facts, such as his own telephone number.[24] Similarly, Frank devoted untold hours to intricate legal problems in cases that, measured by the likely fee, did not warrant the time he committed to them. An associate recalled that Frank "was born to be either a professor or a judge, and not to be a practicing lawyer."[25]

In 1924 unusual circumstances made Frank a suspect in a ruthless murder that shocked the country. Bobby Franks, the son of a prominent Chicago family, was murdered by Nathan Leopold and Richard Loeb, the latter the son of a vice-president of Sears, Roebuck.[26] These two heirs of rich Jewish families played the senseless game of attempting to commit the "perfect crime" by kidnaping and killing their fourteen-year-old neighbor. A pair of eyeglasses found near the body provided a significant clue to the identity of the murderers. While the prescription was common, the hinges were most unusual. Only three pairs had been sold in the Chicago area, one of them to Jerome Frank.[27] When the police inquired about Jerome, they were told he was out of town on business, when in fact he was holed up in a Chicago hotel conducting some sensitive negotiations for Mayor Dever. Before the conclusion of the negotiations, the boys confessed and Jerome was no longer a suspect. Frank later recalled the incident, reflecting on the reputation of the Chicago police for third-degree interrogation methods: "If I'd been taken to the police station, I'd probably have confessed."[28]

In appearance, Jerome had bright, piercing blue eyes, a broad mouth, a high, sloping forehead, an olive complexion, sparse, medium-brown hair, and an average-sized body.[29] The physical activities Frank most enjoyed were horseback riding and swimming. He and Florence occasionally hiked in the Indiana Dunes, ice skated on the lagoons of Chicago's parks, and danced. As one of the founding members of Northmoor Country Club, Frank golfed, though not well. The perennial bags under his eyes, giving him a burned-out appearance, came from mental rather than physical overindulgence.

II

A turning point in Frank's life came in 1928, when he moved his family to New York City out of concern for his daughter, Barbara, who suffered intermittently from a psychosomatic paralysis of the legs.[30] After conventional medical treatment in Chicago failed, she became a patient of Dr. Bernard Glueck, a psychiatrist in New York. Frank took such a liking to Dr. Glueck that he considered undergoing analysis himself, but insisted on reducing the doctor's usual term of treatment from a year to six months. Dr. Glueck told him that a shorter period would be quite impossible, but Frank persevered, suggesting that they meet twice a day. Dr. Glueck reluctantly agreed and the hurried sessions began. Frank's intellectual interest in psychology and Freudian psychoanalytic theory generally stemmed from his student days at the University of Chicago. In the 1920s psychology was still a novel and insecure social science; Freud's theories of the id, ego, and superego generated a pervasive yet skeptical response. It was typical of Jerome Frank to plunge headlong, with infectious enthusiasm, into a new idea or theory. The Freudian psychoanalysis with Dr. Glueck profoundly affected Frank by uncovering the underlying reasons for his own problems in life. Restless and unhappy in the practice of law, Frank waged "an internal Civil War," wasting energy and consumed by conflict.[31] Psychoanalysis resolved some of Frank's unconscious conflicts concerning his parents, particularly his father's insistence on pushing him into a legal career, and enabled him to gain satisfaction from the practice of law. It also provided him with an analytic framework that he later used in structuring his legal philosophy. In later years, when Richard Rovere began work on a "profile" of Frank for *The New Yorker,* Jerome suggested that Rovere visit his analyst to gain insight into his character. Frank wrote a waiver instructing Dr. Glueck to open his file to Rovere. Dr. Glueck nonetheless rebuffed Rovere: "He may be crazy, but I'm not."[32]

Upon moving to New York, Frank joined Chadbourne, Stanchfield, & Levy, a large Wall Street firm, and continued his specialization in corporate reorganization. However, Frank disliked Wall Street practice. He found that the large New York firm operated like "a factory system," and he became disillusioned by practices he considered unprofessional.[33] On moving to New York, the Franks established residence in Croton-on-Hudson, a rural area to the north, within commuting distance of New York City. Jerome took the New York Central Railroad to the city and then rode the subway down to Wall Street. The trip took an hour each way, which Frank put to productive use by writing.

In *Law and the Modern Mind,* published in 1930, Frank argued that the law was neither logical nor predictable, and depended to a substantial degree on the judge's personality and prejudices. Drawing on Freudian psychology, Frank observed that the illusion that the law is certain stems from childhood longings. Although children ultimately discover that their father is fallible, they often retain the childish need for an authoritative father figure. Transferring his own recent experience with psychoanalysis to the legal system, Frank argued that the law acts as a father substitute, providing certainty and infallibility, thereby "dissipating the fear of chance and change."[34] *Law and the Modern Mind* catapulted Frank from the obscurity of corporate law to the forefront of a movement that became known as American legal realism. It led to his appointment as lecturer at the New School for Social Research and as research associate at the Yale Law School. The latter position Frank described as "a fancy title," one of whose unscheduled functions in those years of prohibition was to supply the law faculty with liquor.[35] In addition, the book brought Frank into contact with Thurman Arnold, Felix Frankfurter, Leon Green, Roscoe Pound, Karl Llewellyn, Thomas Reed Powell, William O. Douglas, and Morris R. Cohen.

Shortly after publication of *Law and the Modern Mind,* Frank commenced a lengthy correspondence with Morris R. Cohen which revealed a great deal about Jerome's personality. It began innocuously enough at a dinner party when Frank challenged some points in Cohen's new book, *Reason and Nature,* on the utility of formal logic. The week after the dinner, Frank resumed the debate with a twelve-page typed letter. Cohen responded, telling Frank he had raised no new point and that his method of arguing was annoying because he continually restated the same argument in different language.[36] Cohen's arrows hit the mark, for Frank's writing suffered from redundancy. Furthermore, his emotional and intellectual makeup made him extremely stubborn and unyielding in debate. Frank seemed to be unable to concede a point to an intellectual opponent. He would persevere indefinitely, summoning his indefatigable energy to repeat, rephrase, and refine an argument until his opponent, through sheer intellectual attrition, made a grudging concession. In Morris Cohen, however, Frank faced his mirror image.[37]

Cohen finally proposed that they bury their differences by simply avoiding a prolonged argument on any issue on which they could not agree. Cohen's letter nevertheless continued for six pages to attack Frank and restate his own thesis. Wounded, Frank promised never again to annoy Cohen "by going beyond grunts of approval or disapproval." In the same letter, however, Frank unleashed a couple of barbs that prompted Cohen to deny that he had "issued a fiat against further discussion between us."[38] Thus encouraged, the correspondence continued interminably, with each combatant futilely harping on the same point. Between June 1931 and January 1932, Frank and Cohen exchanged thirty-odd letters, often ten to fifteen pages long, each blaming the other for straying from the point, being obtuse, and resorting to "inexcusable abuses of the privileges of friendly correspondence."[39] Each dwelled on picayune points in an effort to parry criticism or to mount a strategic counterattack. Fired by this reciprocal animosity, their correspondence sometimes lapsed into trivial bickering. Frank argued: "If you did receive my September 3 letter, then your September 5 letter must be considered as asking a new question, which you didn't ask in your August 29 letter. . . . I anticipated that question in the foot-note on page 3."[40] Cohen replied: "Your ingenuity and persistence would be admirable if they were not in the service of such a hopeless cause."[41] The correspondence degenerated so badly that each tried to enlist the support of Felix Frankfurter and Thomas Reed Powell.[42]

Neither Frank nor Cohen would budge; neither, particularly Frank, was aware of making accusations that applied equally well to himself. "Although you spanked me verbally without much mercy, and sometimes I thought unjustifiably," declared Frank, "I surely did not at any time attempt to retort in kind."[43] Frank insisted, quite remarkably, that Cohen had taken their intellectual disagreement personally while he himself amiably continued to view it as "a good scrap about ideas."[44] To Frankfurter, Frank wrote "that Morris is singularly sensitive and that with his friends he occupies a position of curious advantage in that he feels entirely at liberty to thwack them as he pleases while they must be on their guard constantly against offending him."[45] Ironically, Frank never understood that his unbecoming description of his intellectual adversary fitted himself perfectly.

For a man of enormous talent, Frank bruised easily. His insecurity, apparently a family trait,[46] manifested itself throughout his life whenever someone disagreed with him. Frank would struggle to change the person's mind and, if unsuccessful, would personalize the disagreement. The mildest chiding hurt him. At one point, this tendency led Felix Frankfurter to tell Frank: "Every time I have a brush with you I feel like a brute who has hurt a charmingly disporting gazelle."[47] Frank's sensitivity did not cause him to treat others gently. On the contrary, his writing cut and stung, caricatured and satirized. The sharp edge to Frank's writing contrasted vividly with the personal image he projected. Everyone, even Morris Cohen, found Jerome warm and personable.[48] A sparkling conversationalist, Frank inevitably became the center of attention, yet engaged people while drawing out the best in them.[49] Witty, charming, and dramatic, Frank cast a "magic spell" on "everyone who came within his ken. Enthusiasm, far beyond his literal words, seemed to emanate from the man himself and spread its aura over the whole of a livingroom or classroom."[50]

Frank enjoyed clever word games, including puns and charades. In his book *If Men Were Angels*, Frank titled the chapter concerning criticisms of administrative agencies "Old Whine in New Bottles." When his daughter shocked some house guests by using choice language, Frank laid down a household rule: "Children should be obscene and not heard." Once, when playing charades, he acted out the first syllable by moving around the room on his hands and knees, sniffing, growling, and barking. For the other syllable he portrayed, as best as he could, a woman nursing a child. The word: dogma.[51] Frank enjoyed all manner of conversation from scintillating discourse through clever humor, but he dearly loved intellectual dialogue. After meeting an expert in a particular discipline at a cocktail party, Frank would read several of the person's books. At their next meeting, he would invariably challenge the central thesis of the author's work.[52] Frank enjoyed intellectual debate and he displayed both an unquenchable thirst for knowledge and a conviction that reason would ultimately prevail. He believed optimistically in the capacity of reason to persuade—a surprising belief indeed for the author of *Law and the Modern Mind*. Although his book demonstrated his acute insight into human irrationality, prejudice, and frailty, he persisted in conducting his own life as though rationality alone determined beliefs.

III

In 1932, after Franklin D. Roosevelt's election, Frank prepared to leave his Wall Street practice. Writing to Felix Frankfurter, he volunteered to enlist for the duration of the crisis facing the country.[53] With Frankfurter interceding, Roosevelt offered Frank the position of general counsel to the Agricultural Adjustment Administration (AAA).[54] Frank accepted immediately, without consulting Florence, and resigned from his law firm to take a government position paying a fraction of his Wall Street income. Although his law partners thought Frank was crazy, he welcomed the chance to join the New Deal. Moving to Washington ahead of his family, Frank lived first at the Cosmos Club and then at the Wardman Park Hotel.[55] He assembled an awesome legal staff and, with characteristic fervor, devoted enormous energy to drafting legislation, lobbying Congress, negotiating marketing codes and agreements, and defending the New Deal in political speeches. In addition to acting as AAA general counsel, Frank helped draft portions of the National Recovery Act, served as adviser to Federal Relief Administrator Harry Hopkins and Secretary of Agriculture Henry Wallace, and provided the legal ingenuity for the Federal Surplus Relief Corporation.

Frank saw the New Deal as "an elaborate series of experiments" to make the economic system work for the good of the whole country.[56] Selfish parochial attitudes, in Frank's view, endangered the very survival of American capitalism. Through reform, the New Deal would correct abuses and preserve the economic system. Almost immediately, however, deep ideological divisions emerged within the Department of Agriculture. AAA Administrator George Peek favored administering the Agricultural Adjustment Act to protect the interests of farmers, processors, and distributors. Frank agreed that depressed farm prices required protection for farmers, but recoiled from the idea of allowing middlemen to benefit at the expense of consumers. This division produced an initial victory for Frank and the department liberals when Peek resigned. Chester Davis, a hard-nosed bureaucrat with political savvy, became the new administrator. At first he and Frank worked well together, but eventually their smoldering political differences flared into a raging conflagration. Not only did Frank continue to champion the interests of consumers, he also tried to protect tenant farmers and sharecroppers. In February 1935 Davis went to Secretary of Agriculture Henry Wallace and demanded Frank's dismissal. Wallace sided with Davis, and Frank was "purged" along with several others.

Stung by Wallace's refusal to support him, Frank considered leaving the New Deal altogether. Instead, at Roosevelt's intercession, he moved over to the Reconstruction Finance Corporation (RFC) as special counsel. At the RFC he drew on his corporate law experience in handling some complicated matters of railroad reorganization. At the end of 1935, however, Frank decided to move back to New York and resume private practice, this time with the firm of Greenbaum, Wolff & Ernst.

Frank kept a hand in the work of the New Deal, nevertheless, by serving as legal counsel to Secretary of the Interior Harold Ickes, who retained Frank on a per diem basis to handle litigation for the Public Works Administration. Private power companies were challenging the constitutionality of the use of federal money to develop public power companies. Frank squared off against able opposing counsel, including Newton D. Baker, and won important victories for the government before the United States Supreme Court.[57]

In December 1936 Frank met with his law partner Morris Ernst and several liberal lawyers to form the National Lawyers Guild and thereby challenge the American Bar Association (ABA). Disen-

26

chanted with the ABA's conservatism, the guild hoped lawyers would become a "progressive force" for civil liberties, minority rights, and collective bargaining.[58] From the outset, however, the guild was riddled with conflicting political aspirations. Its national executive board of directors was an uneasy melange of liberals and radicals. As the guild became increasingly politicized, Frank found himself in a tenuous position. An abiding liberal, Frank detested communism, but the organization he helped found, and on whose executive board he sat, became dominated by radicals. Frank resigned from the guild in 1940.[59]

In 1937, Roosevelt, on the recommendation of William O. Douglas, appointed Frank to the Securities and Exchange Commission (SEC).[60] A return to Washington to take an administrative position at a substantially reduced salary did not appeal to Frank, but Roosevelt sweetened the offer with a promise of an appellate court appointment.[61] Although his appointment to the SEC raised the ire of conservative businessmen, who saw him as the prototypical New Deal liberal, Frank's prior corporate law practice well equipped him to handle intricate securities questions.

Created in 1933, the SEC determined the adequacy of information contained in registration statements of corporations issuing new securities, oversaw the trading of stocks and bonds on U.S. stock exchanges, regulated about half of the U.S. power industries under the Public Utilities Holding Act, and exercised broad power over corporate reorganizations. During Frank's first two years on the commission, he worked closely with Chairman William O. Douglas.[62] When Douglas left for the Supreme Court in 1939, Frank succeeded him as chairman. He presided over a faction-ridden commission composed of two conservative Republicans, George Mathews and Robert E. Healy, and two staunch Democrats, Leon Henderson and Edwin Eicher. Poised in the middle, Frank held the balance of power over industries regulated by the commission.

Frank did not oppose bigness per se. In 1933 he helped draft the National Recovery Act, which sought to cooperate with business, and in his 1938 book, *Save America First,* he praised the "social value" of the intelligent monopolist. Frank considered the SEC a "conservative institution" whose purpose was to improve the profit system. The need for government regulation, he believed, stemmed from the breakdown of private self-regulation and the consequent failure to maintain the financial stability necessary to secure investor confidence.[63] As chairman of the SEC, he repeatedly called on the securities industry to reform itself, or else face increased government regulation.

The stock market was sluggish during the late 1930s, and Wall Street, particularly the Investment Bankers Association, found a scapegoat in the SEC. Perceiving SEC procedure to be sheer "mental cruelty," some critics blamed Jerome Frank for the administration's red tape. One vitriolic opponent described Frank as "arrogant, nervous, argumentative, unreasonable, even insulting at times, . . . an almost perfect example of the type of person with whom it is virtually useless to try to reach an agreement when there is a difference of opinion."[64] Such criticism, however, was quite atypical and undeserved, as Frank endeavored to work closely with the leadership of the stock exchanges, investment houses, and trade publications. He took pains to explain SEC actions and defend the commission as a friend of capitalism. One of the major accomplishments of the SEC during Frank's tenure was the reorganization of the New York Stock Exchange, which the financial community greatly appreciated.[65] On March 11, 1940, *Time* featured Frank on its cover and described him as "warm-blooded, quick-witted, supersensitive" and the "least hard-boiled, most likeable of the New Dealers."

As SEC chairman, Frank faced the difficult task of administering the Public Utilities Holding Company Act. Many holding companies sprawled across the continental United States, combining gas, electric, and other utilities into massive, loosely controlled, and poorly financed empires. The Holding Company Act tried to bring some semblance of organization and rationality to these unseemly giants, often created overnight by reckless investment bankers. In dismantling various economic organizations, Frank's SEC encountered stonewalling from some holding companies and antipathy from the business community. In time, Frank persuaded utility leaders that simplification and geographical integration would produce economic benefits. As a result, the streamlined holding companies, eventually divested of scattered properties, enjoyed significant economic gains and greater investor confidence.[66]

Frank began working on his second book in 1932. Published in 1938, *Save America First* found Frank unexpectedly urging isolationism for the United States. As the specter of war loomed in both Europe and Asia, Frank believed the United States could do "nothing of substance" except ensure the flourishing of democracy in America.[67] World War I, he believed, had temporarily postponed economic problems in the United States by creating an artificial boom through foreign war purchases. He feared that America would drift into a second World War by once again subordinating its concern with the domestic economy to the more lucrative concern of winning profits in foreign markets. A sharp reduction in foreign trade, Frank reasoned, would correct the nation's economic problems. Frank thought extensive foreign trade would lower the country's standard of living, subject its economy to the booms and depressions of foreign markets, and finally propel the United States into the next European war.[68]

In his inimitable fashion, Frank drew on his extensive knowledge of anthropology, economics, physics, political science, history, and philosophy to reject economic class analysis and determinism. Karl Marx suffered some tough criticism from the man who ultimately urged greater attention to the needs of the poor and broader distribution of the nation's wealth. Ever the capitalist, Frank found that the skewed distribution of wealth in the United States posed a serious challenge to the survival of capitalism. The solution, he contended, lay in intelligent planning, allowing some areas to remain regulated solely by the existing profit system, while reserving other areas for governmental control.[69] Only by modifying its system of capitalism, Frank argued, could the United States hope to produce "an economy of plenty inside the profit system and within the framework of political democracy."[70]

Frank's staunch isolationism ruptured his relationship with the administration. Several years later, Roosevelt, looking back on Frank's contribution to the New Deal, commented: "My memory is charitable today and I do not recall that he ever wrote a book called 'Save America First.'"[71] By 1941, however, Frank recanted and wrote "Confessions of an Ex-Isolationist." He still believed that the United States should be economically independent, but, bowing to changed military circumstances—in particular Hitler's invasion of Czechoslovakia, Poland, Denmark, and Norway—Frank came to recognize the necessity for military cooperation with the Allies.[72]

IV

In 1939 President Roosevelt considered appointing Frank to the U.S. Court of Appeals for the District of Columbia, but Frank's religion became a political issue and FDR refused to buck the rising tide of anti-Semitism.[73] Instead, the administration offered Frank a less visible District of Columbia district judgeship, which he declined, acting partially on the advice of Felix Frankfurter and William O. Douglas.[74] Once again Frank considered leaving government, but at Roosevelt's urging he remained. With FDR's endorsement, he was elected SEC chairman by his fellow commissioners. In 1941 Frank finally received his promised appellate judgeship on the U.S. Court of Appeals for the Second Circuit, but not without new anti-Semitic opposition.[75]

At various points in his career Frank struggled with his role as a Jew. His family, although culturally Jewish, attended no synagogue or temple. While practicing in Chicago, Frank had been invited to join an exclusive Gentile country club, but he refused to limit his association with his Jewish friends. An "almost assimilated Reformed Jew,"[76] he found himself in a difficult position as AAA general counsel when, to blunt political attacks, he limited the number of Jews he hired. Just before Pearl Harbor, Frank published a piece in the *Saturday Evening Post* describing his shift from isolationism to interventionism, and arguing against the view of Jews as a monolithic group. Frank portrayed American Jews as diverse, embracing religious views from Orthodox to Reformed, political sentiments from isolationist to interventionist, and economic positions from wealthy to poor. Jews, he contended, do not differ from any random sample of the American population. Although cultural heritage continues, so does the assimilation process, and "most Jews born in America regard as their significant heros Jefferson and Lincoln, not Moses and David."[77] Zionism troubled Frank, for he believed it engendered anti-Semitic sentiment. He understood the desire to establish a lasting Jewish political state in Palestine, but he scorned "fanatic Jewish nationalists" as "not American Jews but Jewish sojourners in America."[78]

These views prompted his active participation in the American Council on Judaism, which opposed the creation of a Jewish homeland. Publication of the *Saturday Evening Post* article, in particular, provoked anger among many Jewish friends and led Albert Einstein to counsel Frank to recognize how Jewish solidarity helped Jews overcome persecution.[79] Frank eventually changed his mind after many conversations with Judge Simon H. Rifkind, an ardent Zionist.[80] Frank participated with Rifkind, Abe Fortas, Judge Stanley Fuld, Professor Milton Handler, and several others in preparing, in 1947, "The Basic Equities of the Palestine Problem." This lengthy brief advocating a Jewish homeland became a "key document in the establishment of the State of Israel."[81]

Frank served on the Second Circuit from 1941 until his death in 1957. During his tenure the Second Circuit had a reputation as the finest bench in the country. Frank became a provocative judge, who wrote seminal opinions in a plucky and unorthodox style. His most important contribution was his influence on the U.S. Supreme Court in the areas of civil liberties and criminal procedure. Occasional speculation placed Frank on the U.S. Supreme Court, but he was never appointed.[82] Frank generally enjoyed excellent rapport with his judicial colleagues, though he and Charles Clark, both strong-willed and thin-skinned, antagonized each other. While it was typical of Frank to assume that such intense judicial differences would not affect their personal relations, it took the efforts of both men to preserve their friendship.[83]

Despite the pressures of his Second Circuit duties, Frank managed to continue writing about law, government, philosophy, and simple justice. Frank published his third book, *If Men Were Angels,* in 1942. He took its title from *The Federalist Papers* and dedicated it to William O. Douglas.[84] To the criticisms of the New Deal's reliance on administrative agencies Frank mounted a vigorous defense. His central theme was that administrative agencies act consistently with democratic rule. Agencies operate within the parameters of power delegated to them by Congress. They exercise this power with care and responsibility, mindful that they exist to serve the public. In addition, they perform valuable tasks, such as investigative fact-finding. Frank viewed the criticism that administrative agencies are undemocratic, yielding broad discretion and legislative power, as coming from persons who politically opposed the agencies' actions.

If Men Were Angels was an extremely weak book. Large portions merely repeated Frank's ideas on legal realism or restated the positions of others, such as Holmes. The book was loosely organized and frequently digressive. Although Frank could be a lucid and clever writer, *If Men Were Angels* consisted largely of quotations with little new analysis. One early chapter even reprinted a ten-page excerpt from an attorney general's committee report.[85] Redundant, petulant, and defensive, the book reflected poorly on Jerome Frank by demonstrating how savagely he could attack anyone who did not share his views completely, such as Roscoe Pound. It also revealed Frank's sensitivity to criticism, for the book placed great emphasis on salvaging Frank's roles on the SEC and as a legal realist.

In his next work, *Fate and Freedom,* dedicated to his daughter and published in 1945, Frank regained his writing flair, his intellectual rigor, his humility, and even his sense of humor. Almost pure philosophy, *Fate and Freedom* attacked the theory of determinism, whether scientific, historical, economic, or philosophic. Marx, Hegel, Toynbee, Freud, and Einstein each received special criticism for trying to confine an unruly world to well-ordered theories. Displaying an abiding skepticism, Frank cautioned readers to doubt not only these thinkers but his own interpretations as well.[86] Demonstrating his enormous eclecticism, Frank penned an ode to the power of individuals to "affect the shape of the future."[87]

In 1949 Frank published *Courts on Trial,* a major critique of American trial courts and a significant work of legal philosophy. Identifying weaknesses in the fact-finding process, *Courts on Trial* secured Frank a unique niche in American legal realism. Fact skepticism thereafter became synonymous with Jerome Frank. Dedicated to Learned Hand, "our wisest judge," *Courts on Trial* argued that the application of legal rules depended ultimately on an accurate determination of the facts. Facts, however, "are guesses" as to what really happened. While the process for determining facts could be greatly improved, American law considers a trial a fight between adversaries rather than an effort to ascertain truth. Law schools offer little help in developing fact-finding skills as they focus on appellate court decisions to the neglect of trial courts, which actually find the facts.

As a Second Circuit judge, Frank had chambers at the Foley Square Courthouse in New York City. He and Florence set up residence in a sprawling, five-bedroom apartment at the corner of Riverside Drive and West 84th Street, in which they maintained separate bedrooms.[88] They led different lives, often eating separately, and Jerome made important decisions—such as to join the New Deal—without consulting Florence. Occasionally there were other women in Jerome's life, but work claimed most of his energy. He was "happiest writing" and worked most evenings and every weekend.[89] He usually arose in the morning around seven and took a room-temperature bath in water drawn the night before. After fixing himself an egg or a bowl of dry cereal and reading the *New York Times,* he set off for the office. He would arrive home around six, take a single cocktail, have dinner promptly at seven, and then begin work. Possessing extraordinary powers of concentration that he could maintain for hours,[90] he often wrote while standing at a piano, oblivious of commotion around him. His refusal to be distracted once so exasperated Florence that she went to a movie alone in order to frighten him. Upon returning several hours later, she realized that Jerome had not even noticed her absence.[91]

A chronic insomniac, Frank rarely slept more than five hours a night. Reading and writing filled his time. His prodigious appetite for books and his speed-reading ability amazed even William O. Douglas, who himself was known for his photographic memory.[92] During the writing of *Fate and Freedom,* his law clerk remembered fetching books for Frank. "Sometimes he would tell me what books he wanted. Sometimes he would just say he wanted books. It got so I would scoop up an armful of just about everything except cookbooks. When he got interested in physics, I would scoop whole armfuls of physics books off the shelves, and he would read through them alphabetically by authors."[93] Along the way, public libraries constantly berated him for not returning books. Frank paid little heed to the ownership of the books he possessed and would as readily lend the library's books to a friend as he would his own.[94] His motives were innocent, but absent-mindedness afflicted him. Having asked his secretary to come to the office on a Sunday, Frank might fail to show up. Not fussy about dressing, unconcerned with styles, too busy to get haircuts, Frank had the "slightly travel-worn air of a shambling, sub-leonine cat."[95] His preoccupation with conversation made him a poor driver. He always drove used Cadillacs, but in such a jerky and erratic fashion that his friends urged him to take taxicabs.[96]

Not only did Frank read quickly, but he remembered almost everything he read. He could quote long passages from books and legal documents that he had not read in years. A friend of his daughter Barbara, visiting the Franks one summer at their rented house on Martha's Vineyard, mentioned Guy de Maupassant at breakfast. Each morning during the succeeding weeks the judge would synopsize a different de Maupassant work, sprinkling the description with ample quotations from the original. In discussing the story, Frank offered not simply his own interpretation but also a range of literary criticism. "You would have thought, listening to him," the visitor remembered, "that he had spent the whole day before and the whole night preparing for those breakfast lectures. But I knew for a fact that there wasn't a bit of de Maupassant in the house."[97]

Frank resumed his association with the Yale Law School, which in 1946 appointed him a visiting lecturer. Until his death Frank offered an extremely popular course on fact-finding, emphasizing the themes he was to develop in *Courts on Trial*. Meeting three hours on Friday afternoons, often outdoors, the course required Frank to commute from New York City. "Jerome could never tear himself away from his Law School friends without first staying for dinner— and then, 'Well, I guess I could take a later train; now as that old fascist, Plato, put it . . .'—and eventually a last-minute dash to the station for the final train, with the good talk still going high."[98] Enjoying the college ambience, Jerome and Florence moved to New Haven in 1951 to live in a large, late-Victorian house on Everit Street. Frank was never too busy to read a faculty manuscript, puzzle out a legal problem, or encourage students. "Like a wise father, never bored and never condescending, he made their enthusiasms his enthusiasms and their problems his problems."[99] An easy grader, Frank the teacher enjoyed playing the ham actor. He once began his course by storming into the classroom with a false moustache, monocle, walking stick, and British accent. Berating a student accomplice about some injustice, Frank chased him from the room. Returning a few minutes later sans disguise, Frank asked the class to write about what they had just witnessed in detail. The widely diverging accounts dramatically illustrated to his fact-finding class the unreliability of eyewitness accounts.[100]

Frank was a visiting lecturer at Brandeis University and at the New School for Social Research as well as at Yale,[101] and a strong didactic strain infused all his activities. From his judicial opinions, books, and articles to his speeches and conversation, Jerome Frank was always a teacher. His exuberance unfortunately marred his writing, which was plagued by redundancy. At times Frank consciously repeated himself, believing that his novel concepts needed reiteration.[102] At other times he recognized his fault, as when he told Felix Frankfurter, "Gosh, I wish I had a tenth of your gift of succinct statement"—no doubt the only time anyone ever accused Frankfurter of brevity.[103] But sometimes Frank did not have an inkling of his tendency to repeat. While preparing an SEC opinion, Frank once had his special assistant review a long introductory section. The assistant boiled it down and offered a much shorter version to Frank, who responded, "It's fine, it's fine. I'll attach it as a summary."[104]

V

In the late 1940s and early 1950s, some federal judges were caught in the wave of anticommunist hysteria that swept the United States. Jerome Frank detested communism. From his work at the AAA through his antideterminist tract, *Fate and Freedom*, Frank placed himself solidly in the camp of American liberalism. The revelations about his former associates Lee Pressman and Alger Hiss shocked him. He naturally believed Pressman's admissions before the House Un-American Activities Committee, but he doubted the validity of the accusations against Hiss. Frank's doubts came largely from Pressman, his former friend, law firm associate, and AAA section chief. Under oath, Pressman implicated John Abt and Nathan Witt, his law partners, but absolved Hiss.[105] Frank could discern no possible motive for Pressman's testimony except that Hiss was not in fact engaged in communist activities. Frank could never understand the charge against Hiss, despite the fact that he had come to dislike Hiss intensely. The falling out occurred just after the New Deal purged Frank from the AAA. Hiss came to Frank to tell him that he had been offered Frank's position as AAA general counsel and to ask Frank whether he should accept the post. The prospect outraged Frank. Since Hiss had been closely identified with Frank's policies, his acceptance of the position would make it appear that the AAA dispute arose from a personality conflict rather than from a sharp difference of policy. To Frank, integrity dictated that Hiss refuse the position. That Hiss even considered accepting it lowered Frank's opinion of him. It bespoke unprincipled ambition for professional advancement.[106] Frank still held this opinion years later when, during Hiss's perjury trial, Frank declined Hiss's request to serve as a character witness.[107]

Judge Frank played a significant role in reviewing and upholding the convictions and death sentences of Julius and Ethel Rosenberg. In addition, in *United States v. Sacher*[108] he affirmed the contempt convictions of the lawyers in the infamous 1950 trial of Communist leaders for violating the Smith Act. This was not Frank's noblest hour. His performance in these cases contrasts sharply with the scrupulous regard for fairness exhibited in his last book, *Not Guilty*, published posthumously in 1957, coauthored with his daughter, Barbara, and dedicated to Florence Kiper Frank. Echoing a passionate theme in Frank's writing, *Not Guilty* presented a lay audience with documented case histories of instances in which the legal system wrongly convicted innocent persons of crimes. *Not Guilty* tried to prove by illustration the fact-skepticism theory that Frank had developed in *Courts on Trial:* people suffer because witnesses are wrong, memories are fallible, and documents are lost. These realities of human behavior may produce genuine hardship in civil cases, but they yield horrible injustice in criminal cases.

VI

On January 13, 1957, at the age of sixty-seven, Jerome Frank died of a heart attack suffered the previous day. His last illness, though short, was long enough to enable Charles Clark, often Frank's Second Circuit antagonist, to rush to the New Haven Hospital to comfort Florence. Afterward she remembered Clark as "singularly kind" during the difficult period following Jerome's death.[109] It seems perfectly fitting that the man so often exasperated by Frank would respond with such compassion. Jerome Frank kindled both loyalty and love in his friends. Learned Hand, for whom Jerome had a fawning devotion, lamented to Florence the loss of "his just and gentle nature, his irrepressible insistence upon giving all of himself to what he undertook, and the absence of any self-seeking in his work."[110] Many eulogies carried powerful praise.[111] While Frank endured a heart murmur during his last seven years and died from his heart condition, he suffered concurrently from leukemia for his last five years.[112] Although he knew the illness was incurable, he kept it a secret from Florence and Barbara.[113] Only two or three close friends knew he was dying. He worked to the end, completing *Not Guilty* two days before he died. To Charles Clark he remained "as infectiously gay, as charming, as hard working as ever."[114] Frank's housekeeper, Mary Strickland, knew he was ill by the way he ate and walked. When she made his bed she saw his pills, and cab drivers told her of taking Frank to the hospital for blood transfusions.[115] Knowing he was dying, Frank set about putting his affairs in order, and inquired about a federal annuity for Florence.[116] During these last years he continued to radiate warmth, as when he comforted Edmund Cahn during a serious illness.[117] After Jerome's death, the Franks' regular laundryman told Florence: "When I read about him in *The* [New Haven] *Register,* I found out how bright he was, and all—Mrs. Frank, you never would have known it."[118]

Chapter Two

JUDICIAL POWER AND THE LEGITIMACY OF LAW

> The myth that the judges have no power to make new law . . . is a direct outgrowth of a subjective need for believing in a child's world.
>
> —Jerome Frank

I

Since the founding of the nation, the United States has struggled with the proper role and political power of its judges. The colonial aspiration for "a government of laws, not of men," reflected confidence in law as objective and impartial. Justifications for the exercise of judicial power usually rested on the argument that judges "declare" the law by reference to past decisions, positive legislative commands, or principles of natural law. Thus judges do not exercise independent will or political choice, but instead serve as conduits for the application of rules of law.

Sir William Blackstone's *Commentaries on the Laws of England,* published between 1765 and 1769 and the most widely read lawbook in the American colonies, argued that human law is valid only if it conforms to the natural law of the creator. Judges are "the living oracles" of the law and their decisions "are the evidence of what is common law." To Blackstone, the common law is "from time to time declared in the decisions of the courts of justice."[1] This declaratory theory found ready acceptance in the American colonies. Despite the break from England, most colonies adopted the common law because they conceived it as a body of universal principles. But the colonists resisted the adoption of British statutes, which represented the will of Parliament and thus lacked the objective and universal quality of the common law. The colonists did not fear judicial power because they conceived the task of judges as the discovery and application of preexisting common law principles.[2]

The effort to render law neutral and apolitical continued into the 1820s, when the codification movement sought to make law scientific, rational, precise, and certain, thereby limiting judicial power.[3] In the 1840s, such prominent judges as Joseph Story reaffirmed that judicial decisions are merely evidence of the universal common law, despite increasing skepticism as to whether judges' decisions actually reflected political and economic choices.[4] Story also contributed significantly to the treatise tradition, which tried to maintain the dichotomy between law and politics. Story, along with Chancellor James Kent, Joseph Angell, and others, wrote lengthy treatises portraying the law as a science based on natural law principles, as a collection of rational rules, not the embodiment of policy choices.[5] One treatise writer described his task as discovering "the inner principles which perhaps not even the judges saw when they decided the cases."[6]

During the second half of the nineteenth century, natural law theories declined but the idea of law as a science continued. One writer in 1880 captured this shift:

> The mistake made by the [natural law theorists] was merely in taking for granted that these principles were perfectly known to them, and that the law of reason, of nature, or of God . . . was the standard of *jus* for all time.
>
> We can improve upon [their theory] not by rejecting their belief in the existence of [natural] law, but by recognizing the fact that it must be learned, like the laws of the physical world, inductively. The decided cases of the past are so many observations upon the practical working of these laws, from which the true theory is to be inferred. . . . The true office of precedents [is] data from which we may obtain by induction the jural rule which they prove to exist.[7]

The notion of law as a science powerfully influenced legal education. After 1870, Harvard became the archetypal American law school with the genesis of the case system.[8] Dean Christopher Columbus Langdell postulated that law was a science to be studied inductively, proceeding from primary sources (appellate court decisions) to first principles (rules). By careful selection, classification, and arrangement of cases, an entire area of law could be simplified and mastered. The only tools necessary to the enterprise were reported decisions, mostly old English cases, which would illustrate the rational evolution of the law.[9] Harvard law professor Thomas Reed Powell recalled graduating from Harvard in 1904 "with the impression that somehow or other the eternal principles of the common law are encased in the Year Books and that all we needed was right reason to find from them the law on any point today. It never occurred to me that we could aim at a goal and get there. I thought that the past had determined all."[10]

Under the declaratory theory, as modified by the theory of law as an inductive science, judges moved automatically from general rules to specific applications. The judiciary neither made law nor promoted public policy, but searched diligently through past decisions to discover the applicable rule of law. A self-executing process of analogical reasoning produces the controlling precedent. Thus judges functioned mechanically, exercised little discretion, and performed only nonpolitical duties.

The declaratory theory came under attack during the Progressive era, when it became impossible to disguise the inevitably political and redistributive functions of law. Judges issued so many injunctions against striking workers that the "labor injunction" became a hot political issue and "government by judiciary" a disparaging reference and popular political slogan.[11] As Progressives attempted to curb the powers of the giant trusts, to check the corruption of urban political machines, and to establish minimum wages and maximum hours for workers, courts seemed determined to stymie these reforms. During the 1890s, the U.S. Supreme Court struck down a 2 percent federal income tax; upheld the contempt conviction of Eugene V. Debs, president of the American Railway Union; and found that the Sherman Antitrust Act did not apply to a company with a 98 percent market share of the nation's refined sugar sales.[12] Faced with a clash between two forms of conservatism—the traditional preference for a well-ordered society ruled by precedent and the belief in a laissez-faire economic system—the bench and bar opted to ignore precedent and repel challenges to existing economic arrangements. To hold the federal income tax unconstitutional, the Supreme Court had to distort 100 years of uniform precedent.[13]

These judicial decisions cast doubt on the impartiality of judges. As the bench increasingly became identified with vested economic interests, Progressives initiated a movement to remove judges from office and overturn judicial decisions.[14] Also contributing to the disintegration of the declaratory theory was the splintering effect of a federal system with forty-odd sovereign courts. It became increasingly difficult to insist that the rules of law preceded judicial decisions or that judges merely discovered them when state courts repeatedly reached plainly inconsistent results on identical legal questions.[15]

Nevertheless, efforts to preserve law as scientific and apolitical continued into the twentieth century. Such treatise writers as Austin Scott, Samuel Williston, and John H. Wigmore contributed major tomes.[16] A companion development, the "restatements of law" sponsored by the American Law Institute, began in the 1920s. The restatements sought to rid the law of inconsistent rules by systematizing and simplifying the common law. Although designed to eliminate the idea that social and economic pressures shaped the law, the restatements ironically comprised reform-oriented rules rather than existing rules.[17] As such attempts to preserve the scientific facade of the law floundered, the declaratory theory came under increasingly heavy attack.

The challenge, dubbed by Morton White the "revolt against formalism,"[18] occurred in philosophy, economics, history, and political science as well as law. The revolt challenged major nineteenth-century thinkers whose highly structured and systematized thought emphasized science and abstract principles. The leaders of the revolt against formalism were suspicious of abstract theories divorced from reality. They insisted on evaluating philosophy, logic, economics, history, and law in a social context. They drew on the pragmatism of William James, for whom truth was not static but dynamic: an idea "*becomes* true, is *made* true by events."[19] Since knowledge is acquired by active participation rather than by passive observation, hypotheses must be tested against experience.

Oliver Wendell Holmes, Jr., became one of America's most respected and influential legal philosophers. From 1870 to 1932, Holmes's books, articles, and judicial opinions elaborated his subtle, complicated, and paradoxical jurisprudence.[20] One well-known strand of his thought took aim at the declaratory theory. Holmes repudiated formal logic—the syllogism—as a sufficient explanation for legal doctrine because one can give a logical form to any conclusion.[21] "A page of history is worth a volume of logic" for understanding the considerations of expediency and community policy that control every important legal principle.[22]

> The life of the law has not been logic; it has been experience. The felt necessities of the time, the prevalent moral and political theories, intuitions of public policy, avowed or unconscious, even the prejudices which judges share with their fellow-men, have had a good deal more to do than the syllogism in determining the rules by which men should be governed.[23]

Pragmatism pervaded Holmes's jurisprudence. Since the justification for a legal rule is a desirable social end,[24] "it is revolting to have no better reason for a rule of law than that so it was laid down in the time of Henry IV. It is still more revolting if the grounds upon which it was laid down have vanished long since, and the rule simply persists from blind imitation of the past." Policy considerations measure the utility of legal rules; the final assessments are made by judges, who "exercise the sovereign prerogative of choice."[25]

Holmes criticized the courts' frequent use of moral categories and precepts to describe legal principles. He separated moral obligation from legal duty. While the law may be "the witness and external deposit of our moral life," a moral obligation becomes a legal duty only when the courts enforce it.[26] Holmes found inadequate the theoretical perspective of John Austin, who insisted that law is the command of the sovereign.[27] Austin's preoccupation with legal abstractions bore little resemblance to the law as practiced or as obeyed. Holmes insisted that "[g]eneral propositions do not decide concrete cases."[28] Focusing on the way the law actually worked, Holmes asserted that a legal duty exists only if a court provides a remedy. For Holmes, the law consisted of "prophecies of what the

courts will do in fact, and nothing more pretentious."[29] This pragmatism enabled Holmes to recognize that "all life is an experiment"
with shifting values and social arrangements.[30] Holmes's abiding
skepticism infused his philosophy of judicial restraint. "To have
doubted one's own first principles is the mark of a civilized man."[31]

Roscoe Pound, a Nebraska biologist turned law professor and
Harvard Law School dean, continued Holmes's attack on the declaratory theory. In a plethora of articles written between 1905 and
1920, Pound developed his theory of sociological jurisprudence.[32]
Drawing sustenance from William James and John Dewey, Pound
wrote:

> The sociological movement in jurisprudence is a movement for prag-
> matism as a philosophy of law; for the adjustment of principles and
> doctrines to the human conditions they are to govern rather than to
> assumed first principles; for putting the human factor in the central
> place and relegating logic to its true position as an instrument.[33]

The major problem confronting American law, according to
Pound, was "mechanical jurisprudence," which he characterized as
"the rigorous logical deduction from predetermined conceptions
in disregard of and often in the teeth of actual facts."[34] A rigid and
sterile form of reasoning, mechanical jurisprudence hid policy
preferences behind its premises and assumptions. Artificial categories, such as "liberty of contract," prevented judges from facing the
social reality that employers and employees do not possess equal
freedom and bargaining power. For Pound, mechanical jurisprudence stemmed from lawyers' sincere belief in this style of reasoning, not from a contrived effort to mask the law's preference for
the status quo. Pound believed that legal reform was an intellectual
problem caused by the system's lapse into a period of decay rather
than by a collision of ideologies and economic interests. He saw law
as a science of "social engineering," with lawyers and experts making the policy decisions. The antidemocratic implications of government by an elite corps of experts did not trouble Pound, who
had no plan for widespread social reform. He sought to purify and
modernize the common law, which was threatened by adherence to
an obsolete, mechanical jurisprudence.[35]

For Holmes and Pound, then, jurisprudence was an intellectual matter unconnected to political struggle. Holmes's Olympian skepticism kept him above the fray, and Pound's social engineering did not endorse political change. Progressives, however, seized on their philosophies as ammunition for reform. And later, in the 1920s and 1930s, there emerged a band of writers concerned with legal philosophy not simply for its own sake but as a vehicle for political reform. Denominated "legal realists," these thinkers did not share a coherent philosophy so much as an antipathy to the declaratory theory and its political values.[36] "Realism" was not a technical philosophical term, but was used, as in art, to describe fidelity to nature or an accurate representation of things as they are, not as one wishes them to be.

II

Jerome Frank pioneered American legal realism with the publication in 1930 of *Law and the Modern Mind,* his first and most important book. Describing as a myth the concept that law is fixed and predictable, he attacked Langdell's depiction of law as an inductive science as well as the theory that judges discover preexisting law. Frank demonstrated how judges select among competing rules and precedent. Citing a series of Supreme Court antitrust decisions, Frank noted how over time the legal rule had changed but the Court's language remained the same. Lawyers and judges, he said, constitute a "profession of rationalizers" who employ fictions to disguise change. Legal reasoning borrowed heavily from Plato and Aristotle, who, Frank disdainfully commented, would have "pictured the 'hatchetness' of hatchets as more real than any hatchet." From Aristotle came scholasticism, with its tendency "to infer existence from a name and to exalt universals at the expense of particulars." From the Aristotelian tradition came the syllogism or formal logic, the method of legal reasoning purportedly used by courts. A syllogism, however, provides merely a logical structure, not the premises. Since the courts select the premises, judges may decide cases any way they choose and camouflage their preferences behind flawless syllogisms.[37]

If logic does not compel certain results, then how *do* judges decide cases? To Frank, they begin with the desired conclusion and search for premises to substantiate it. Oriented to achieving certain results, judges rationalize their decisions by finding facts and selecting rules that justify the desired conclusion. By manipulating those facts and rules, judges enjoy unfettered discretion. But what persuades judges to reach one conclusion rather than another? Rules of law, admittedly, are one variable, yet not the most important. Political and economic attitudes and values shape the judge's outlook, but often are not relevant in cases between litigants of the same economic class. Most important, according to Frank, are the "uniquely individual factors" that are the product of the judge's "entire life-history." Thus "the personality of the judge is the pivotal factor in law administration," and the law in a particular case may vary according to the judge's own "hunch" or "intuitive flash of understanding."[38] Since it is impossible to ferret out the obscure influences that produce the judge's decisions, "it is fantastic, then, to say that usually men can warrantably act in reliance upon 'established law.' "[39]

Frank thought that legal rules had a very limited role in the determination of judicial decisions. Rules neither directly decide cases nor authoritatively compel any given result. Instead, judges "manipulate the language of former decisions" to reach the desired result.[40] Since there is no way to force a judge to follow an old rule or to predict when a result will be rationalized by a newly formed rule, it is impossible to predict future decisions on the basis of earlier rulings. No law exists until a court issues a decision in a concrete case. Until that point, law is merely the guess of lawyers as to what result a court will reach. Hence law is either "actual law, *i.e.*, a specific past decision," or "probable law," a prediction of the future. At best, rules merely serve the conscientious judge as a check on his tentative conclusion.[41]

Frank reveled in unfettered judicial discretion, which he thought "virtually impossible to delimit." Since most people act without regard to or knowledge of legal consequences, he ridiculed the practical importance of certainty as highly overrated. Unfortunately, "judges have failed to see that, in a sense, all legal rules, principles, concepts, standards—all generalized statements of law—are fictions." By deluding themselves about the necessity of searching for past decisions to control present opinions, judges often produce "injustice according to law"—excessive preoccupation with stare decisis at the sacrifice of sound and good results. For Frank, the creative hallmark of the law is judicial discretion or the power to individualize abstract rules.[42]

He criticized the American jury for maintaining the appearance of certainty in the law while surreptitiously individualizing cases. In theory the judge prescribes the legal rules and the jury finds the facts; in reality the jury does anything it wants. Defenders of this unpredictable system insist that the jury can nullify rules that the judiciary is hesitant to overturn. Frank spurned this defense as a cumbersome method of reforming a system dependent on the capriciousness of the petit jury. "Proclaiming that we have a government of laws, we have in jury cases, created a government of often ignorant and prejudiced men. . . . The jury makes the orderly administration of justice virtually impossible."[43]

Frank recognized his debt to Roscoe Pound, but criticized him for stopping short. Although Pound lambasted mechanical jurisprudence, he still insisted on the need for, and the reality of, certainty in property law and commercial transactions. Frank viewed Pound's dichotomy as artificial and the "presumed reliance" on legal rules as largely mythical. Pound ultimately clung to "rule-fetishism" or mechanical jurisprudence.[44]

Frank similarly parted company with Benjamin N. Cardozo. Although in the realist camp, Cardozo longed for "a rationalizing principle" to eliminate "discord and disorder."[45] In *The Nature of the Judicial Process* Cardozo described how judges, including himself, tried to accommodate the law's twin needs of continuity and change. Cardozo, as the law's most brilliant and eloquent rationalizer, became Frank's bête noire. As a judge on the New York Court of Appeals from 1913 to 1930, Cardozo overhauled New York law, especially in torts and contracts, placing it in the vanguard of social and economic reform. His formidable reputation as a common law judge stemmed from his skill at making past decisions appear to support a present quantum leap forward. Cardozo honed the technique of harmonizing and reconciling precedent to make startling changes appear routine, logical, and inevitable.[46] His cleverness threatened Frank's efforts to demystify judicial discretion and power, prompting Frank's challenge in *Law and the Modern Mind* and a subsequent essay that Frank published anonymously, criticizing Cardozo's judicial style for obfuscating judicial realities.[47]

In *Law and the Modern Mind* Frank attempted both to expose the basic myth of legal predictability and to explain its remarkable persistence. When lawyers and judges pretend that the law is certain, are they engaging in professional hypocrisy? No, answered Frank, for even lawyers and judges believe the basic myth. For a partial explanation of the source of this widespread illusion, Jerome Frank turned to the nascent discipline of psychology.[48] Frank explained that in infancy the child's wants are satisfied almost instantly. The world appears rational and orderly and the child develops a sense of omnipotence. As the years pass, the child becomes aware of his or her inability to control surrounding events. Beset by fears of the unknown, the child expects the parents to control the universe. Initially this dependence alleviates the child's uncertainty, as the mother embodies tender protection and the father personifies certainty, security, and infallibility. In struggling for existence, the child relies on an omniscient and omnipotent father who determines rules of conduct. But evidence of the father's fallibility slowly accumulates and the child becomes disillusioned. Yet the urge to find certainty and security continues.

> The Law—a body of rules apparently devised for infallibly determining what is right and what is wrong and for deciding who should be punished for misdeeds—inevitably becomes a partial substitute for the father-as-Infallible-Judge. That is, the desire persists in grown men to recapture through a rediscovery of a father, a childish, completely controllable universe, and that desire seeks satisfaction in a partial, unconscious, anthropomorphizing of Law, in ascribing to the Law some of the characteristics of the child's Father-Judge.[49]

To overcome the blindness of legal uncertainty, adults must relinquish their childish need for an authoritative father. Jerome Frank's "modern mind is a mind free of childish emotional drags, a mature mind."[50]

Frank seriously intended his father-substitute notion to jar the emotional block thwarting thought about the law, but he also intended the concept to provide "a useful figure of speech." He engaged in "deliberate overemphasis," believing that a "new vocabulary sometimes freshens or revives thinking."[51] Later, however, he regretted having dwelt on the father-substitute, for he thought this emphasis detracted from *Law and the Modern Mind*'s essential theme—the judge's personality as the key to decision making.[52] Critics attacked the father-substitute idea as a crude and rather simplistic explanation. Even fellow realists such as Karl Llewellyn were amused by Frank's doctrinaire account.[53] Frank thought that friend and foe alike had misread his book and caricatured his position as simpleminded.[54] In fairness to Frank, it should be noted that he wrote a deliberately tentative essay and repeatedly stressed that the father-substitute notion was merely "a partial explanation."[55] His recognition of other factors, however, was offhand, usually dashed off in a footnote, while he dwelled incessantly on his psychological explanation. He did consider another explanation— that the quest for certainty arose from religious impulses—but dismissed it as insufficient and subordinate to his psychological thesis.[56] Frank attached overwhelming importance to his father-substitute theory and readers legitimately criticized his preoccupation with it.

A hallmark of Frank's legal realism was his bold and innovative use of sources outside the law. He sought to understand how law works by looking beyond narrow legal rules and drawing creatively on the insights of other disciplines.[57] Psychology had special utility as the best instrument available for the study of human nature, and Frank's own experience with psychoanalysis greatly influenced *Law and the Modern Mind*. Freudian psychology permeates the father-substitute notion, and the child psychology of Piaget informed his analysis.[58] Frank also relied on the philosophic writings of Plato and Aristotle, the work in logic of F. C. S. Schiller and John Dewey, the linguistic theories of C. K. Ogden and I. A. Richards, and the anthropology of Bronislaw Malinowski.[59]

Frank pioneered in using social science analysis to study the law, but his effort never took hold. A problem in interdisciplinary study is to select among competing methodologies from the companion field. Frank did not consider himself a behaviorist, nor was he committed to viewing the world through Freudian-tinted glasses.

To Frank, the time had "not yet come to adopt any one psychological point of view in the field of law."[60] He used elements of many disciplines without ever adopting completely any particular system. On occasion his ecletic style led him to borrow from conflicting approaches, such as Freudian and gestalt psychology, without appreciating that each theory had its own coherence and demands. The efforts of Frank and the legal realists to engage in social science analysis was primitive and incomplete.[61] However, Frank lent credibility to psychology as a serious discipline at an early and critical stage in its development and he generally encouraged the use of social science methodology in the analysis of legal problems.[62]

Shortly after Frank published *Law and the Modern Mind,* Felix Frankfurter accurately criticized him for not articulating any substantive program of reform.[63] While concerned with reform, *Law and the Modern Mind* is oriented overwhelmingly toward changes in the legal process. The book never specifies or even hints at what substantive alterations should be made. Frank thought that his "prime purpose was to urge a *revised* description of how decisions are made." He thought that "greater awareness of how judges actually do their work will affect their doing it. How, I do not venture to say."[64] Frank called for a change in attitude, for adopting the approach of the creative scientist, ever ready to retest hypotheses.[65] The experimental method would make law more pragmatic and realistic.

In his writings Frank constantly urged readers to confront problems. His openness was partly influenced by Freudian psychology, which seeks to trace problems to their roots in early childhood and in unconscious urges. He believed that an understanding of ego psychology was necessary before one could hope to control harmful impulses. Frank trusted free people to govern themselves intelligently if they possessed complete information on which to base their decisions. As a liberal, Frank believed in the possibility of meaningful reform. He assumed, perhaps naively, that people have goodwill, are honest, and are receptive to change. He did not think that economic class, group interests, or professional training and values seriously limited reform.[66] While Frank thought the economic bias of judges "terrifically strong,"[67] he spurned a Marxist interpretation of law as reflecting a struggle between economic classes. Frank thought that most cases involved suits between members of the same class, so that the class struggle was neutralized.[68] His view of class conflict was extremely crude, and he never understood how a system of dispute resolution could be part of a bourgeois ideology. At bottom, he did not share the Progressive view of a society split by irreconcilable differences.[69] In Frank's consensus vision, personal idiosyncrasies formed the largest impediment to social progress.

His thesis that the judge's personality is the key factor in decision making assumes that hidden biases control even routine cases. He trivialized his argument, however, by making judicial decisions turn on whimsical irrelevancies, such as the color of a person's hair. If he had placed his analysis on historical and demonstrable grounds, such as racial, ethnic, or sexual prejudice, or perhaps economic class and interests, he would have been on firmer terrain.

In *Law and the Modern Mind* Frank exaggerated the degree of judicial discretion and unpredictability in the legal system. By concentrating only on court-made law, he slighted the role of the legislature in enacting statutes and thereby circumscribing judicial discretion.[70] He failed to recognize that detailed rules by statutes, orders, and regulations serve to channel judicial decisions. While rules do not completely coerce judges into particular results, norms of professionalism demand that judges pay allegiance to legal rules. It is incumbent on judges either to apply a relevant rule or to explain why it is not controlling. Only the willfully perverse judge completely ignores all written rules.

In arguing that law is unpredictable, Frank carefully cast his analysis in terms of future judicial decisions. One cannot know a particular result because one does not know which judge will hear the case, or if state or federal law will govern, or whether the Supreme Court is divided on the question.[71] Frank and the realists stressed law as it worked in practice, not as it appeared on the books. Legal "rights" and "duties" had no independent existence, but depended on enforcement by courts. If courts refused to enforce "rights" and "duties," then "rights" and "duties" did not exist.[72]

Even Frank desired legal certainty. He hoped that exposing the frailty of existing devices for securing certainty would lead to the creation of better ones.[73] Ultimately "the child will grow up."[74] After Frank sent Cardozo a copy of *Law and the Modern Mind,* the judge replied, "Being as yet not wholly adult, but in truth a hopeless juvenile, I did what any juvenile would do: I looked at the index to see the references to myself. I have consulted these with hope and trepidation and am now strutting about the house, convinced that I am no hobblededog, but in truth a grown man." On the merits Cardozo thought the book "a valuable piece of work. . . . But is the flux quite as bad as you picture it—are we really so utterly adrift? Perhaps."[75]

Ironically, Jerome Frank was guilty of the same rigidity he denounced in others. Because he could demonstrate that rules do not translate into absolutely predictable court decisions, he assumed that they had negligible value. Frank ignored the role of probability in guiding men and women to adapt their behavior to comply with legal rules. The law affects people not merely by producing court orders but also by shaping their expectations of what will probably occur if a rule is violated. Commercial law offers an example of rules enacted into law to place the legal imprimatur on conduct in the marketplace. The customary behavior of business became the legal norm.[76]

A more simple illustration may prove the point. In every state it is illegal to drive through a red traffic light. The realist, asking what impact or predictability this rule has, finds very little, for suppose the light is stuck on red; or the vehicle is a police car, fire engine, or ambulance; or an emergency exists; or the brakes fail; or the driver stops, looks carefully, and proceeds to turn right. Further, how does one know that the light was red? Suppose witnesses testify that the light was green, and the judge or jury believes this testimony and acquits the driver. Even a clear and precise legal rule allows the judge wide discretion in applying or devising exceptions and in finding facts. Therefore, under Frank's analysis we are remitted to the personality of the judge as the operative factor. Concededly, these exceptions prevent absolute predictability as to what will happen in individual cases. But the reality is that automobile drivers normally stop at red lights. In a complex civilized society, most people adhere to legal rules most of the time. Whether motivated by fear of punishment, moral principles, fear of injury, avoidance of shame, ridicule, social disgrace, or belief in democratically enacted rules, people establish law by voluntarily conforming their behavior to legal rules.

Law and the Modern Mind challenged central tenets of the American legal system. Conventional wisdom portrays the common law system as one of slow growth guided by stare decisis. Reasoning from past experience to present problems, judges apply the law. The democratic system prides itself on being a government of laws, not of men, remembering the maxim that "where law ends, tyranny begins." Under the American system of separation of powers, the legislature makes the law and the judiciary applies it. In rejecting these ideas, *Law and the Modern Mind* presented a potentially explosive attack on the political status quo.[77] By exploding the myth of the role of stare decisis and by exposing judicial power and discretion, Jerome Frank tried to disabuse both the profession and the public of the idea that judges follow the law. But if judges do not obey the law, then why do people obey judges? Frank raised a serious challenge to the legitimacy not only of court decisions but of law generally. If the law does not embody principles of natural law and if it is not the expression of democratic sovereignty, then from where does law derive its legitimacy? If law depends on "the personality of the judge,"[78] on an act of will of very human and biased people, then its arbitrary character deprives it of any rightful claim to allegiance and obedience. By exposing the political aspect of law, Jerome Frank revealed law's inevitable role in the distribution of wealth and power.

Law and the Modern Mind, a bold and innovative foray into legal philosophy by a previously unknown corporate lawyer, excited the legal world of the 1930s. Neither wholly original nor a complete philosophy, Frank's realism expanded the ideas of Holmes and Pound in framing an extreme version of judicial relativism. Frankfurter observed in 1931 that "so far as the underlying ideas are concerned, [Holmes] saw them all and said most of them fifty years ago."[79] Frank concurred: "Everytime I re-read one of his essays I am struck by the fact that most of our current discussion is either a bad re-hash of what he said or more or less adequate foot-notes thereto."[80] Frank sold short his originality. While Holmes had first exposed the deceptive role of the syllogism in explaining the growth of the law, Frank revealed that judges willed law. Holmes, as well as Pound, continued to believe that law was a science; Frank, by contrast, saw law as one of the "social arts."[81] Pound's "social engineering" rubric conveyed far too much precision for Frank.[82]

As a reformer, Jerome Frank had two options available: he could attack the process that formed law, asserting that legal reasoning was not mechanistic and formalistic; or he could challenge the legal results, the substantive doctrine as politically unsatisfactory and as producing an inequitable distribution of wealth and power. Frank opted to challenge the conventional wisdom on legal reasoning by questioning the autonomy of law—the claim that law exists apart from power, will, and politics.[83] Legal deductions and analogies inescapably require choices, and those choices frequently are political. Jerome Frank collapsed objectivity in law, partly by analogy to science and history. If these seemingly exact disciplines contained a large dose of subjectivity, then law could make no greater claim to objectivity.[84]

Debunking legal doctrine made good sport but necessarily required efforts to explain law in other terms. Many legal realists turned to empirical studies and social science explanations for the current shape and content of the law.[85] They accumulated data with the curious expectation that the facts would speak for themselves. Lacking any broad conceptual picture of law, they became apologists for the political status quo.[86] On a political level, *Law and the Modern Mind*'s failure to offer a program of reform subjects Frank to the criticism that he tore down without offering a positive substitute.[87] On a jurisprudential level, Frank failed to appreciate the role of the legislature in confining judicial discretion, the impact of rules in coercing compliance, and the degree of probability in predicting legal decision.

III

Reactions to *Law and the Modern Mind* and to legal realism generally came from two directions. One group of writers bristled at realism's smugness and attempted to reassert the primacy of the rule of law. Roscoe Pound, Mortimer Adler, Morris R. Cohen, John Dickinson, and Herman Kantorowicz gamely tried to restore faith in the efficacy of legal rules. Other critics mounted a challenge to realism's relativism. Robert Hutchins, Jerome Hall, Lon Fuller, and Felix Cohen challenged realism's ethical subjectivity and its lack of a theory of values. A natural law revival condemned realism as morally bankrupt.

A major event in the legal world, *Law and the Modern Mind* excited and challenged, quickly becoming a controversial contribution to American legal realism.[88] Shortly after its publication, Roscoe Pound published "The Call for a Realist Jurisprudence" in the *Harvard Law Review*.[89] Without mentioning any legal realist by name, Pound lashed out at the new jurisprudence for focusing only on the law as it exists and ignoring law as it ought to be. He identified five characteristics common to realism: faith in quantities of data having independent significance; belief in exclusive reliance on a single methodological approach (for instance, psychology); a dogmatic confidence in psychological premises; emphasis on individual cases as opposed to general principles; and a conception of law as serving the interests of business instead of broad social ends. In chiding the realists as dogmatic and as wedded to a priori categories, Pound evoked a response from Karl Llewellyn, writing in collaboration with Jerome Frank.[90]

Llewellyn attempted to refute Pound on every point. He compiled a list of the twenty most prominent realists, carefully examined their books and articles, and assessed whether the writing supported any of Pound's five characteristics. He concluded that Pound unfairly and inaccurately described the new movement in jurisprudence by lumping together men of quite disparate ideas and by exaggerating the rigidity of a school of thought whose keynote was flexibility. Llewellyn and Frank made a concerted effort to avoid the thrust of any of Pound's barbs, including the telling and legitimate ones. Pound's essay had particular applicability to Frank, who epitomized Pound's displeasure with the new jurisprudence.[91] Llewellyn and Frank's reply succeeded only in escalating the rhetorical level and in making further dialogue strained. By not joining issue, they confused understanding of the realist movement and contributed to a succession of tedious and uninformative law review articles.[92]

The excitement engendered by *Law and the Modern Mind* prompted the *Columbia Law Review* to publish a symposium on it. The contributors were Karl Llewellyn, who was enthusiastic and supportive but dubious about its psychological thesis; Walter Wheeler Cook, a fellow realist who offered resounding applause and a staunch defense of Frank; and Mortimer J. Adler, who bitterly attacked Frank.[93] Adler came to prominence as an Aristotelian philosopher at the University of Chicago.[94] Frank's ready acceptance of James, Dewey, and Schiller and his castigation of scholasticism nettled Adler into writing a stinging denunciation. Adler challenged Frank's loose use of philosophical terms and accused him of writing an "utterly authoritarian and dogmatic" book. To Adler, Frank confused the structure of formal logic with the truth or falsity of its premises and postulates. One must analyze the logic of an argument apart from the factual accuracy of its premises. An argument may be logically impeccable yet incorrect because one or more of its premises is not true. Formal logic concerns the analysis of and relationships among propositions, not an evaluation of the choice of premises. Frank's psychological musings, thought Adler, did not bear on the truth or falsity of the contested premise. Frank was thus "an extreme nominalist" who denied the existence of anything except particulars; universals existed only in the mind.[95] Frank considered the nominalism charge "a verbal brick bat." He retorted, "I don't happen to believe that there are such things as hippogriffs, but that doesn't mean that I believe there are no horses."[96]

Philosopher Morris R. Cohen of City College of New York continued the sharp criticism of Frank. Initially Cohen had written Frank that the book would have been better without the psychological explanation, but it was "an extraordinarily good book anyway."[97] Now in print, Cohen, like Adler, thought Frank had overstated his case against formal logic. Cohen believed that logic could apply even in a world in flux. The relativism of James, Dewey, and Bergson infuriated Cohen, who considered their positions extreme and foolish reactions to changes in the world about them.[98] Einstein's theories did not topple Cohen's faith in the world as understandable. While to some observers Einstein's work on relativity fragmented any sense of objective knowledge, Cohen found to the contrary that "the general theory of relativity established the 'absoluteness of the laws of nature.'"[99]

Einstein's theory thus became a new way of making sense out of the physical universe. Cohen claimed that "nonmental, logical invariants were both intrinsic to nature and compatible with the radical contingency of the physical world." In jurisprudence, Cohen denied ethical relativism and called for a scientific natural law. He distinguished between the "uniformities" of human conduct, or "descriptive sociology," and the norms for deciding legal issues. Realists, by blurring the distinction between the way people behave and the behavior that law would sanction, denied any standard by which to criticize existing law.[100]

A dinner party at Judge Julian Mack's in 1931 began an unusually lengthy series of exchanges between Morris Cohen and Jerome Frank. Other guests included Cardozo, Harold Laski, Thomas Reed Powell, and Felix Frankfurter, who "dragooned" Frank into commenting on Cohen's recently published *Reason and Nature*.[101] Discussion was heated, with Frank and Cohen doing most of the jousting and the others occasionally joining in. After the party, Frank sent Cohen a twelve-page explication of his position. Cohen had maintained that a psychological description of the reasoning process does not determine whether the conclusion is true: psychology does not affect logic. Frank stressed that knowledge of the background of a thinker's ideas allows readers and critics to detect errors. Formal logic may be misused to mask the background, thus drawing attention to the accuracy of the syllogism and diverting it from the correctness of the premises.[102] Psychology may unearth the motivation behind the thinker's choice of premises—both values and facts. The selection or finding of facts conforms to the desire to reach a given conclusion, thus obscuring the choice behind the syllogistic form.

On July 3, 1931, Cohen responded that Frank had confused three things: factual truth, logical relationships, and the reliability of testimony. Psychological motivation does not determine truth or falsity: a fact is true or false wholly apart from a person's motives.

Cohen was correct and Frank agreed, but the exchange continued. Frank returned to the idea that logic plays a small role in law because the "facts" vary with the fact-finder, who finds facts to support his preordained conclusion. Frank had floated this idea in *Law and the Modern Mind* but, spurred by Cohen, he elaborated it further.[103] It ultimately became the focus of his other major book, *Courts on Trial.*

The other major reaction to realism focused on the ethical implications of its relativism. Edward Purcell has convincingly demonstrated that realism was part of a social science movement, known as scientific naturalism, which rejected the idea that absolute rational principles govern the universe.[104] A priori truth did not exist; only empirical investigation could produce truth. Scientific naturalism scorned the idea that ethical ideals have a rational justification in, for instance, a "natural law." By denying that reasoning may establish the truth of ethical propositions, scientific naturalism evaporated the rational basis for moral ideals. By accepting as valid only those ideas empirically proven, it left all ideas open to constant change and revision with each succeeding wave of data. By refusing to accept as authoritative a religious or a rational explanation for values, scientific naturalism left the origin of values in social and economic pressures. Since no value could have greater "validity" than any other, a "sweeping ethical relativism" pervaded scientific naturalism.[105] The theoretical underpinnings came from many disciplines, but the development of non-Euclidean geometry proved most important. When Einstein published *The General Theory of Relativity* in 1915, he raised new doubts about the validity of synthetic a priori knowledge. Euclid's geometry, while internally consistent and logical, failed on empirical investigation. Thus non-Euclidean thinking carried the suggestion that all rational, deductive systems of thought are true only if empirically validated.

Legal realism created problems for traditional democratic theory by rejecting the role of logic and precedent, by exposing broad judicial discretion, and by embracing the empiricism and relativism of scientific naturalism. How can judicial subjectivity be harmonized with democracy's boast of a government of laws and not of men? If the actions of government officials constitute law, is there any moral or ethical basis for criticizing those acts? If ethics are relative, can any barbarity be declared evil? These intellectual problems for democratic theory became gnawing political issues during the 1930s, after the rise of Mussolini's Fascists and Hitler's Nazis.[106] If law is what the government does, then Nazi atrocities constitute law. Ethical relativism came under savage attack in the face of momentous injustice. American legal realism seemed morally bankrupt if it offered no satisfactory way to criticize totalitarianism.

The dilemma prompted a renaissance of natural law thinking in the United States. Robert Hutchins, president of the University of Chicago, urged that "law is a body of principles and rules developed in the light of the rational sciences of ethics and politics."[107] In the face of the totalitarian threat, natural law justified democracy as the only type of government that combined law, equality, and justice. A chorus of other scholars chimed in to berate realism as ethically indefensible. A number of Catholics revitalized Thomist philosophy, urging its special relevance to combat totalitarianism.[108] God, country, philosophy, and rationality went together to demonstrate the rightness of the battle against fascism.

Realists might have expected opposition from adherents of Aristotelian philosophy, but criticism came also from erstwhile sympathizers. The rift with Roscoe Pound opened rather than closed,[109] and new fissures appeared as Jerome Hall and Lon Fuller, two prominent young legal philosophers, condemned realism as leading to Nazism. Fuller's attack began as early as 1934 when he cautioned against "making an orthodoxy of the sterile and uninspired behavioristic philosophy." He discerned that realism began as a reform movement but quickly embraced a reactionary principle. In separating "what the law is" from "what the law ought to be," realism offered no way to eliminate the cleavage. Existing law could be changed to conform to the "ought," or the "ought" could acquiesce in the "is." Since the realists never articulated what ought to be, they effectively collapsed the ought into the is, thereby affirming the status quo.[110] By 1940, Fuller scorned realism as "demonstrably incapable of sustaining a nation in time of crisis" and as having "accelerated the disintegrative forces which threaten modern society."[111] Realism justified the substitution of brute force for justice.[112]

Needless to say, these charges stung and the realists became defensive. Frank resented the characterization of realism as unconcerned with values and ethics, for he considered the major purpose of his jurisprudence to improve the judicial process.[113] Frank wanted judges "to do justice," but he did not think that legal rules necessarily embodied normative concepts.[114] While Frank refused to equate law and morals, he simultaneously insisted that the law was concerned with values.[115] He saw his stint as a government attorney as a preoccupation with values and the embodiment of realism in practice.[116] Frank believed in "the necessity and desirability of the 'ought' in thinking about law," but he considered it imperative to separate temporarily what is from what ought to be. "You can't do much with 'oughts' until you know something about 'ises.' "[117]

Felix Cohen, a lawyer, ethicist, and Morris' son, also attacked *Law and the Modern Mind* for failing to distinguish sharply "between the existent and the desirable."[118] While Cohen was persuaded by Frank of the utility of distinguishing between objective description and ethical judgment, he considered description only the first step. So simple a question as "is there a contract?" posed both a question whether the court *will* enforce the agreement and a question whether the court *should* enforce the agreement.[119] Cohen found completely unacceptable Frank's insistence on law's unpredictability, for law then becomes "simply noises" and no more intelligible that the pious incantations of formalism.[120] To Cohen, "a judicial decision is a social event," the outcome of social forces. Interpreting law as the product of individual personality and calling on judges to individualize cases denies that law is the product of social determinants. Judicial decisions lack social significance if they are viewed simply as the unique product of a concrete moment.[121]

Felix Cohen credited realism with unmasking formalism and permitting "ethics to come out of hiding," but realism failed to offer any criterion for assessing the ethical, political, or social consequences of legal decisions. Every description is an evaluation and only a critical theory of values can make sense of facts. "Legal criticism is empty without objective description of the causes and consequences of legal decisions. Legal description is blind without the guiding light of a theory of values."[122]

Frank agreed that facts neither are objective nor speak for themselves. "A 'fact' is a synthesis. An observation or description is selective or interpretative."[123] He also considered ethical criticism important, but he thought it impossible to control the application of ethical norms because the fact-finding process is so subjective. Through the power to manipulate the facts, the judge and jury may circumvent the law's ethical standards and substitute personal values. Ultimately, Jerome Frank did not think that rules mattered.[124]

Frank began moving toward fact skepticism almost as soon as the ink dried on *Law and the Modern Mind*. Indeed, even that book partly blamed the fact-finding process for the lack of predictability. After its publication Frank defended his stance on legal uncertainty by elaborating on his position that in "contested cases" the facts are always in doubt.[125] Pushed by criticism from Mortimer Adler, Morris Cohen, Felix Cohen, and John Dickinson, Frank increasingly turned to fact skepticism to defend himself. In dwelling on the uncertainty of facts, Frank collapsed the traditional dichotomy between law and facts.[126]

IV

During the 1930s and 1940s Frank published a steady stream of books and articles on philosophy, jurisprudence, legal education, and law reform, culminating in the publication of *Courts on Trial* in 1949.[127] A major jurisprudential work, it carved out for Frank a unique niche in the realist movement. In *Courts on Trial*, Frank turned his focus to the trial courts and, motivated by a reform impulse, wrote for a lay as well as professional audience.

While reiterating the main themes of *Law and the Modern Mind*, Frank refined and elaborated his ideas on the judicial process. Continuing to insist on the lack of predictability in law, Frank exposed the frailty of the fact-finding process. At trial a witness reports his or her memory of events in the past. Even if the witness is completely honest, memory may be faulty, the original observation erroneous, or the present recollection misstated. Conscious or unconscious partisanship makes the "facts" even less certain. In addition, "facts" depend on accurate documentation, often unavailable. Finally, "facts" are found by the presentation of testimony to a judge or jury, but the judge and jury are witnesses as well and suffer similar human weaknesses. Findings of fact, then, are the opinions of the judge or jury about the opinions of witnesses.[128]

Returning to the question of judicial discretion, Frank asked rhetorically, "Are judges human?" He continued to believe that the social, economic, and political backgrounds of judges shaped their court decisions. Yet he insisted that many cases defied easy labeling and others turned on "obscure idiosyncrasies" in fact-finding. Personal biases color the judge's reactions to witnesses. Unpredictability further undermines the certainty of legal rights. If a court refused to enforce a legal right because it erroneously found certain facts, then, Frank argued, the right did not exist. "Legal rights should therefore be viewed from the angle of their actual enforceability." Frank's skepticism had changed since the publication of *Law and the Modern Mind.* Instead of focusing on the ambiguity of legal rules and the breadth of judicial discretion to select among competing doctrines and precedent, Frank now located the source of uncertainty in the fact-finding process. He now thought the rules had "great importance" but were often skewed by defective fact-finding. The application of any legal rule depends on the facts, and "facts are guesses." The American legal system cavalierly assumes that the adversarial system, pitting two antagonists against each other, will produce the truth. Jerome Frank derided this method as a "fight theory" in which partisanship often blocks access to vital evidence and distorts rather than uncovers the truth. Frank proposed that the government assume responsibility for making available all important evidence at civil trials, that judges assume an active role in examining witnesses, that exclusionary evidence rules be discarded, and that criminal defendants have broad pretrial discovery. Frank continued his attack on the jury system begun in *Law and the Modern Mind.* The capriciousness of jury-made law maximized legal unpredictability. Frank advocated concrete reforms: special verdicts, specially selected juries, professional fact-finders, revision of the rules of evidence, the recording of jury-room deliberations, and training for jury service.[129]

Frank's concern for fact-finding made him extremely critical of

American legal education. To Frank, the case system, developed at Harvard under Langdell, not only epitomized a purely mechanical legal philosophy but also evidenced a concern with rules to the exclusion of facts. He derided Langdell as "a brilliant neurotic," a recluse who loved to pore over dusty books in the bowels of the Harvard Law Library.

> He slept, at times, on the library table. One of his friends found him one day absorbed in an ancient law book. "As he drew near," we are told, "Langdell looked up and said, in a tone of mingled exhilaration and regret, and with an emphatic gesture, 'Oh, if only I could have lived in the time of the Plantagenets.' "[130]

From Langdell came the idea that the raw material of law consisted of reported decisions. Students studied upper-court opinions, dissected their meaning, and arrived at the law's first principles. Quarantined in the law library, students were not trained to act as real lawyers.

In *Courts on Trial* Frank repeated his plea, first voiced in 1933, that legal education become clinical.[131] The law faculty should be composed largely of persons with substantial experience in practice. The so-called case system should include the complete record of cases, including briefs and trial transcripts, not merely the appellate court opinions. Law schools should expose students to "litigation laboratories"—the trial and appellate courts. Learning from the medical school model, law schools should establish legal clinics that would enable students to engage in supervised law practice. Current legal education rigidly separates theory from practice and focuses only on analysis of appellate court opinions. "It is like the difference between kissing a girl and reading a treatise on osculation."[132]

Since Frank attached critical importance to the fact-finding process, he urged that trial judges receive special training to equip them for their tasks. To maximize fairness, the judge should try to control his or her biases, but since prejudices are often unconscious or deeply buried, Frank proposed that every judge undergo psychoanaylsis. Psychology had the capacity, Frank believed, to free men and women from blind fears. With typical ebullience, Frank thought that if people know their prejudices, they would work to counteract them. Frank detested masks and charades. He urged his readers to be alert to his own hidden biases. He also lashed out at "the cult of the robe," the judges' practice of wearing robes to conceal their human character and distance themselves from the people. Robes conjured up the specter of priests and kings, authoritative figures who pronounce an absolute and infallible law. Frank urged judges to discard their robes as an anachronistic symbol in a democratic society.[133]

Frank broke ranks with his former realist allies. Bound together by skepticism, realists divided into "rule skeptics," led by Llewellyn, and "fact skeptics," led by Frank. The rule skeptics, according to Frank, failed to carry their skepticism far enough. By slighting trial courts and fact-finding, they adhered to the magical desire for legal certainty. Frank acerbically suggested that Llewellyn, instead of traveling to Montana to investigate the Cheyenne legal system, should take a subway ride from Columbia Law School to the trial courts in New York City. Frank also criticized such realists as Herman Oliphant, who stressed that one can best understand the law by observing what judges decide and disregarding the reasons they offer for their decisions. Oliphant thought behaviorism, as advocated by J. B. Watson, held the key to legal predictability. Frank scorned behaviorism as one more determinist philosophy. "Descartes . . . said, 'I think, therefore I am.' Watson says, 'There are white rats, therefore I don't think.'"[134]

Response to the legal realist emphasis on judicial discretion came from Harold Lasswell and Myres McDougal. They believed in the feasibility of "scientifically" predicting court decisions and advocated training lawyers to shape the law consciously to achieve desired results. Notions of good public policy would dictate court decisions. Frank welcomed their attitude toward judicial discretion, but considered misguided their effort to create a legal science of prediction. The unpredictability of the fact-finding process posed an insurmountable stumbling block.[135]

In 1949, in a new preface to the sixth printing of *Law and the Modern Mind,* Frank responded to criticism that he slighted ethical values by castigating natural law: "I do not understand how any decent man today can refuse to adopt, as the basis of modern civilization, the fundamental principles of natural law, relative to human conduct, as stated by Thomas Aquinas."[136] At first blush Frank seems to have retreated dramatically from the harsh criticism he leveled against natural law in the first printing of *Law and the Modern Mind.* Frank, however, did not endorse an absolute and undeviating natural law, but an "intuitive awareness" that a few universal principles of justice—such as "seek the common good"— derive from human nature. From these basic principles, one may deduce secondary precepts; for example, that "one should not kill or steal." While the principles and precepts are undeviating, the applications are tentative and uncertain. The broad ideas of justice remain constant while precise moral principles depend for their justification on particular circumstances. Thus Frank saw merit in Thomistic natural law because it offered broad moral principles without pretending to supply clear and objective rules in specific cases.[137]

Nevertheless, Frank continued to ridicule the idea that natural law offers a series of fundamental principles from which one can rationally deduce morally correct results in concrete cases. He considered natural law inescapably vague, often "a mask for the sheerest expediency," and susceptible of use by "either side of almost any cause." Indeed, if the guide is the law of nature, social Darwinism with its ruthless self-assertion demonstrates why nature should be tempered by civilized ethical concerns. Frank endorsed natural law only on the most general level as, at best, only "a standard of justice and morality for critically evaluating the manmade rules."[138] Natural law offers no help for improving the accuracy of the fact-finding process.

Courts on Trial sparkled with the inimitable style of Jerome Frank. Witty and didactic, contentious and unsettling, the book displayed extraordinarily broad knowledge. It drew on philosophy and psychology, history and historiography, literature and literary criticism, science and medicine, sociology and anthropology, classical music and aesthetics.[139] Basically optimistic, it exhibited concern for justice and confidence that people have good will and will act justly if their psychological fetters are removed.

The accusation that realism is bereft of concrete proposals for change cannot be leveled against *Courts on Trial,* which offered a blueprint for major reform of the trial courts. A self-described reformer, Frank proposed changes in legal education, the jury system, the rules of evidence, and the training of judges, prosecutors, and police. The legal system has adopted many of Frank's ideas, including special verdicts in many jury trials, the necessity for a clinical component in legal education, and liberal discovery for criminal defendants. Some suggestions, such as that trial judges assume a more active role in the fact-finding process, continue to generate discussion and controversy, while other proposals—for instance, that judges undergo psychoanalysis—were hopelessly naive and bore no relation to economic costs or practicality.

In the nineteen years between publication of *Law and the Modern Mind* and *Courts on Trial,* Frank turned away from the broad political implications of his first book. *Law and the Modern Mind* had called into question the legitimacy of law. *Courts on Trial* borrowed heavily from *Law and the Modern Mind* and from articles Frank published in 1931 and 1932.[140] Although he still recognized the enormous discretion of judges, he concentrated on improving the performance of trial courts and not on exposing the political power of judges. Frank became mired in detail and focused on concrete reforms that would improve the accuracy of the fact-finding process. Along the way he slighted *Law and the Modern Mind*'s emphasis on judicial discretion. To be sure, *Courts on Trial* had a wide audience and raised problems regarding the administration of justice, but it placed to one side the question of the legitimacy of the system.

V

Critics commonly write of a postrealist world, dismissing legal realism as a short-lived, misguided effort by lawyers to play social scientists and philosophers. There have been significant developments since the heyday of legal realism. In the 1940s Myres McDougal and Harold Lasswell tried to create a policy-oriented science of law.[141] The 1950s witnessed an attack on realism for politicizing the law and made an effort to reassert the autonomy of law as a process of reasoned elaboration. Judicial review was compatible with democratic principles if judges neither found nor made the law, but reasoned toward it and then articulated the reasoning process.[142] In 1961 H. L. A. Hart published an important book, *The Concept of Law,* which offered a revised positivism and described judicial discretion as circumscribed by the legislature. In the 1970s John Rawls, Robert Nozick, and Ronald Dworkin presented theories premised on individual rights and distributive justice.[143]

Yet the ghost of American legal realism lingers on, since the political character of law seems irrepressible. Published a half century ago, *Law and the Modern Mind* addressed problems still unresolved. For many students, legal education, especially during the first year, is a process of discovering how judges manipulate legal rules. Case analysis teaches how to unravel the rhetoric of a decision and expose what the judge is *really* doing. The contemporary law student learns that legal rules are pliable instruments of the judiciary.

In constitutional law, the U.S. Supreme Court's 1973 decision in *Roe v. Wade,* establishing abortion rights, rekindled an old controversy about the propriety of substantive due process.[144] Recent literature has debated the legitimacy of the Court's engaging in constitutional policy making as opposed to constitutional interpretation.[145] Notwithstanding the efforts to harness the Court, the judiciary's political power identified by the realists remains unhampered. Bob Woodward and Scott Armstrong's 1979 book *The Brethren* contains an unsettling account of the way the U.S. Supreme Court decides cases. Justices lobby each other, consider how a vote in one case will affect another justice's vote in another case, and pay attention to political repercussions. The portrait that emerges is of an intensely political struggle, in which personal values and beliefs weigh far more heavily in the balance than do reasoning and precedent.

In political science, the behavioralist school studies judges' votes and the results reached, neglecting the written opinions that purportedly justify the decisions. This school of thought finds computer programs and elaborate charts and graphs more useful in predicting judicial behavior than doctrinal analysis of court opinions. Another theoretical school has turned to economics to explain the character of legal doctrine. The "law and economics" school, like legal realism, finds judicial rhetoric an inadequate explanation for judicial decisions. This school argues that judges intuitively, sometimes explicitly, reach results that maximize social wealth. Whatever the reasons that judges assign to their opinions, the results generally conform to efficiency principles of economics.[146] A final example of realism's vitality comes from the writings of the members of the Conference on Critical Legal Studies. As the political heirs of realism, they insist that legal reasoning "provides only a wide and conflicting variety of stylized rationalizations from which courts pick and choose."[147] The critical legal scholars have raised anew the issue of whether law is autonomous and has legitimacy beyond bare political power to command compliance.[148] The issues first raised by Jerome Frank remain alive and well.

Chapter Three

"PRINCIPLES ARE WHAT PRINCIPLES DO": LAWYERING IN THE NEW DEAL

I don't say that "most law is bunk." You remember the farmer who was asked if he believed in baptism and who replied, "Believe in it? Hell, I've seen it."

—Jerome Frank

I

The New Deal greatly increased the number of attorneys in government service and for the first time made government employment attractive to the most able graduates of American law schools. Through the 1920s high-ranking graduates of national law schools chose first to practice on Wall Street. Service as a government attorney lacked prestige, offered less interesting legal problems, and usually attracted only persons who failed to obtain positions in corporate law practice.[1] But the New Deal found many Harvard and Yale law review editors selecting government service as their first choice. For some Jews and other new immigrants the government offered employment at a time when elite corporate law firms discriminated against them.[2] But the New Deal also began to attract many lawyers of impeccable Anglo-Saxon lineage.[3] For some lawyers the government simply offered employment at a time when the private sector was stagnant. Yet this circumstance does not account for the ability of government service to compete effectively with Wall Street for the allegiance of Ivy League law review editors.[4]

For some the New Deal held the allure of power and responsibility. For others it awakened a nascent sense of professional and social responsibility anaesthetized by a generation of exclusive service to the interests of corporate America. By the beginning of the twentieth century, lawyers had surrendered a measure of professional autonomy by defining their responsibility as solely to the client. The concept of the lawyer as a public figure who owed allegiance to the public weal receded in the face of rising commercial and industrial business opportunities.[5] The New Deal restored a measure of professional responsibility and independence by enlisting lawyers in the effort to combat the depression. It thus occasioned a measure of idealism rarely witnessed in the social history of the American bar. For many attorneys the lucre of New York did not match the excitement posed by the problems confronting Washington.[6]

The New Deal dramatically expanded the number of federal legal positions, thus creating the option of a career as a government attorney.[7] The conventional portrait of the legal profession is of the lawyer in private practice. This model is far from accurate. Examination of the entire legal profession reveals significant numbers of attorneys acting as judges, prosecutors, salaried employees of private business, and legislators. Others serve federal, state, county, and municipal governments on legislative staffs, in executive agencies, and in legal aid and defender associations. The last half century has witnessed a vast transformation in the social history of the bar. This process began in earnest with the influx of attorneys in the New Deal.[8] While the New Deal attracted extremely talented young attorneys and offered opportunities to Jews and other recent immigrants, anti-Semitic sentiment occasionally limited hiring opportunities. New Deal attorneys brought to government service techniques and styles of law practice recently developed in the private sector. Government legal staffs modified these practices, thus enabling young lawyers to enjoy substantial responsibility and to move from one federal agency to another.

According to revisionist historians, FDR's administration was willing to experiment but sought no major transformation of the American economic system.[9] The politics of the national administration set real limits to the possibilities of social reform through the legal and political system. Still, the New Deal aroused hope that lawyers and legal means would stop the country's deterioration.

Lawyers responded with imagination and creativity in the drafting of legislation, with shrewd litigation strategies grounded in the philosophic insights of legal realism, with originality in the formation of policy, and with keen administrative ability in translating new ideas into working programs. In refashioning the governmental landscape, lawyers became indispensable to the functioning of the modern regulatory state.[10]

In many ways the New Deal experience of Jerome Frank epitomized this shift in the social history of the bar. He and numerous other legal realists entered government service as officials in newly created agencies, and used the flexibility and creativity inherent in their philosophic approach to wrestle with and subdue monumental economic and legal obstacles. Frank was equally adept at formulating an approach to a complex problem and at tackling the tedious legislative drafting and political jawboning necessary to ensure its success. He well understood and substantially fulfilled the dual demands made of the New Deal lawyer: that he be a generalist in terms of substantive issues and also a highly skilled technician. In both respects, legal realism served him well.

II

Jerome Frank entered the New Deal after successful careers in Chicago and New York City. Despite his success, he had tired of Wall Street practice. "I didn't like it. It was quite different from anything I'd been accustomed to. It was a factory system. The whole attitude of the big Wall Street law office went against the grain."[11] After Roosevelt's election Frank wrote to Felix Frankfurter: "I know you know Roosevelt well. I want to get out of this Wall Street racket. More important, this crisis seems to me to be the equivalent of a war, and I'd like to join up for the duration."[12] Through Frankfurter's intercession, Jerome Frank was appointed, at a substantially lower salary than he had received in private practice, general counsel to the Agricultural Adjustment Administration.[13]

When Roosevelt entered the White House, the economic outlook was bleak. National income had dropped 50 percent in four years while unemployment hovered at close to 25 percent. Thousands of banks had failed while others closed their doors to prevent a stampede of customers seeking to withdraw savings. Many people doubted that democratic government could avoid economic collapse. Faith in capitalism declined while violence, even revolution, seemed possible. Farmers were particularly hard hit by the Depression: 1932 farm income was less than one-third the 1929 level and prices for farm products had dropped more than 50 percent. Unable to meet mortgage payments, many farmers faced bank foreclosure—a process sometimes interrupted by violent mobs.[14]

The agricultural situation made a special call on Roosevelt's attention, and he responded by proposing an Agricultural Adjustment Act, which Congress quickly passed. Falling farm prices had caused farmers to increase production in order to offset declining prices. But this strategy merely drove prices down faster and further. The act was intended to increase farm income by controlling production through the Agricultural Adjustment Administration (AAA). It offered farmers benefit payments for adjusting their plantings according to a national scheme. The act also empowered the government to maintain prices by purchasing crops, to lease land and withdraw it from cultivation, and to enter marketing agreements restricting the quantities of products being marketed.[15]

AAA General Counsel Frank assembled a staff of brilliant and dedicated young attorneys.[16] One of them, future Supreme Court justice Abe Fortas, later recalled that everyone worked twenty hours a day: "I did not unpack my suitcase for about 3 days, getting a few hours of sleep each evening, fully dressed, on a couch in the office. . . . The world was then being reconstructed from the chaos left by President Hoover's administration. Jerry and the rest of us—including Rex Tugwell—could see the new world and feel it taking form under our hands."[17] Frank's extraordinary staff included Alger Hiss, a former law clerk to Justice Holmes and subsequently the subject of investigations by the House Un-American Activities Committee (HUAC) as well as of two criminal trials for perjury. Future Democratic presidential candidate Adlai Stevenson, then a young Illinois attorney, also joined Frank's AAA staff. From the Yale Law School faculty Frank recruited for special assignments Wesley Sturges, a future dean of Yale, and Thurman

Arnold, who subsequently headed the Justice Department's Antitrust Division, served as U.S. Court of Appeals judge, and founded the Washington law firm of Arnold and Porter. Staff members who became distinguished private practitioners included Frank Shea, of Shea and Gardner, and Sigmund Timberg, later a renowned international lawyer. Frank also tapped Telford Taylor, who became a Nuremberg war-crimes prosecutor and eventually a Columbia law professor. Out of prestigious law firms Frank hired Lee Pressman, Nathan Witt, and John Abt—all members of Harold Ware's underground Communist Party group during the 1930s. Pressman later served as general counsel of the Congress of Industrial Organizations, Witt as executive secretary of the National Labor Relations Board, and Abt as general counsel of the Communist Party of America. During the McCarthy period all three were hauled before HUAC and Witt and Abt refused to testify, relying on the Fifth Amendment privilege against self-incrimination.[18]

Felix Frankfurter assisted Frank in assembling this formidable legal staff. Frankfurter had long functioned as a kind of one-man employment agency. Previously his placement efforts had resulted in positions for young Harvard graduates in corporate firms; now Frankfurter's recommendations often led to legal positions in the New Deal. His efforts produced the first government legal staff of unquestioned competence.[19] Its quality was enhanced by an arrangement that Frank hammered out with Jim Farley, Roosevelt's patronage boss. They agreed to alternate AAA appointments. Since Farley did not care what position his appointees filled, Frank named all the talented lawyers and Farley controlled the clerical and supporting positions. Frank's quality staff went beyond those names made famous by history, and many unknown AAA lawyers had exceptional ability. While remarkable, the talented AAA legal staff was not alone among New Deal agencies. Others that benefited from extremely able legal staffs were the Interior Department, the Federal Trade Commission, and the Petroleum Industries Board.[20]

Government law practice varied significantly from practice in the private sector. During the nineteenth century important changes had occurred in the practice of law. From the stereotype of Daniel Webster orating fluently for hours evolved a new model of law practice. Centered in a law office rather than a courtroom, the new lawyer counseled clients on avoiding rather than pursuing litigation. The change in style of law practice was spurred by the enormous corporate growth of the late nineteenth century. To accommodate the needs of the giant corporations, law firms mushroomed in size in the early twentieth century. These new firms patterned themselves on the model of the firm of Paul D. Cravath.[21]

Cravath believed that the best recruit for the firm came from a law review editorship at an Ivy League school. Newcomers should receive training by working under the careful supervision of a senior associate or partner. Under this tutelage, young lawyers developed the skill of analyzing a legal problem in terms of its component parts. Members of the firm were expected to develop areas of specialization, but not before receiving broad exposure to diverse areas of law. Cravath thought that a large firm offering the talents of specialists in different areas best served the array of client problems. Accordingly, his firm expanded dramatically. Each associate was carefully weaned; as his competence grew, so did his responsibility. Not until the young attorney demonstrated mastery did he receive greater responsibility. This process, reinforced by a hierarchical staff organization, led to the gradual but steady advancement of hard-working and able associates. In the end, the Cravath system provided a finely tuned system of legal experts aided by industrious young associates.[22]

The New Deal gained the benefit of this kind of training by hiring Jerome Frank and many others from prestigious corporate firms.[23] They brought to government the techniques and organizational skills of private law office management. Frank's legal staff resembled the Cravath model in some respects but significantly departed from it in others. Like Cravath, Frank sought high-ranking law review students and organized his staff into divisions, each headed by an experienced attorney. This hierarchical organization resulted in legal documents—codes, licenses, and legislation—which were the products of group effort, not of a single legal mind. But unlike corporate law firms, the New Deal permitted young attorneys to assume major responsibility and power quickly. Legal staffs mirrored the pragmatic character of the New Deal. The urgent need for action during the worsening depression left

flexible the positions young attorneys could assume.[24] As Abe Fortas later observed, the New Deal offered a rare moment when
"there was practically no obstacle between thinking up an idea and
putting it into effect."[25]

In another respect the style of New Deal lawyering departed
substantially from that of the private sector. Unlike the Cravath
model, where the ultimate goal of exposing young attorneys to a
variety of substantive areas was to produce a proficient specialist,
the New Deal lawyer retained the generalist's ability to handle any
and all legal problems. A New Deal attorney often handled legal
problems that cut across a wide range of substantive legal areas.
Frank, for instance, after beginning his work as general counsel in
the Agricultural Adjustment Administration in 1933, served in
1935 as a special counsel to the Reconstruction Finance Corporation, a post that focused on problems of railroad reorganization. At
the end of 1935, when the New Deal faced the threat of losing
major power company cases, Secretary of the Interior Harold Ickes
appointed Frank special legal counsel to the Public Works Administration. In 1937 he became a member of the Securities and Exchange Commission, and in 1939 assumed the chairmanship of
that agency, a position he held until 1941 and his appointment to
the Second Circuit Court of Appeals. Through these years Frank
served the New Deal in other capacities. As a brain truster, he
helped in marathon sessions to draft a version of the National
Industrial Recovery Act. He also played a major role in the creation
of the Federal Surplus Relief Corporation and the Commodity
Credit Corporation.[26] From 1933 through 1935, he served informally as an adviser to Harry Hopkins when Hopkins headed the
Civil Works Administration and the Federal Emergency Relief
Administration. He typified the many New Deal attorneys who
bounced from agency to agency.[27] To some degree this pattern of
professional advancement stemmed from accidental but important
personal relations. Given the chaotic nature of the New Deal, persons worked with and through friends and acquaintances. On his
arrival in Washington, for instance, Frank lived with Henry Wallace
and Rexford Tugwell for some months. Their initial acquaintance
arose from the immediate need for housing, but friendship and

patterns of professional interaction developed, with Frank becoming a close adviser to Wallace and Tugwell.[28]

The style of the New Deal assumed the omnicompetence of lawyers. The New Deal used brilliant lawyers who, as generalists, were creative problem solvers. Today this pattern of professional advancement occurs less frequently. The federal legal service no longer encourages mobility from agency to agency, from one substantive area to another. At the end of the 1930s, legal positions began to be subject to civil service requirements.[29] Thus the New Deal constituted a distinctive moment in the history of the American bar. It relied on brilliant though unspecialized lawyers to bring fresh perspectives and imaginative proposals to bear on the social and economic crises of the time. In some areas prior legal experience was simply unavailable, and New Deal lawyers created whole new areas of substantive federal law, such as securities regulation through the Securities and Exchange Commission. The vast growth of administrative law epitomizes the legal universe shaped by New Deal lawyers.[30] New Deal lawyers worked at an intense pace. Marathon brainstorming sessions on drafts of important legislation, such as the National Industrial Recovery Act, were routine. Frank recalled that the initial idea for the Commodity Credit Corporation was scribbled on the back of an envelope and resulted in a $100 million appropriation written into law within five minutes.[31]

New Deal lawyers' lack of familiarity with certain businesses aroused consternation. In particular, there was the feeling that the Agriculture Department was run by city slickers who lacked any understanding of agriculture.[32] To some degree this was true. There is an anecdote about Lee Pressman, who was charged with responsibility for negotiating an agreement between the AAA and the macaroni industry. Given the plight of farmers, Frank insisted that the AAA should not give any business an antitrust exemption unless there was assurance that farmers would reap a portion of the benefits. At a crucial point in the negotiations, Pressman is reported to have asked in a raised voice, "But what will this code do for the macaroni growers?"[33]

Frank was sensitive to these charges but thought they were

mostly ruses designed to torpedo the actions of the AAA. He himself had acquired considerable experience in agricultural industries, particularly meat packing, during his corporate practice in
Chicago. But Frank did not care whether attorneys on his legal
staff had similar experience. For him a critical legal mind was the
only essential trait. "The very nature of being a lawyer is that you
pick up your context very quickly and apply techniques that either
have been used elsewhere or that you imagine."[34]

III

In the AAA Jerome Frank constantly faced attacks on the
grounds that he was a city slicker and a Jew, but the most frequent
charge was that he was a radical. Critics frequently accused Frank
and others of sabotaging American principles of government and
the economic system. Nothing could be further from the truth.
Above all else, Jerome Frank and the New Deal generally tried to
keep intact the contours of a profit system. In the light of later
events, it is remarkable that Alger Hiss, Lee Pressman, John Abt,
and Nathan Witt gathered under one roof. At the time, however,
these men of impeccably traditional credentials did not reveal left
leanings. Even in hindsight, very little has been brought out to
suggest that Alger Hiss was radical during his AAA years; as for
Pressman, Abt, and Witt, their Communist activities were limited
and apparently in no way affected their performance as attorneys
for the AAA. Indeed, Jerome Frank was very much surprised to
learn that his good friend Pressman had Communist leanings. He
found the charge incredible and its accuracy even more puzzling.[35]
Those who criticized Frank as "radical" failed to distinguish between total rejection of the economic system and a reexamination
of economic postulates. A collision occurred in the New Deal between two views as to how much reworking the American capitalist
system would require to survive. Frank saw a dichotomy between
those concerned with the general social welfare and those concerned with particular selfish interests.[36] To Frank the New Deal
would "permit the profit system to be tried, for the first time, as a
consciously directed means of promoting the general good." Ac-

cusations of radicalism came from persons who, Frank thought, were "real dangers to the social order" because of their "stubborn and blind refusal" to accept "needed revisions of traditional business practices."[37] "We are working like crazy men trying to save the capitalist system and the big capitalists are denouncing us as communists."[38] Their denunciations were fundamentally misplaced.

Frank's service on the Securities and Exchange Commission demonstrates that he was an ardent reformer but not a radical. He told Adolph Berle that the SEC existed "primarily to preserve the capitalist form."[39] During his term of service as commissioner and then as chairman of the SEC, the major tasks of the commission were to supervise the reorganization of public utility holding companies under the 1935 Holding Company Act and to reorganize the New York Stock Exchange. Frank wrote one iconoclastic book urging economic isolationism and another justifying government regulation to make business more competitive.[40] Frank was a confirmed capitalist of the liberal persuasion who abhorred determinism of any stripe.[41] Yet the New Deal ultimately purged Frank for advocating too much reform.

Ironically, Frank has been criticized for the opposite reason: that he prevented reform.[42] But it is a mistake to blame lawyers and legalism for stifling political reform during the 1930s. Roosevelt and his administration never aspired to transform the system of corporate capitalism, to alter significantly the distribution of wealth, or to change the allocation of political power. The New Deal hoped merely to soften the hard edges of an unbridled profit system. According to the New Deal economic world view, unabashed greed during the 1920s had brought the American economy to the brink of disaster. It tottered under the impact of fraudulent securities, poor banking practices, monopolistic industries, price gouging, and myriad other ruinous economic practices. Overreaching by corporate America, aided by lawyers, had precipitated an economic crisis that threatened to engulf private enterprise capitalism. As the stock market collapsed and the Depression worsened, lawyers tried to harness corporations.[43] The New Deal achieved enough significant changes to ensure the survival of corporate capitalism.[44] New Deal lawyers shared these limited aspirations. Thus limits to the New Deal came not from a philosophy of

77

legalism that hampered change but from a widely shared agreement that there would be no major alteration in the political system.[45]

Ethnic and religious prejudice has occupied a dominant place in American social history, yet its role in legal history has only recently been identified. Jerold Auerbach, in tracing the dominance of "elite" lawyers, unearthed material indicating that prominent law firms on Wall Street and elsewhere discriminated against Jews and other immigrant groups.[46] Religious and ethnic discrimination closed many doors for Ivy League law review graduates until the New Deal provided an avenue of professional mobility and success. Yet even the New Deal engaged in religious discrimination. Historians have documented the turn to anti-Semitism midway through Roosevelt's New Deal,[47] but it was far more pervasive than has been recognized, and ironically and tragically involved Jews themselves.

Anti-Semitism assumed subtle guises. One newspaper proclaimed it did not oppose Jews as such, but only Jews who were "notably inexperienced in farming."[48] Adlai Stevenson gave voice to another variant when he wrote to his wife that Jerome Frank, his boss as general counsel, "has none of the racial characteristics [of Jews]," but "there is a little feeling that the Jews are getting too prominent—as you know many of them are autocratic and the affect on the public—the industries that crowd our rooms all day— is bad." In Stevenson's judgment other Jews on Frank's staff, "though individually smart and able, are more racial."[49] Frank did not think his fight with AAA administrator George Peek stemmed from anti-Semitism but thought Peek so angry that he might "lend himself to that cause." Peek apparently opposed Frank's appointment as general counsel and complained to Wallace that appointing a Jew and city slicker would antagonize farmers.[50] Peek criticized the AAA legal staff: "There were too many Ivy League men, too many intellectuals, too many radicals, too many Jews."[51]

Anti-Semitism affected the composition of Jerome Frank's legal staff, prompting him to limit the number of Jews hired. In writing to Felix Frankfurter for staff recommendations, he lamented: "One of my problems, as you can well appreciate, is the possibility of having too many Jews on the legal staff. Unfortunately, most of these capable young fellows from Harvard to Columbia, and even

Yale, bear that disability." As Frank augmented his staff, he wrote again to Frankfurter inquiring whether he could recommend other men "who would not suffer because of religious disabilities."[52] On another occasion, Frank intentionally selected one of three candidates for a legal position precisely because he was not Jewish, thus antagonizing his assistant, Frank Shea, who accused Frank of being anti-Semitic.[53]

In one remarkable memorandum Frank described himself as "embarrassed" by the number of Jewish lawyers at the AAA. Despite assurances from the Administration that Frank should continue to recommend the ablest persons of whatever creed, Frank wrote to his three assistants charged with making most recommendations: "I have again and again urged you . . . if possible to recommend lawyers who were not Jews."[54] In another memorandum, to Secretary of Agriculture Henry Wallace, Frank reviewed prospective candidates for the legal staff, assessing their backgrounds, their references, and, as to each, whether they were Jewish. "[Lee Pressman] is an exceptionally able lawyer, and I should greatly like to have him as one of my assistants. However, he is a Jew."[55] The New Deal placed Jews in the sardonic position of acting as self-censors and discriminators against fellow Jews in order to avoid political repercussions.

According to Frank, some newspapers used anti-Semitism as a red herring for broader political attacks on the New Deal.[56] At one point Frank entered into an angry exchange with General W. I. Westervelt, head of the AAA Processing and Marketing Division, accusing him of leaking anti-Semitic stories to the *Kiplinger Letter*.[57] Later Frank remembered this incident as the only occasion when anti-Semitism affected him personally.[58] Frank's recollection was inaccurate. In 1939, Roosevelt considered appointing Frank to the U.S. Court of Appeals for the District of Columbia but did not do so because of the number of Jews he had recently appointed to the bench.[59] The problem arose again two years later, when FDR considered Frank for the Second Circuit Court of Appeals. In the midst of that controversy Frank wrote to Harry Hopkins:

The press also learned—obviously not from me—that, when such a vacancy occurred [in 1939] he [Roosevelt] failed to fulfill that promise

79

solely because I was a Jew and too many Jews had been, recently, put on the bench. . . . I was publicly humiliated by that publicity. . . . The tale spread all over New York—and may soon break into print that I won't be appointed—again because I'm a Jew.

Frank was angry over and disappointed by this new instance of anti-Semitism. He lamented to Hopkins that failure to appoint him would be interpreted as meaning that "when it comes to selecting a Jew for the judiciary I can't make the grade. I've been a good soldier. . . . But just because I'm loyal and won't start a rumpus . . . is no reason why I should again be publicly humiliated."[60] Ultimately, of course, Roosevelt did appoint Frank to the Second Circuit.

IV

Roosevelt responded to the social and economic crisis by relying significantly on positive law to combat social unrest. The frenzy of the "hundred days" created a great need for legal help because, to a degree previously unmatched in American political history, the New Deal relied on new legislation. This legislation had to be formulated, drafted, and then navigated through a sometimes reluctant Congress. Statutes were augmented by a bewildering array of regulations, codes, licenses, agreements, and legal opinions. Lawyers were charged with defending these laws in litigation before frequently recalcitrant courts and with coercing compliance from an obdurate private sector.

Efforts to gather support for New Deal legislation were not confined to lobbying on Capitol Hill. Jerome Frank and other members of his AAA staff frequently made political speeches to concerned farm groups. Fireside chats were not limited to Franklin Delano Roosevelt; cabinet-rank officials as well as lower ranking administrators and members of legal staffs often spoke on radio. It was imperative that the administration explain to the public, especially farmers and others in rural districts, the aims and purposes of new legislation. Jerome Frank in particular showed a crisp awareness of the role of the press in molding public opinion. His files contain literally hundreds of letters to columnists, editors, and publishers about issues of public importance. Even slight criticism in print of administration actions prompted Frank to retort.

These functions, while important to the effectiveness of the New Deal, were hardly unique to New Deal lawyers. Lobbying, drafting legislation, negotiating agreements, and defending or initiating litigation had all been done by nineteenth-century American lawyers.[61] The career of Louis Brandeis, as private attorney and as public ombudsman from 1897 to 1916, illustrates how these tactics previously had been used to marshal support. Brandeis used political endorsements and newspaper editorials, along with a host of more traditional legal techniques, to affect public opinion and thereby political results.[62] What was distinctive to the New Deal was the quantity and quality of legal help tapped by the administration.

Lawyers did more than legal work. While many attorneys served as administrators, filling cabinet-level and other high-ranking executive positions, others became legislators. On occasion some lawyers acted as advisers to high New Deal officials.[63] In these instances administration officials sought good judgment and counsel; the lawyers' contribution did not depend solely on specialized legal skills or talents. Early in his administration Roosevelt relied on the so-called brain trust to find ways to cope with the worsening depression.[64] Some brain trusters were lawyers, others economists, political scientists, or sociologists. At the broadest level of policy formation, lawyers contributed ideas but not always specifically legal skills. One did not need an attorney to suggest industrial and agricultural reforms as a means of combating economic depression and social unrest.

But when it came to drafting statutes and implementing policy, Frank and the other New Deal lawyers played a key role. The New Deal uniquely depended on attorneys to translate new ideas into workable programs. That meant dealing with people whose ideologies or economic interests were threatened by proposed reform. It was one thing to agree on the best course of action; it was quite another to drag recalcitrant businessmen into actual compliance. That was the task of New Deal lawyers.

New Deal lawyers needed to anticipate objections to augmented governmental power, and to draft legislation that would meet those objections yet still fulfill policy goals. Challenges to New Deal legislation occurred on the grand level of constitutional power and on the more mundane plane of statutory construction as vague language created loopholes for the devious. Above all, New Deal programs had to exact compliance from the business community. Even the National Industrial Recovery Act, a "voluntary" act, had important coercive aspects.[65] Thus New Deal lawyers had to assess not only whether a proposed act was a legitimate exercise of constitutional power, but also whether it was workable. Would a person of ill will and bad motives still need to comply with the act? The New Deal lawyer performed a unique function as legal strategist. Harry Hopkins, head of the Federal Emergency Relief Administration, feared that legal technicalities would bog down his policies and so relied informally on Jerome Frank for legal advice rather than appoint a full-time attorney. Eventually Hopkins did hire Lee Pressman, after Pressman had been fired during the purge at the AAA. Hopkins gave Pressman one instruction: "The first time you tell me that I can't do what I want to, you're fired. I'm going to decide what I think has to be done and it's up to you to see that it's legal."[66]

Brilliant lawyers, such as Frank, understood that doing battle with opposing groups and interests necessitated careful attention to strategy. As Frank told AAA Administrator Chester Davis, "I want to win cases and have our job stand up in court."[67] Therefore, he insisted from the outset that he and his staff pass legal judgment on any document that required Secretary Wallace's approval.[68] This process involved the legal staff at an early stage and ensured repeated consultation and legal overview. Those persons who opposed Frank's policy predilections asserted that his staff often obstructed the flow and efficiency of the AAA. Frank defended his staff for performing what he saw as its three functions: first, to draft instruments; second, to indicate legal difficulties that might arise; and third, to use "ingenuity" in suggesting ways to avoid legal obstacles. "Skill in that third function involves equal skill in the other two functions; a lawyer who is a careless draftsman or who is unable to recognize legal difficulties is unable to suggest methods of circumventing legal obstacles. None of those three functions can be discharged by robots."[69]

As counsel for the government in several railroad reorganization cases, Frank encountered able opposing counsel and showed his sophistication in shaping legal arguments. His maneuvering sometimes rivaled the intricacy of a master chess player's game plan.[70] Even though the Supreme Court held the Agricultural Adjustment Act unconstitutional in *United States v. Butler,* there still remained room for an able attorney to construe narrowly the Court's decision and salvage some power for the AAA.[71]

Frank's strategic abilities also figured prominently in cases challenging the constitutionality of the Public Works Administration (PWA). The PWA could initiate construction projects, allow other federal agencies to develop projects, and offer a combination of loans and grants to state and local governments. Conceptions of the proper role for public works ranged from stimulating heavy industries to providing relief and employment to building aesthetic national monuments. The PWA constructed roads, sewer and water systems, schools, courthouses, hospitals, dams, and even aircraft carriers. It generated an enormous need for workers, constructed its projects honestly and efficiently, and left a durable legacy of impressive accomplishments.[72] In the PWA cases, Frank arranged for the submission of amicus briefs and coordinated the advice and support of experts in the legal academy.[73] Frank became counsel only long after the litigation had commenced. At that point he found that the cases were on appeal but had not been adequately tried. His predecessor had demurred to facts that made damaging admissions that the administrator, Harold Ickes, had abused his statutory powers in a number of ways. With those facts admitted, Frank clearly saw grave peril to the legality of the statute, "since there would be such a bad 'atmosphere' as to arouse marked hostility on the part of the most liberal Justices when the cases were argued in the Supreme Court." By careful legal maneuvering, Frank had these cases remanded to lower courts for findings of fact. At these trials—which Frank won—he established evidence flatly contradicting the factual assertions to which his predecessor had previously demurred. Having removed "the bad atmosphere," Frank emerged victorious in the Supreme Court. He later said, "I strongly suspect that, but for those trial tactics, PWA and the valuable policy it represented would have been judicially destroyed."[74]

Awareness of strategic options did not necessarily translate into court victories. Indeed, several factors hampered the effectiveness of AAA lawyers. Frank desired as much autonomy as possible for his brilliant legal staff in litigating AAA cases, but for a long time the Department of Justice would not permit him independence. At one point Lee Pressman complained to Frank, "The situation with respect to the Department of Justice has gone from bad to worse. Not only have they insufficient personnel to handle the situation (and poor personnel at that) but they are delaying matters considerably before getting around to them, are revising our pleadings, etc., causing considerable delay."[75] Yet Attorney General Homer Cummings reaffirmed that the Department of Justice would maintain control of litigation for all agencies. In addition, while the legal staff included some seasoned veterans, others had little or no practical experience either with litigation or with agriculture. The exigencies of the moment required Frank to rely on these neophyte attorneys to oppose skilled trial lawyers. Finally, all the strategy and experience in the world could not overcome the antipathy of a federal judiciary that perceived FDR as the devil incarnate. While legal realism may have attuned Frank to political reality, it could not alter that reality.[76]

V

American legal realism, through the writings of Jerome Frank, Karl Llewellyn, William O. Douglas, and others, emphasized flexibility as the operating principle of the American judicial system. This recognition helped realist lawyers to understand why the law lacked predictability and certainty. While there was no necessary logical correlation between legal realism and New Deal liberalism, prominent legal realists, including Jerome Frank, William Douglas, Thurman Arnold, Herman Oliphant, Wesley Sturges, Walton Hamilton, and Felix Cohen, served Roosevelt's administration. Their legal philosophy fitted well with the experimental and flexible nature of the New Deal.[77]

Jerome Frank understood clearly this relationship and guided his actions at the AAA by his underlying philosophy of legal realism. The success he enjoyed as a New Deal lawyer was partly a function of the philosophical sophistication he brought to bear on traditional legal work. Legal realism, to Frank, clarified and somewhat justified judicial result orientation.

> Many judges . . . tend to commence their thinking with what they consider a desirable decision and then work backward to appropriate premises, devising syllogisms to justify that decision. . . . Those who sympathize (whether or not avowedly) with experimental jurisprudence have found it easy to work for the New Deal. It is not only because they are less procrustean and more flexible in their techniques. It is because legal institutions and devices are constantly viewed by them as human contrivances to be judged by their every day human consequences. Accordingly, the experimentalists are stimulated by the opportunity to help contrive new governmental agencies to be used experimentally as means for achieving better results in agriculture, industry, labor conditions, taxation, corporate reorganization, municipal finance, unemployment relief, and a multitude of other subjects.[78]

Frank and other New Deal lawyers attempted to make law more responsible to social needs; a conscious jurisprudence shaped their activities.

Constitutional historians have sometimes portrayed the Supreme Court during the New Deal as an especially anachronistic and reactionary body that thwarted the major reforms propounded by Roosevelt.[79] Even ardent supporters of the New Deal, however, saw that some major legislation was in danger of exceeding the constitutional powers of the federal government. Frank believed that only an actual court decision could determine an act's constitutionality, and that the decision would turn on the facts found and on the precise legal issue presented and decided.[80] It was impossible to know in advance whether a court would declare a particular action legal or illegal. Thus a finding of constitutionality might depend on how carefully a defense of the statute was constructed. In fixing prices and prorating goods among distributors and shippers, the AAA invited challenge as to whether or not this kind of federal regulation was a legitimate exercise of the interstate commerce power. Frank recognized that the validity of AAA licenses and agreements would depend to a substantial degree on supporting economic data. He insisted that government economists have supporting data, for "it is only with such economic justification that we can hope to support the same legally."[81] His position reflects a central tenet of legal realism—that social and economic variables substantially affect legal doctrine and judicial results.

In a similar vein, Frank believed there was a strong correlation between political and popular support on the one hand and judicial response on the other. In the early New Deal, district courts, including some conservative judges, sustained the powers of the government under the stress of the national emergency. As Frank put it, federal judges thought "the world was coming to an end and the New Deal would save it."[82] Courts had at that time resolved dubious questions in favor of the New Deal. As enthusiasm for Roosevelt and his administrative programs waned, however, the judicial response changed. At that point the uncertain constitutionality of New Deal measures made it imperative for Frank to avoid taking cases to the U.S. Supreme Court. Avoiding litigation became essential in order to permit the New Deal to continue to function.[83]

To implement AAA policies, Frank steadfastly maintained that a good portion of any price increase actually go to farmers and, simultaneously, that the consumer not be gouged through windfall profits of middlemen. Others in the AAA, particularly Administrators Peek and Davis, were content if the farmer received an increase in price. As one of them bluntly commented: "What in the hell have we got to do with the consumer. This is the Department of Agriculture!"[84] Frank understood that one could not neatly separate legal questions from political reality. A strong correlation between administrative implementation and subsequent judicial scrutiny required the AAA to ensure against undue profits to middlemen. Otherwise Frank predicted "hostility" from judges concerned with the interest of consumers.[85] Judicial belief that the AAA failed to protect consumers would affect court decisions on questions of constitutionality and on interpretations of statutory powers. Frank, the legal realist operating as New Deal attorney, understood that judges were not only human but political, and that a lawyer's job was to convince courts that the agency was doing a good job.

Frank criticized legal counsel for the National Recovery Administration for failing to appreciate that antimonopoly judges, such as Justice Brandeis, would be unsympathetic to such an autocratic organization as the NRA, and that the pace and mood of the country—the strength of the country's support for the New Deal—had a decided though unquantifiable impact on court decisions. While Frank at the AAA prodded economists to supply supporting data, the legal staff at the NRA was less attuned to principles of legal realism. Jerome Frank participated in litigation strategy sessions for defense of the National Industrial Recovery Act. In his judgment it was poorly handled:

> They got themselves euchered [sic] into the position where they took up that "sick chicken" case which was one of the silliest. [NRA administrator Hugh] Johnson was regulating barbershops; he was regulating everything. He had paid no attention to what was essential and what wasn't. He paid no attention to the problem that was bound to face us in the courts with respect to interstate commerce. It may be that—and I feel fairly confident of this—if the codes had been fairly handled—the way we had contemplated, with a few codes—and if it had been administered with an idea to increasing production, it wouldn't have been declared unconstitutional.
>
> But you had in the Supreme Court not only men who were opposed to any governmental interference but you had Brandeis who was a fanatic on the subject of protecting the consumer. When you used high-handed monopolistic powers this way, you were bound to offend him.[86]

In a revealing exchange of letters with Felix Frankfurter, Jerome Frank expounded his concept of New Deal lawyering and its relationship to legal realism. Frankfurter cautioned Frank to avoid novel arguments and broad implications, for "the essence of 'functionalisms' and 'realism' in advocacy is to win a case and not to vindicate new philosophic insight."[87] Frank replied that he had presented traditional and narrow arguments in the important Public Works cases. His strategy was to

> assert on behalf of the government no more power than is necessary to justify the precise action heretofore taken by it. You ought to know that I do not believe in trying to vindicate abstract principles and that

to me the important thing is to win *particular* cases. Also, you should know, without my telling you, that I do not believe in such a thing as an abstract judiciary, and that I am convinced that particular cases are won by appealing to the particular attitudes of the particular judges by whom those particular cases are determined.[88]

Unpersuaded, Frankfurter labeled Frank a "romantic intellectual who finds it not wholly easy in view of your brilliance and wide reading to use language that will make the Sutherlands of this world feel that you are their kind of fellow. Please note that I do not say the McReynoldses."[89] Frankfurter continued to chastise Frank's legal realism:

May the Lord forgive me if I have thought erroneously that you have been a little too much under the influence of the notion that courts decide the way they want to decide apart from what they say is the way they have decided. In other words, not the least propelling force of a good deal of the bar and the bench is the simple-minded effort to square a present case with past formulations. And even sophisticated judges like Learned Hand and Mack and Cardozo and Brandeis and Holmes, pay considerable allegiance to that form of intellectual loyalty.[90]

Frank replied:

I have been writing briefs for 21 years for upper and lower courts, and have been moderately successful. . . . My notion in brief-writing has always been that one must use the particular kind of jargon and articulate one's idea in terms of the particular kind of precedential language that, so far as one can conjecture, will be most pleasing to the particular tribunal to which the argument is addressed. My belief is that the appeal to the man inside the ermine will fail signally if that man likes to think—as most judges like to think—that the appeal ad hominem cannot touch him. Therefore, the appeal ad hominem must in most cases be artfully concealed and take on the guise of traditional judicial cant.[91]

The exchange continued as Frankfurter wrote: "I still continue to think that you are wrong in thinking, as I believe you think, that most of the law is bunk, but that you dish up bunk because other people like to feed on it. All of which has nothing to do with your skill as an artist in making the judges believe that you like the fare which you serve them."[92]

Frank responded:

I don't say that "most law is bunk". You remember the farmer who was asked if he believed in baptism and who replied, "Believe in it? Hell, I've seen it". I think "law" is damned real. But I do not believe that it works the way it appears, on the surface, to work. I think that many legal ceremonials could be eliminated. But while they exist, they play an important part in their effects on human lives. Therefore, as lawyer, I want to be well up on them and meticulously practice them. To use highbrow terms, I think that, pragmatically, practice, procedure and substantive law inter-mingle or, to put it differently, "substantive law" is merely one of the implements used in a court fight,— one of the implements of persuasion used to induce a court to issue an order which will be backed by armed force, if necessary, to compel some one to do what your client wants him to do.[93]

Not surprisingly, Frank felt wounded by Frankfurter's criticism. "Your impression of me as a brilliant but naively brave spirit might be pleasing if expressed in an epitaph—but I'm still alive."[94]

The New Deal relied on the services of prominent American legal realists who understood clearly that law was a social institution. They created administrative agencies and devised constitutional arguments to sustain their powers. They understood political hostility and its conscious or unconscious impact on judges and accordingly framed arguments aimed at winning cases rather than vindicating abstract principles. The experimental nature both of the New Deal and of American legal realism coalesced to allow brillant legal minds an opportunity to apply their legal philosophy in defense of Franklin Roosevelt's efforts to combat the Depression.[95]

VI

The New Deal period saw an enormous growth in administrative law and "alphabet" agencies. The work of lawyers molded the modern regulatory state; it was naturally lawyers that drafted, shaped, and created these new agencies.[96]

Jerome Frank's career reflects the scope and character of the New Deal legal imagination. An example is his role in the birth of the Federal Surplus Relief Corporation. The economic problems confronting Roosevelt's administration included a surplus of cotton, wheat, hogs and other commodities at the same time that malnutrition and hunger plagued those without jobs or money. The administration moved to curtail crops and cut back on the raising of hogs and other animals in an effort to reduce the surpluses. According to traditional laws of supply and demand, this action would raise prices and ease the economic plight of American farmers. But turning fields under and slaughtering pigs in the face of massive human deprivation posed a political dilemma and liability. As baby pigs were slaughtered to reduce the glut of hogs on the market, cries of outrage assailed the administration. Several people suggested the obvious solution of giving the surplus food to hungry people. Eleanor Roosevelt asked the AAA to send meat to miners in West Virginia; the National Corn-Hog Committee called for the sale or donation of surplus food to relief agencies; economist Mordecai Ezekial urged that the Federal Emergency Relief Administration (FERA) put surplus food to good use. On September 11, 1933, FDR wrote to Henry Wallace: "Will you and Peek and Harry Hopkins have a talk and possibly prepare a plan for the purchase of surplus commodities such as butter, cheese, condensed milk, hog products and flour, to meet relief needs during the course of the winter."[97] While it is difficult to ascertain exactly who first conceived the notion of distributing surplus food to the starving, the absurdity of destroying hogs while people went hungry was widely perceived.

At the AAA, Jerome Frank suggested to Rexford Tugwell that Harry Hopkins ought to use the surplus hogs, but opposition arose from the farm leaders and George Peek, who argued that Hopkins, as administrator of the FERA, would therefore reduce his meat purchases, thus making the program self-defeating. Since the destruction of surplus food aimed to rebalance the laws of supply and demand, these food programs would move in the wrong direction. Frank persevered and asked Hopkins whether he was buying any meat; he was not. Nonetheless opposition continued. One Sunday Tugwell and Hopkins came to Frank's home to prepare for a meeting with Roosevelt the next day. They discussed ways to distribute food and agreed to a joint venture between the AAA, which would buy the products, and the FERA, which would pay for processing them (since the AAA lacked funds for that purpose). Frank proposed the Federal Surplus Relief Corporation (FSRC), and they discussed directors for it. The next day Roosevelt approved the proposal and instructed Frank to proceed.[98] At this point, they were really no further than the idea itself; all agreed that Hopkins should have the food to distribute, but how to do it remained unclear. According to Tugwell, Frank "supplied the legal ingenuity."[99] Frank recounted:

> I was bothered that if we organized this corporation, the Controller General would step in and say we had no right to organize, although the Corporation itself would really be a conduit. I was worried that he would raise hell and cause all kinds of difficulties. So I did something that maybe was politically immoral. I organized the corporation. It cost about $35 to organize it and I paid it out of my own pocket. I never got the money back. Fortunately the next session of Congress appropriated money to this corporation which legitimized it. It stopped being a bastard and changed its name later to the Federal Surplus Relief Corporation.[100]

Frank created a government corporation with independent status. More recently, this legal form has become common—witness the Legal Services Corporation, the Corporation for Public Broadcasting, and Amtrak—but in 1933 it was highly unorthodox.[101] Moreover, congressional enabling legislation had authorized all past government corporations.[102] Frank chartered the corporation in Delaware in order to give it independent legal status and invest it with the broadest possible powers.[103] He then served as general counsel to the FSRC for two years, until November 1935.[104] The FSRC was the federal government's first effort to distribute surplus food to needy persons. It might have had a short and uneventful life had not Frank used the independent corporate form. The FSRC clearly represented a major departure in governmental policy toward surplus agricultural products. All previous efforts had aimed at alleviating the plight of the farmer; this program, by contrast, took the form of a relief program for the destitute. The FSRC would have collapsed at the termination of the FERA in 1935 had the corporate form not allowed the food assistance program to continue beyond the life of its parent agency.[105]

Frank's legal creativity was again called into play with regard to the marketing agreement of the meat-packing industry. The Agricultural Adjustment Act permitted the secretary to grant an exemption from the antitrust laws to the extent that the marketing agreement effected the declared policy of the act. The agreement proposed by the meat packers contained all kinds of special exemptions but little in the way of promises other than vague assurances that the farmer would be compensated adequately. Frank argued that permitting this antitrust exemption would not further the declared policies of the AAA unless the secretary were empowered to inspect the books and records of the meat-packing firms in order to ensure that some portion of the increased profits went to the farmers. Frank inserted a clause in the agreement permitting the secretary to inspect corporate books and records. "I suppose I got the idea from corporate accounting, or one thing or another, or from my previous legal training."[106] Now the AAA could police the industry and prevent windfall profits. Frank's proposal attempted to translate the act's vague policy objectives into a realistic program.

Frank also helped to create the Federal Register, which publishes regulations of federal administrative agencies. Marketing agreements with the AAA bound all members of a particular industry or area. Often, however, these agreements were hammered out with select members of the affected group. This process posed a major legal problem: how could the government constitutionally impose an agreement on persons who had not participated in its formulation? Procedural due process with its requirement of notice presented an awesome legal obstacle. While Frank and others muddled through by giving legal notice to newspapers, governors, mayors, and others in the affected area, they were quite aware of the dubious legality of that form.

This legal problem beset a number of government agencies and legal staffs. At a cocktail party, Frank discussed with Erwin N. Griswold, later dean of Harvard Law School, the problem of locating government regulations that were not published in any single or comprehensive way. Later Frank recalled, "Let me say first that the most important things that happened in Washington in those days were over cocktails. Martinis did an awful lot to stimulate thinking. Maybe some of the Republicans would say that it sounded that way."[107] Frank and Griswold pursued the matter with others in government and ultimately proposed to Roosevelt that regulatory information be gathered in a central publication. Opposition came from right-wing groups that viewed a government reporting system in competition with private enterprise as a socialistic endeavor totally at odds with American democratic principles. Griswold later wrote an article in the *Harvard Law Review* about government ignorance of the law. Justice Brandeis, to whom Griswold had sent a copy of the article, prodded a government attorney during oral argument on a regulation that had been attached to the wrong piece of paper. The embarrassment caused by Brandeis' action finally prompted the president to encourage Frank to assemble a committee to produce a draft statute addressing the problem. Subsequently enacted by Congress, the Federal Register has become an important source of constructive notice satisfying the constitutional command of procedural due process.[108]

The policy of the AAA, at least as Frank envisioned it, was that any profits that resulted from a marketing agreement that exempted an industry from the antitrust laws ought to go partly to farmers, partly to consumers, and partly to industry. But these savings proved difficult to assess. The formula that industry wished to use to determine profit was "fair return on fair value." Decades of experience had shown this formula to be meaningless.[109] An alternative effort to assess "cost of production" had proved equally unsatisfactory. Drawing on the ideas of economists in the AAA, Frank created a new approach that he called "savings in actual expenses": any change in profits from those of a base-period year was attributed to exemption from the antitrust laws.[110] This method would have simplified the task of assessment, yielded a workable formula, and produced a "savings fund." The AAA would then allocate this savings fund among consumers, farmers, and industry. Once more Jerome Frank creatively blended law and economics to try to make the AAA effective.

VII

Lawyers served the New Deal in executive and administrative positions where their express role was to create and shape policy. But government attorneys also often determined policy while acting as lawyers, and this role has largely been ignored.[111] Law and policy are inescapably intertwined, yet historians have mistakenly perceived lawyers as concerned only with legal questions. Jerold Auerbach, for instance, in arguing that a philosophy of legalism set limits to the New Deal, incorrectly identified Jerome Frank as typifying this attitude.[112] Auerbach saw Frank as indifferent to substantive policy and as focusing only on narrow technical, legal questions.

To answer legal questions, lawyers needed to understand policy objectives. To draft legislation, attorneys had to know the purposes behind proposed bills. Faced with uncertain objectives, lawyers might identify the competing choices for administrators to select among, or might choose one and proceed accordingly. With the emergence of administrative due process in the New Deal, lawyers enjoyed a kind of "veto power" on how an agency might proceed.[113] Thus lawyers acted not merely as technicians but also as policy makers.

This function created conflict, sometimes severe, with administrators. An example is the struggle in the AAA between George Peek, and later Chester Davis, on the one hand, and Jerome Frank and the legal staff, aided by Blaisdell and Tugwell, on the other. Peek and Davis attempted to portray Frank as an overreaching lawyer encroaching on their domain as administrators. They correctly saw Frank urging and shaping important questions of policy but mistakenly accused him of exceeding his proper function as a lawyer. They did not appreciate the policy function performed by lawyers, whether in or out of government, in shaping and creating legal doctrine. The initial conflict leading to Peek's resignation and the ultimate purge of Frank and his supporters centered on such ideological differences.[114] Ultimately Jerome Frank's ouster represented a repudiation of his policy objectives. Frank wished to aid tenant farmers and sharecroppers and also to protect consumers in AAA actions. George Peek and Chester Davis thought raising farm prices would ultimately benefit the entire economy, including consumers. Their allegiance, however, was to farmers, not to consumers.

As a good lawyer, Frank understood his role as counsellor and insisted on approving the legality of all documents signed by Secretary of Agriculture Henry Wallace.[115] In this way Frank insulated the AAA from some legal challenges. At the same time this role involved the general counsel at an early and crucial stage of policy formation and implementation. Much of Frank's and his staff's time was occupied in drafting codes, licenses, and agreements for various commodities and businesses regulated by the AAA. It was Frank's province to ensure harmony between the AAA and NRA and to enforce the codes, licenses, and marketing agreements pertaining to agriculture. He was thus able to exert considerable influence over the policy direction of the AAA. Given the ideological split between Frank and the administrators, Peek and Davis interpreted this influence as meddling in their business. Frank insisted that correct interpretation of the act demanded an understanding of the policies the act embodied. If, for example, a marketing agreement failed to fulfill the act's policies, Frank would withhold legal approval. Furthermore, he would develop counterproposals that would better effectuate the act's policies. He justified this practice by referring to Wallace's request that he "do more than be a lawyer."[116] To Felix Frankfurter, Frank expressed his feeling that the general counsel should formulate theories and techniques to defend the constitutionality of the act and should protect consumers and labor in connection with agreements and licenses.[117]

Yet Frank was sensitive to charges of interfering with policy matters properly within the domain of the administrators. After Ezekiel, an Agriculture Department economist, had apparently accused Frank of expressing policy views "under the guise of a legal opinion," Frank wrote to Chester Davis that he "leaned over backwards to avoid any such inclination. . . . I can think of nothing more unfair to you than the employment by me of such a device. It would mean that, where I feared you would disagree with me on a question of policy, I would be throwing a monkeywrench into the machinery by converting my judgment on pure policy into a judgment about the law."[118]

On one occasion, after Jerome Frank and Abe Fortas had prepared a legal opinion with respect to the cottonseed oil refining industry, in which they had urged a number of changes in the code in order to implement the policy of the act, Frank followed the legal opinion with another memorandum a week later, interestingly captioned "Policy Memorandum for Mr. Davis supplementing attached legal memorandum." It purports to draw hard and fast lines between law on the one hand and policy on the other. Repeatedly Frank noted that "I am not giving a legal opinion that those provisions on their face, are unlawful, but I am making the above suggestions as *policy suggestions* for your consideration." He attempted to segregate carefully law from policy and did not, by subterfuge, push his policy predilections. Frank's directness appears to have been in harmony with the rest of his career and philosophy. As the author of *Law and the Modern Mind* with its plea for the modern mind free from childish ways, Frank tried often to be direct and open about his possible motivations, both conscious and unconscious. Nonetheless, in this instance Frank was swept away by his own ideas of policy. Indeed, he and Fortas were urging certain policy dispositions not favored by the then current administrator of the AAA. While protesting that his legal judgment was not an attempt to influence policy, he also asserted:

> Of course, it is true that a lawyer's opinion is only a guess as to what the courts will decide, and that in forming his guess the lawyer cannot avoid taking into account to what extent the courts are likely to be influenced by the economic desirability of a particular statute, contract or other instrument. To that extent consideration of policy influences a lawyer's opinion on almost anything, but that factor should not play at all a dominant role in a lawyer's thinking. With respect to marketing agreements under the Agricultural Adjustment Act questions of policy to a somewhat larger, although still restricted, sense become questions of law since the statute expressly authorizes the Secretary to enter into such agreements only if they effectuate the "declared policy" of the Act.[119]

On another occasion, after insisting that "it goes without saying" that policy was for the administrator to determine, Frank expressed a view contrary to the policy of the administrator.[120] Frank actively sought to influence policy. Early in his tenure as general counsel he put forward a comprehensive view of the principles he thought should govern the development of marketing agreements. While he called them "tentative suggestions," he clung tenaciously to them during succeeding months and years.[121]

At one point, after insisting to Davis that he would accept whatever policy Davis settled on, Frank continued immediately to assert that "insofar as a policy question has an obvious legal aspect—as for instance whether a license or agreement violates 'the declared policy of the Act'—it will still be necessary for me to consider that policy question."[122] This reservation gave Frank ample opportunity to push his policy views under the aura of legal judgment. Section 8 of the AAA allowed the secretary to enter marketing agreements only "in order to effectuate the declared policy" of the act. Frank took the position that to be legal, a marketing agreement must effectuate that policy. But what was that policy? As the attorney charged with interpreting the act, Jerome Frank naturally had to assess the policy objectives. Not unexpectedly, he decided the act intended protection for both farmers and consumers.[123] When the meat packers sought a marketing agreement with the AAA, Frank used the preamble to urge the secretary to reject the agreement, which offered "nothing but the vaguest hopes" that farmers would receive any price increase or that consumers would be protected.[124] Since "the declared policy of the Act" was an issue in every code and license, this back-door route allowed Frank to urge on the administrator whatever position Frank preferred.

In his effort to aid consumers Frank seized on the AAA preamble, which indicated a desire to help consumers. Frank urged Tugwell and Ezekiel to grant consumers special representation. Secretary of Agriculture Henry Wallace ultimately agreed and created a Consumers Counsel within the AAA. This division, staffed by Fred Howe with assistance from Thomas Blaisdell and Gardner Jackson, aligned itself with Frank over the next couple of years.[125] Although Frank later recalled that the preamble was not "transparently clear," he often relied on it to justify a major policy choice.[126]

The blend of law and policy emerged clearly in a battle Frank waged for the insertion of his favorite "books and records" clause in the Cottonseed Code of Fair Competition. The code came to

Frank for his assessment of legality and he used the opportunity to push once more his views on the protection of consumers. He tied his policy preferences to possible legal challenges to a code lacking the "books and records" clause. Frank argued that under Section 3 of the NIRA a code could grant exemption from the antitrust laws only if it was "not designed to promote monopolies or to eliminate or oppress small enterprises."[127] To Frank, a "books and records" clause was absolutely necessary to enforce the code and to prevent violations of Section 3. The missing link in his analysis was that a code of fair competition without such a clause would still be valid so long as it did not in fact promote a monopoly or oppress small businesses. The absence of a "books and records" clause did not transform a legal code into an illegal code.

Several important policy factors informed Frank's legal judgment. Abundant evidence suggested that the cottonseed industry had previously violated the antitrust laws. Indeed, the Department of Justice and the Federal Trade Commission currently had the industry under scrutiny for antitrust violations.[128] Frank believed that the absence of an effective enforcement mechanism would permit unscrupulous businesses to reap windfall benefits at the expense of both farmers and consumers. He was probably right in urging the insertion of a "books and records" clause, for the clause would have given the administrator effective means to supervise industry and thus afford protection to farmers and consumers. It is clear, however, that his argument for the clause rested on policy rather than strictly legal grounds.

Preoccupation with policy ultimately led to Frank's ouster as general counsel of the AAA. The AAA had decided upon acreage reduction as a major tool for reducing farm surpluses. This decision created a problem particularly in the South, where there were many tenant farmers and sharecroppers. When the AAA reduced acreage on large corporate farms, how would apportionment, if any, occur among those who were cultivating portions of the larger farm? At a time when unrest and incipient unionism stirred tenant farmers, acreage reduction provided a vehicle for larger farmers to evict troublesome tenants. Paragraph 7 of the Cotton Acreage Reduction Contract provided that the reduction would occur among all tenants, and the farmer would "insofar as possible, maintain on his farm the normal number of tenants and other employees; [and] shall permit all tenants to continue in the occupancy of their houses on his farm."[129] Paragraph 7 thus hedged the issue of whether the contract required the farmer to keep the *same* tenants or only the same *number* of tenants. The ambiguity stemmed from the intentionally vague contract language, which aimed to finesse the conflict between those who wanted to offer some protection to tenant farmers and those who did not.[130] Thus the stage was set for a major conflict over AAA policy.

For a year the Cotton Section of the AAA had been interpreting paragraph 7 to permit the eviction of tenants. When this situation came to Frank's attention, he set in motion a procedure for the Legal Division to issue a new interpretation. Meanwhile, sharecroppers on Fairview Farms Company land in Arkansas petitioned Secretary Wallace to intercede on their behalf in an eviction proceeding. He referred the petition to the Committee on Violations of Rental and Benefit Contracts. By a 2-to-1 vote the committee decided that it was inadvisable for the secretary to enforce paragraph 7 in accordance with the interpretation being prepared by the Legal Division. Frank then protested to Wallace that the committee's report was fundamentally "a legal argument as to the correct legal interpretation. . . . I assume that . . . the legal opinion of the Office of the General Counsel will be accepted rather than the legal opinion of representatives of the Cotton Section and the Comptroller's Office." Frank rigidly separated legal questions from policy questions and asserted that his legal judgment was final, conclusive, and not a matter of policy. Yet he recounted subsequently that paragraph 7 was "awkwardly stated."[131]

The Legal Division's opinion, drafted under Alger Hiss's supervision and signed by Jerome Frank, ultimately concluded that paragraph 7 required farmers to keep the identical tenants.[132] At the same time, Frank prevailed on Victor Christgau, AAA acting administrator in Davis' absence, and on Paul Appleby, Wallace's assistant, to send a telegram to AAA officials in Arkansas. The telegram, stating that the issue of interpretation was being reviewed by Wallace and that the AAA officials should avoid making any interpretation, created considerable opposition from large farms throughout the South. The American Cotton Cooperative Association protested to Henry Wallace that the opinion reversed the general understanding that crop allotments follow the land rather than the tenants. The association saw the impending reinterpretation as a breach of faith with the cotton growers. On the other hand, Frank's representative in the South wired back to Washington a picture of human greed and exploitation. Hundreds of supporting affidavits swore that the termination of tenant farmers came as a result of their participation in the Southern Tenant Farmers' Union.[133]

Frank won the battle and lost the war. Through these turbulent two years Wallace had consistently supported Frank's actions and policy choices. In this instance, however, Frank misjudged the support for sharecroppers and tenant farmers. On his return to Washington, Davis discovered not only the telegram but also hundreds of protests from landlords and others regarding the proposed reinterpretation. Davis went to Wallace, demanding power to dismiss Frank and others who shared Frank's views. Frank and Davis had collided before, but in this instance Davis seized the opportunity to rid himself of troublesome supporters not only of sharecroppers and tenant farmers but also of consumers.[134] Frank had exposed his political flank by intentionally reducing his contacts with Wallace.[135] While Frank, Pressman, and Tugwell each considered Frank's interpretation to represent Wallace's point of view, by this point in time Wallace may already have been stung by the presidential bee.[136] Frank's other powerful political ally, Rexford Tugwell, was recuperating from influenza out of town and in any event had reduced his AAA responsibilities. Davis, a skillful agriculture politician, had powerful support from southern senators.[137] Wallace yielded, describing Frank's interpretation as "not only indefensible from a practical agricultural point of view but also bad law." He described Frank and the others as "*New Republic* liberals."[138] Davis fired Frank, Francis Shea, Lee Pressman, Gardner Jackson, and Victor Rotnam. He also abolished the office of AAA general counsel. Alger Hiss escaped the purge because Davis liked him and thought he was merely being loyal to Jerome Frank.[139]

The AAA purge revealed limits of New Deal policy as an agent of social change. Such pragmatic politicians as Roosevelt and Wallace understood that they were treading on thin ice in giving major political support to a dissident tenants' union. The political ice would not support such a social transformation. Jerome Frank was fired for attempting to push the New Deal further than the administration was willing to go. The purge also revealed the interrelation between law and policy. Ultimately, Frank's ouster centered on whether or not the administration would give vigorous support to sharecroppers, tenant farmers, and consumers. While tricky legal questions often lurked in the records, at bottom the conflict concerned a policy choice. To answer even technical, narrow legal questions one must often understand broader policy objectives. This was most evident when an issue focused on the "declared policy of the Act." But even in such an instance as the enforcement of a contract negotiated under AAA powers, law blended with policy and legal judgment with political judgment.[140] Jerome Frank is a single but vivid illustration of lawyers' ability to push clients, whether private corporations or government agencies, in one direction or another.

Frank and many other lawyers who served the New Deal were not narrow technicians wedded to a philosophy of legalism and of process. Process mattered little if substantive goals were frustrated. Attorneys exerted major influence on policy not merely as advisers and administrators but also as lawyers. Such able lawyers as Jerome Frank, absorbed by substantive policies, bridged the gap between means and ends, between process and result. New Deal lawyers did not accept social ends and experiment only with legal means. "Principles are what principles do" for Jerome Frank and for the New Deal.[141]

Chapter Four

ON BARKING UP TREES:
THE JUDGE AS AN ACTIVIST

It is comforting to know that one is not a solipsistic fool.
—Felix Frankfurter

I

The preeminent role of the United States Supreme Court in distributing political power, in shaping federal-state relations, and in promoting individual rights has fostered a rich historical literature on that institution. Most constitutional studies, however, treat the Court as if it operated in a vacuum. Such titles as *Freedom and the Court* and *Nine Men against America* suggest a Supreme Court divorced from all outside influence.[1] More sophisticated studies, remembering Mr. Dooley's advice that "th' supreme coort follows th' iliction returns," portray the Court as a political institution responding to contemporary pressures.[2] Although sensitive to the impact of broad political forces, these works still describe a court removed from professional and institutional influence. Few studies recognize the contributions of the legal profession—counsel, the bar, law reviews, and lower courts—to the work of the Court.[3]

The Supreme Court, of course, sits at the pinnacle of the federal judicial system. It must be remembered, however, that the Court operates as only one part of an entire system. Surprisingly, even the best study of the federal judiciary makes no effort to relate the Supreme Court to the other federal courts.[4] We know very little about how other courts interact with and influence the U.S. Supreme Court.

Most works focusing on courts other than the Supreme Court

find state courts more appealing than federal courts, probably because the state supreme courts are, within their own provinces, the final arbiters of legal issues.[5] When one evaluates the social impact of law, a state's tort doctrine may be far more instructive than the nuances of federal patent law. Studies of the lower federal courts are infrequent, in part because the district and circuit courts generally operate within the parameters of U.S. Supreme Court decisions.[6] So, from the perspective of what ultimately becomes law, there seems to be no reason to study the understudies. Lower federal decisions remain authoritative only when the Supreme Court does not speak. If the issue warrants attention, the Court will eventually hear it.[7] Final resolution by the Supreme Court blunts the impact of truly original lower-court judges, whose contributions are destined to be temporary.[8] As a result, the "inferior" role assigned by the United States Constitution to the lower federal courts precludes the production of jurists of the stature of Lemuel Shaw, Oliver Wendell Holmes, and Benjamin Cardozo.

Nevertheless, it is necessary to examine the lower federal courts if one is to discover how law ultimately develops.[9] Inferior courts are a vital part of the process by which the Supreme Court reaches its conclusions. Intermediate appellate judges especially contribute to the maturation of judicial reasoning. Their opinions serve not only to crystallize and narrow legal issues but also to articulate major strands of precedential and policy considerations. The work of a brilliant circuit court judge, willing to express the directions he or she thinks the Supreme Court should take, provides a vivid illustration of the interaction of two levels in the federal court system. As a judge, Jerome Frank developed a highly refined concept of his role in relation to the Supreme Court.

Jerome Frank served on the United States Court of Appeals for the Second Circuit from 1941 until his death in 1957. During this period the Second Circuit was one of the most illustrious courts in the nation's history. Sitting with Frank was Learned Hand, who first became a federal judge in 1909 and is universally regarded as one of the greatest judges in American legal history. Justices Holmes, Stone, and Frankfurter each proposed that Learned Hand be appointed to the U.S. Supreme Court. Also on the court were Augustus Hand, Learned's first cousin and an intellect of substantial ability, and two former deans of the Yale Law School, Thomas Swan and Charles Clark, often called the father of the Federal Rules of Civil Procedure. Finally, John Marshall Harlan served on the Second Circuit in the 1950s before his appointment to the Supreme Court. This formidable array of legal talent had responsibility for federal appeals from the district courts in New York, Connecticut, and Vermont. During Frank's tenure, the Second Circuit had the heaviest case load of any federal appeals court.[10]

As a result of a major revision of the Internal Revenue Code in 1939 and the passage of New Deal labor legislation, the Second Circuit had an important role in determining tax policy and interpreting labor law. Oversight of appeals from New York City, the nation's commercial hub, enhanced the Second Circuit's power. Because the New York Stock Exchange and other major exchanges are located in New York City, litigation based on their transactions came before the Second Circuit. The U.S. Supreme Court reviewed only a small number of securities cases during this period, thus ensuring even greater influence for the Second Circuit's decisions. Commercial litigation involving the country's largest banks came before the Second Circuit, either because New Deal banking legislation authorized federal jurisdiction or because diversity jurisdiction permitted a federal forum for actions between citizens or corporations from different states. New York City also housed publishing houses, movie companies, the American Society of Composers, Authors, and Publishers, theater companies, music studios, and the home offices of major corporations. Thus copyright, trademark, and patent law problems often found their way to New York's federal courts. Finally, the presence of the country's most prestigious law firms ensured careful presentation of novel legal problems. These several factors made the Second Circuit the nation's "top commercial court."[11]

Often Frank's opinions followed the traditional format of careful exposition, frequently in minute detail, of the legal issues, the governing precedent, and the social policies. But frequently Judge Frank wrote discursive essays about an array of matters that had little or no connection to the legal issue. Frank did not conceive of law as an autonomous field whose results were explainable solely in terms of legal factors. He strove to show how ideas from disparate fields affected law, how extrinsic forces shaped legal doctrine. His opinions contained much *obiter dictum* because, for Frank, a judicial opinion was not merely a narrow instrument for the resolution of a precise issue. Drawing on his legal realism, Frank thought courts were a critical instrument in democratic government which must "do justice" and be open to scrutiny, and whose judges should didactically explain their results. Frank's resulting judicial opinions were, to understate it, idiosyncratic. In the 1940s and 1950s, only Jerome Frank would refer to *Gulliver's Travels* and *Alice in Wonderland*, discourse on the history of science, comment on economic theory, rely on Aristotle's philosophy, or describe recent advances in gestalt psychology—all in the context of a judicial opinion.[12] When he first ascended to the bench this style received much comment, often sharply critical. Felix Frankfurter and Jerome Frank exchanged lengthy letters discussing the functions of judicial opinions. One interchange especially captures the flavor. Frank wrote:

> My aims, so far as I can articulate them, in writing opinions, when they are "essayistic," are these: (a) To stimulate the bar into some reflective thinking about the history of legal doctrines, so that they will go beyond the Citator perspective of doctrinal evolution; (b) To induce them to reflect on the techniques of legal reasoning, (e.g., to consider the nature and value of stare decisis, or the use and value and limitations on the proper employment of fictions); (c) To recognize that the judicial process is inescapably human, necessarily never flawless, but capable of improvement; (d) To perceive the divers "forces" operative in decision-making, and the limited function of the courts as part of government.
>
> And, underlying it all, is a strong desire, not easily curbed, to be pedagogic—not in a didactic manner but in a way that will provoke intelligent questioning as to the worth of accepted practices in the interest of bettering these practices. The Holmes' approach was, of course, differently motivated. He wrote for the few. If what he said was over the heads of the many, he didn't care—or, rather he preferred it that way. Don't misunderstand: I don't mean that I'm a Holmes, or that I can compete with him. I do aim to teach; he did not.[13]

Frankfurter responded: "You are teeming with ideas and the world needs their expression. But that is no reason why you should take a simple case which Holmes would have disposed of in a page and a half and use it as a peg for an essay on mercantilism."[14]

One aspect of Frank's personality was his reforming zeal. As evidenced by his work in the New Deal, he enjoyed reevaluating old customs and practices, and hoped to reshape them to meet current needs. As a judge Frank retained this fervor to redo, but it posed a dilemma. How could an intermediate appellate court judge improve the law while operating within confines set by the Supreme Court? Frank's relation to the Supreme Court was much like that of an advocate—urging, persuading, coaxing, and cajoling the Court to move in desired directions. At the same time, he recognized the institutional limits imposed by his subordinate position and gracefully accepted those bounds. Consequently, Frank developed methods to push the Court while simultaneously bowing to its superior authority.

II

As a judge on a lower rung of the judicial ladder, how did Frank defer to authority without losing his ability to prod the Supreme Court? Examining prior decisions poses squarely the tension between an adherence to tradition and a desire to reform.[15] If, as a member of a Second Circuit panel, Frank confronted an issue not previously decided by either the Supreme Court or the Second Circuit, then obviously he enjoyed complete discretion in voting to resolve the question. If Frank wrote for the panel, a petition for a writ of certiorari necessarily implied a challenge to his opinion. When Frank wrote in dissent, however, he implicitly appealed to the Supreme Court, as the only body with power to modify the Court of Appeals judgment, to review the decision. Indeed, the Supreme Court is more likely to grant a writ of certiorari if a judge dissents below: merely writing separately calls special attention to the case.[16] Writing as strong and cogent a dissent as possible enhances the likelihood of Supreme Court review, so Jerome Frank painstakingly elaborated his dissenting positions.[17] He also used a split among the circuits to his advantage, since a conflict between courts of appeals may tip the balance in favor of review.[18] On occasion Frank emphasized the split and demonstrated its precise nature, thus appealing to the Court to settle the matter.[19] In one criminal case, Frank explicitly addressed the Court: he concurred "with the hope that the Supreme Court would review our decision and consider the question."[20]

On issues previously decided by the Second Circuit, stare decisis bound Frank either to acquiesce, to distinguish, or to overrule. As a judge, he took seriously his obligation to confront decisions.[21] This posture carred a certain incongruity. In *Law and the Modern Mind* Frank had ridiculed the quest of lawyers and judges for certainty in the law. Although his jurisprudential writing depicted judges as having nearly unfettered discretion, his judicial position demanded that he abide by the customary rules of play.

A quirk in Second Circuit procedure enabled Frank to put additional pressure on the Supreme Court to review certain Second Circuit decisions. The circuit made no regular provision for en banc hearings until 1956, after Charles E. Clark became chief judge.[22] To prevent different panels from reaching conflicting results, thereby producing inconsistent decisions within the same circuit, the practice of deferring to earlier decisions of Second Circuit panels developed. Frank acquiesced in this practice even when he disagreed with the earlier decision or had not even participated in it.[23] The absence of an en banc procedure meant that a majority of the entire Second Circuit might disapprove a decision yet abide by it. Reversal was even more difficult, since presumably only the original panel could freely reconsider its prior decision. Although Frank opposed en banc hearings, he found other routes to seek reversal.[24]

Both Frank and Learned Hand viewed the Supreme Court as sitting partially to resolve intracircuit as well as intercircuit conflicts.[25] As a result, Frank might bow to the earlier decision while voicing doubts as to the warmth with which he embraced it: "Whatever we might now hold if this were for us a novel question, we need not consider, for the matter is governed in this circuit by our decision in . . ."[26]

Frank also employed less subtle techniques in pleading for Supreme Court overhaul of Second Circuit precedent. Occasionally he expressly disapproved the earlier decision, although still following it, and solicited Supreme Court review.[27] In other cases, Frank considered intervening Supreme Court opinions treating subsidiary questions, and even comments by single justices, as sufficient warrant to reject well-established Second Circuit decisions.[28] Thus the presence of a higher tribunal and the possibility of reversal by it provided justification for Frank's resistance to applicable Second Circuit precedent.

In *In re Luma Camera Service, Inc.*, for example, Frank went to extreme lengths by simultaneously following and parodying an earlier decision. Federal bankruptcy law allowed a trustee in bankruptcy to obtain a "turnover order" commanding individuals who possessed property of the bankrupt to turn over such assets to the trustee. Failure to do so might result in imprisonment for contempt. Prior Second Circuit cases had presumed that an individual, once shown to be in possession of a bankrupt's property, remained in possession indefinitely, regardless of actual possession. The rule sought to prevent fraudulent transfers. Frank perceived this as a fiction that operated very unjustly, but firm Second Circuit precedent held otherwise. In *Luma Camera Service*, Frank accepted the inevitable force of these earlier decisions, but not without expressing his disagreement.[29] Frank ridiculed the very result he reached, and implored the Supreme Court to accept the case for review and overturn these Second Circuit precedents:

> Although we know that Maggio cannot comply with the order [because he did not have the property], we must keep a straight face and pretend that he can, and thus affirm orders which first direct Maggio "to do an impossibility, and then punish him for refusal to perform it." Our own precedents keep us from abandoning that pretense which, in this case, may well lead to inhumane treatment of Maggio and which, in other turnover cases, has brought about a revival of those evils of the debtors' prison which legislation like the Bankruptcy Act was supposed to abolish. . . . It is an open secret that Maggio is being punished as if for a crime, but we are precluded from so acknowledging.
>
> To eliminate the unfortunate results of the unreasonable fiction we have adopted, it will be necessary for the Supreme Court to grant certiorari and then to wipe out our more recent precedents.[30]

After such an impassioned plea, was there any doubt that the Supreme Court would grant certiorari? Indeed, one might ask if the

Supreme Court enjoyed freedom of choice. Here was an opinion by an able judge, joined by Learned Hand, that cried out for reversal. Frank did not merely identify a split in the circuits; he sharply attacked the rule, intimated it was inhumane, and expressly sought Supreme Court review. Quoting Frank's parody of turnover proceedings, the Court granted certiorari and reversed.[31] Judge Frank did not reject the applicable precedent: his concept of his role as circuit judge dictated that he abide by prior rulings. But he also perceived his role as permitting him to place the onus on the Supreme Court to correct the past errors of his own court.

Frank's attitude toward Supreme Court precedent reveals how a circuit judge may defer to a higher judicial authority while simultaneously exhorting the Court to adopt a desired position. When confronted by Supreme Court decisions, Frank felt duty-bound to adhere to them because he visualized himself as "merely a reflector, serving as a judicial moon."[32] He had little patience for those who, either by subterfuge or simple act of will, refused to follow higher authority.[33] It mattered not whether he agreed with those decisions: "[W]here the [Supreme Court] has directly enunciated a specific rule we must then follow it, even if we think it wholly wrong. Thus I happen to feel very strongly that the Supreme Court has been wrong in [certain cases] . . . nevertheless I have felt that we are obliged to follow those rulings."[34]

There are methods by which lower court judges may ignore or disregard relevant but distasteful Supreme Court authority.[35] Frank's intellectual integrity precluded resort to devious means to slight rules he disliked.[36] By temperament he was not inclined to give niggardly constructions to decisions he opposed, but instead opted for candor. His approach was to admit the binding force of the precedent, apply it fairly to the case at bar, but articulate reasons why the rule seemed misguided. Jerome Frank honed to a fine edge the art of following a Supreme Court case while criticizing its doctrine and urging the Court to reexamine it.[37] Typically he acknowledged the effect of stare decisis but lamented the unjust consequences of the rule. Frank described the old rule's deficiencies in detail and suggested possible routes the Supreme Court could take to modify it. He might conclude with an explicit call for review by the Court. Such a plea was usually gratuitous, since by that point

Frank had revealed his opinion that the Court should take the case.[38]

On occasion Frank adamantly insisted that a doctrine needed overhaul or replacement. In *Hammond-Knowlton v. United States* he criticized the judicial doctrine requiring strict construction of statutes waiving sovereign immunity. The Supreme Court, however, denied certiorari.[39] An identical issue reached Frank later, but not before the Supreme Court had, by Frank's own admission, reaffirmed the doctrine. Nonetheless, while adhering to precedent, Frank again criticized the doctrine: "We must here, once more, follow the niggardly rule and deny to a citizen a right to recover money which his government wrongfully obtained from him and which unjustly enriches it."[40]

Frank displayed no hesitation in following a doctrine he believed unwise or even unjust. Given his position as a judge on an intermediate tribunal, no other option existed. Although his duty bound him to accede to the views of the higher court, it did not prevent him from questioning the wisdom or the constitutionality of past rulings. This judicial style advanced the process by which old doctrines receive new scrutiny and are either approved or discarded; elaboration of reasons that supported change contributed to the Supreme Court's understanding of the need to reconsider past decisions.[41]

Although Frank might have aired his views in another forum, his assertive style and personality rejected any armchair posture of legal reform. A generic law review discussion would not substitute for the concrete judicial opinion, which provided a fulcrum to propel the upper Court to reform its law. Frank preferred the occasion for change to be imminent, not in the nebulous future. A letter to Learned Hand captures the creative spirit that Frank applauded in judges:

> Let me congratulate you on *The Evergreens v. Nunan*. It is, I think, the finest kind of inventive judicial product. For it involves a real flash of genius in the contrivance of new judicial tools. I know that you pretend to jeer at the idea that courts should do justice. But here, in the interest of doing greater justice, you have given the judiciary a perfected instrument.[42]

Frank perfected a "new judicial tool" in the technique of following Supreme Court precedent while evaluating it. The apex of its
use occurred in *United States v. Roth,* the lower-court decision in the
famous Supreme Court obscenity case.[43] By concurring separately
in *Roth,* Frank revealed how cautiously he approached his task.
Frank considered the federal legislation unconstitutional. Although the Supreme Court had never resolved the constitutional
question, several decisions had assumed the statute's validity. Frank
declined to describe earlier Supreme Court comments as mere
dicta, even though this dodge might have produced the result he
desired. The collective thrust of the Supreme Court cases tended to
sustain the legislation. Frank therefore voted to uphold the convictions and contented himself with a concurrence. But what a Hercu-
lean concurrence! Frank analyzed the constitutional issues with a
coherence and lucidity that have not yet been surpassed. His insights included the recognition that the federal statute impinged
on protected First Amendment activity by punishing the mailing of
material that induced thoughts or desires but not conduct.[44] Frank
also argued that the legislation lacked a firm factual basis showing
that the reading of obscene materials had an effect on conduct.[45]
Moreover, he perceived a constitutional difference between regulation affecting adults and that affecting children.[46] In addition,
Frank noted that the legislation burdened the judicial system with
troublesome legal process issues because it permitted prosecutors
and juries to wield enormous discretion and anomalously asked
judges to serve as literary critics to exclude true classics from prosecution. This last burden prompted Frank's wry query whether the
task would produce a "Legal Restatement of the Canons of Literary
Taste." Drawing on implications from past cases, Frank not only
unraveled the constraint on free speech posed by such statutes but
also articulated an early statement of the void-for-vagueness doctrine.[47]

Frank's judicial effort in *Roth* identified and illuminated major
issues requiring resolution by the Supreme Court. That Frank anticipated so many later cases indicates how seminal his effort was.
While his *Roth* concurrence has withstood the test of time, its
preparation created anxiety and insecurity for Frank. His col-

leagues on the Second Circuit thought his opinion a fine essay, but "really quite out of place for an inferior court."[48] During its preparation, Frank corresponded with Justice Frankfurter concerning the role of inferior judges vis-à-vis the Supreme Court. Frankfurter wrote:

> Of course you should respect your Lords and masters here, but you need not anticipate a ruling that is not almost explicitly indicated or find a trend where there is none. Don't let me stir you up again, but I think the decision in *Spector Motor*, 139 F. 2d. 809, was, as L. Hand pointed out, inexcusable. This business of anticipating what this Court will do grossly misconceives the nature of the deliberative process here and improperly deprives this Court of the illumination to which we are entitled when an issue is not foreclosed—I am not begging the question in saying this. We have a right to expect, and are badly in need of, such illumination and discriminating discussion from Courts of Appeals and, more particularly from a judge like you. After all, while you are what the Constitution calls "an inferior court" and therefore must duly respect the superior, your brain is yours and is to be exercised. You are not intellectually enslaved where your superior hasn't commanded. It is the duty of this Court to be clear in its commands. You are a free agent until the command is clear.[49]

Frank responded: "I shall remember that statement in writing an opinion in which I'm engaged, on the federal obscenity statute."[50] Nagging doubts persisted, and Frank wrote Frankfurter that he would like to insert in his upcoming *Roth* concurrence the following: "We are an inferior court. Yet we have received intimations that the Supreme Court does not resent, but welcomes opinions from its inferiors on subjects as to which it, as the superior, has not given fairly unequivocal commands." He asked if Frankfurter would think such a statement improper.[51] Frankfurter penned back on the bottom of the letter:

> You have not received any such "intimations" because I'm not empowered to give any for the Court. What I wrote you was not an "intimation" but my own strong, explicit conception of the duty, not merely the permissible scope, but the duty of lower court judges, where the U.S.S.C. has not spoken clearly. Why not express this view, if it is also yours, in your own way for your authority.[52]

While striving to follow conscientiously the Supreme Court's lead, on occasion Frank refused to apply some of its decisions. When may a lower court judge disregard an explicit ruling of the highest tribunal?[53] At one point, the conventional wisdom decreed "never," for the task of lower-court judges was simply to follow blindly the past rulings of higher courts.[54] More recently, that position has encountered resistance, partly as a consequence of the Supreme Court's increased willingness in the twentieth century to overrule its own decisions.[55] With some Supreme Court rulings destined to be overruled, should an intermediate court, in the interim, attempt to discern the likely future fate of past rulings? Or must the obituary await a formal interment?

Diametrically opposed answers have been given to these questions. On the one hand, Judge Joseph Hutcheson advanced the classic common law distinction between holding and dictum, and insisted that only explicit Supreme Court holdings could govern his actions.[56] "Holdings" mark the path lower-court judges must follow; "trends" offer uncertain guidance through a dark thicket. On the other hand, some jurists—with Frank at the vanguard—urged that it served justice poorly to adhere to cases discredited by subsequent events but not yet explicitly overruled.[57] Such adherence saddles litigants facing the application of obsolete decisions with the burden of carrying an appeal to the Supreme Court. Since the reasons for declining review may rest on the state of the Court's own docket rather than its approval of the obsolete ruling, the losing party suffers a serious unjustified loss. The dispute may turn on law that the Supreme Court would reject if it had considered the merits. To avoid this consequence, Frank argued: "Legal doctrines, as first enunciated, often prove to be inadequate under the impact of ensuing experience in their practical application. And when a lower court perceives a pronounced new doctrinal trend in Supreme Court decisions, it is its duty, cautiously to be sure, to follow not to resist it."[58]

Those who agreed with Frank shared the general view that they need not follow discredited cases, but differed regarding how to assess whether a past ruling had been discredited. Learned Hand, for example, dissented from a Clark opinion (which Frank joined) that refused to abide by old Supreme Court rulings on a state's power to tax interstate commerce. But Hand did not quarrel with the general approach urged by Frank.[59] In one dissenting opinion, Hand asserted:

> I agree that one should not wait for formal retraction in the face of changes plainly foreshadowed. . . . Nor is it desirable for a lower court to embrace the exhilarating opportunity of anticipating a doctrine which may be in the womb of time, but whose birth is distant; on the contrary I conceive that the measure of its duty is to divine, as best it can, what would be the event of an appeal in the case before it.[60]

Thus Hand reasoned that although explicit overruling is unnecessary, the "womb of time" is too speculative. Therefore, the problem is to assess the Supreme Court's likely reaction in the particular case rather than to project its long-term direction.

Although Frank and Learned Hand shared similar positions in theory, they differed on the application of the general principle.[61] In several cases Frank was more willing to identify a "new doctrinal trend." Preferring a more limited function for the judiciary, Hand eschewed strong judicial intervention by inferior-court judges.[62] Frank's reforming spirit and exuberant style favored a more assertive reexamination of accepted law and a more active quest for new doctrines.

How broad-gauged was the power claimed by Frank? Surprisingly, he set sharp limits to the "exhilarating opportunity," and carefully operated within them. A "new doctrinal trend" grounded Frank's approach.[63] This rubric demanded more than mere speculation about Supreme Court policy or likely court attitudes. Frank assumed an obligation to describe in detail the recent developments on which he based his belief that a Supreme Court case was no longer authoritative.[64] Whenever Frank refused to accede to a relevant Court precedent, he set forth the intervening developments.[65] Frank's approach required the Supreme Court to generate the initial impetus for change. If the Court had given no clue that a precedent had become suspect, Frank claimed no authority *sua sponte* to suppose it was. Even with regard to doctrines that Frank believed the Court would reexamine, and about which Frank possessed strong convictions, he obeyed the dictates of stare decisis.[66] In *United States v. Rosenberg*, the atomic spy case, for example, Frank considered the death sentence imposed by the trial judge to be excessively harsh, yet he contented himself with a plea to the Supreme Court to reconsider its earlier decisions denying appellate courts the power to modify trial court sentences.[67] Frank felt bound by a line of authority that remained unimpaired, though criticized by law journals.[68] By "new doctrine" Frank meant legal rules and precepts and not merely changes in the social and political climate. For example, when cases challenged an 1896 decision that limited the Fifth Amendment privilege against self-incrimination to protection against punishment for crime,[69] Frank perceived the atmosphere of the 1950s as so vastly changed from that of the 1890s that the Supreme Court would perhaps be willing to guard against social disgrace. Yet this kind of change did not permit Frank to ignore relevant authority.[70]

Although Frank set outer limits to his own discretion, troublesome questions about his approach remain. Does the search for a "new doctrinal trend" include counting noses on the Supreme Court? On closely divided issues, a single vote may spell the difference. Should intermediate judges bet on Supreme Court justices as though they were racehorses? One federal case has been criticized for doing almost that. In *Barnette v. West Virginia Board of Education*, Judge John Parker held unconstitutional a statute mandating a salute to the flag despite a contrary Supreme Court ruling barely two years old.[71] Parker justified his action on the basis of several Court personnel changes and an explicit shift of position by three members of the earlier majority.[72] Although Parker's method was criticized as "an unseemly thing," he was actually merely attempting accurately to assess the current state of the law.[73] His opinion did not degenerate into an irreverent effort to measure the justices' ideological leanings. He avoided crude political speculation on the positions of newly appointed justices, and relied solely on the shifts in position as reflected in the published *United States Reports*.[74] Such shifts were presumably important even to Learned Hand. In Hand's scenario, the judge must gauge the Supreme Court's present reaction to the issue at bar. In close cases, he can intelligently assess the situation only by examining the prior votes of individual justices.[75]

Even though lower court judges may unquestionably identify a "trend," their analysis may fail because the Court merely made a false start, or changed its mind, or deferred consideration until a later time. Indeed, the seemingly ordained "trend" may never develop. In a 1922 case, *Federal Baseball Club v. National League of Professional Baseball Clubs of Baltimore, Inc.*, the Supreme Court held that because major league baseball was not interstate commerce, the sport was exempt from the Sherman Antitrust Act.[76] By the time a fresh challenge reached the Second Circuit twenty-seven years later, the Supreme Court had completely altered its conception of interstate commerce.[77] This shift led Frank to describe *Federal Baseball Club* as an "impotent zombi."[78] When the Court finally reexamined its holding, the anticipated overruling did not materialize.[79] Instead, the Court deferred to Congress. Its prior interpretation of the Sherman Act was an established aberration in which Congress had acquiesced. Congress, should its desire, could easily remove the inconsistency. Even an "impotent zombi" may escape its deserved burial. No degree of caution will eliminate the factor of uncertainty. Once committed *not* to await formal overruling, intermediate judges necessarily face the danger of being reversed or ignored.

Felix Frankfurter criticized Frank for his effort to identify Supreme Court trends. To Frankfurter, that process deprived the Court of the independent judgment of lower courts.[80] Frankfurter underestimated the judicial independence and creativity provided by Frank's approach. Delineating a trend is purportedly an effort to follow what the Supreme Court will do. Yet, because the Court had not yet reached that point, Frank actually urged a particular course on the Court. By tying that step to the Court's own precedent, Frank subtly minimized both his role and the departure from past practice.

When lower courts anticipate changes in Supreme Court rulings, their decisions pressure the Court. Once an inferior court disregards a relevant Supreme Court decision, the losing party will assuredly petition for review, squarely confronting the High Court with a challenge to its earlier ruling. Although denial of certiorari implies no position on the merits in these cases, such denial leaves standing an explicit rejection of an earlier ruling.[81] Because a conflict in the circuits often prompts Supreme Court review, surely such a repudiation carries equal importance. When a prior ruling weakened through intervening events deserves to be discarded, the Supreme Court is the proper court to overrule its own decision. Lower-court repudiation very likely advances the time for reexamination, and thus influences the Supreme Court's decision-making process.[82]

Frank traveled a final avenue in his journey to move the Court forward by creatively applying Supreme Court decisions.[83] When new rulings signaled potentially fundamental shifts in the High Court's doctrines, Frank might affirm and encourage the Court to expand these rulings. *McNabb v. United States,* for example, decided in 1943, marked the beginning of the Supreme Court's efforts to harness police interrogation practices.[84] Along this tortuous path, Frank exhorted the Court to champion the ideals embodied in *McNabb.* His opinions read the *McNabb* principle broadly.[85] Frank also warmly received *Griffin v. Illinois,* which held that an indigent was entitled to receive a free trial transcript to aid in his appeal.[86] At the first opportunity, in *United States v. Johnson,* Frank relied on *Griffin* to challenge a prevailing federal practice that permitted the trial judge to deny an indigent leave to appeal:

> The Griffin doctrine represents an important step forward in the direction of democratic justice. My colleagues, regarding it as a bold step, shudder away from applying that doctrine to a case like that at bar. . . .
> Yet Griffin, splendid though it is, is not exceptionally bold. We still have a long way to go to fulfill what Chief Justice Warren has called our "mission" to achieve "equal justice under the law," in respect of those afflicted with poverty.[87]

Central to Frank's conception of his relation to the Supreme Court was his effort to accept graciously the constraints of his inferior-court position while vigorously pushing the High Court to reexamine old doctrines. His faithful adherence to higher authority revealed a giant intellect who accepted completely his role as a subordinate judge. In his view, the intermediate judge could facilitate the Supreme Court's work. While his carefully crafted opinions illuminated the legal issues, Frank went considerably further in accenting areas that needed Supreme Court attention. His technique of following while criticizing precedent epitomized this approach. Frank did not hesitate to disregard High Court rulings so long as he could identify a "new doctrinal trend" based squarely on more recent Supreme Court opinions. When a new Court decision had potentially far-reaching effects and the policy direction met with Frank's approval, he would craft an opinion that fleshed out the possible implications. In so doing, he provided helpful nutrients to enrich the soil for young doctrine.

The net effect of Frank's devices unquestionably heightened the pressure on the High Court to respond. Although some might deem these approaches an unwelcome interference with the Supreme Court's discretion, no evidence suggests that the Court itself thought so. No decision rebuked Frank for using any of these judicial tools, and Frank's private correspondence with individual justices generally contains no hint of disapproval.[88] Nor should these facts seem surprising. The skills of an able judge such as Frank aided, rather than impeded, the High Court in keeping abreast of current social needs.

III

During his public career before he joined the Second Circuit, Frank developed strong friendships and intellectual associations with several persons who later ascended to the Supreme Court. These personal relations continued after Frank donned judicial robes, and the remaining correspondence provides a fascinating study of the informal ways in which two levels of the federal judiciary can interact.[89]

Frank was closest to William O. Douglas and Felix Frankfurter. Douglas and Frank shared many insights about the legal system and, with others, spearheaded the legal realism movement. Their friendship blossomed, especially as both assumed key positions in the budding New Deal. It was Douglas that persuaded Franklin D. Roosevelt to appoint Frank as a commissioner of the SEC and later suggested that FDR name Frank to the Second Circuit. Through the New Deal years the friendship of Douglas and Frank matured;

a personal relationship grew from shared philosophic and ideological perspectives.[90]

Frank enjoyed a less intimate relationship with Felix Frankfurter. While still a Harvard Law School professor, Frankfurter had played a key role in assembling talented persons to work in Roosevelt's administration—one of whom was Frank. Thus began a relationship keynoted by prolific correspondence: over the next twenty-five years, Frank and Frankfurter exchanged hundreds of letters.[91]

Frank's relations with Hugo Black and Robert Jackson were cordial but less familiar than those with Douglas and Frankfurter. Once again the New Deal tied the knot that bound the men together. With Black, a United States senator from Alabama, and Jackson, the United States attorney general, shared political concerns set the backdrop for friendly personal relations. These four future justices provided the nucleus of Frank's informal association with High Court personnel.[92]

Once Frank was on the bench, his contacts with Supreme Court justices assumed myriad forms. Correspondence ranged over many topics that had nothing to do with the business of the courts. Frank might share with Black observations on broad political events, with Douglas reminiscences about SEC days, with Frankfurter comments on the Zionist movement. The letters covered a broad spectrum of topics, with a heavy emphasis on the world of ideas. More germane to the legal system, Frank often exchanged views with Frankfurter on recent books.[93] With Black he debated the merits of trial judges' use of special verdicts to check jury discretion.[94] To certain justices Frank also sent letters recommending applicants for law clerk positions. Usually blessed with his seal of approval, a number of his law clerks later clerked for justices. Frank's gregarious personality brought him in contact with many persons clerking for his fellow members of the Second Circuit. He also evaluated their performance for friends on the Supreme Court. Conversely, justices might write Frank—as did Stanley Reed—soliciting prospective clerks.[95]

On one occasion Frank tried to persuade several justices to lower their barrier against public comment on legislation. After several

Supreme Court cases had broadened the scope of habeas corpus remedies challenging state court convictions, proposed federal legislation sought to nullify those decisions.[96] Writing to Black, Douglas, and Frankfurter, and personally seeing Chief Justice Warren, Frank urged that the justices express disapproval of the bill's attempt to undo Supreme Court rulings. Nothing came of his efforts, as Black and Frankfurter both thought that public comment would exceed the proper bounds of their judicial office.[97]

Frank's relations with the justices provoked a minor dispute with Charles Clark, his Second Circuit colleague. For some time Clark and Frank had split over the circuit's "harmless error" rule. While Clark supported it, Frank crusaded against it as particularly unjust.[98] The dispute erupted after Clark became convinced that Frank

has been down lobbying with the Supreme Court law clerks against what he likes to term the dreadful "Second Circuit rule" of harmless error, and that the law clerks are all emotionally upset—so much so that it is confidently believed the Supreme Court only awaits an appropriate vehicle for Felix to write a scathing condemnation of us for our brutality.[99]

After Clark voiced to Frank his objections at a court conference, Frank denied that he had "improperly engaged in propaganda activities with the Supreme Court law clerks."[100] To support his position, Frank sent Clark two letters from Supreme Court clerks explaining what had happened. Frank had been in Washington and had lunched with several clerks at the Supreme Court. They had discussed the "harmless error" rule, but the clerks did not seriously think that Frank had sought to lobby them. Rather, the topic had a "social and intellectual" interest for them, and in any case Frank's responses did not differ from his published opinions.[101]

Returning the two letters to Frank, Clark denied knowledge of the lobbying accusation, but continued:

It is my understanding that you have sent copies of your [recent "harmless error"] opinion to various persons in or about the Supreme Court, and that this was done in previous cases. This does seem to me inappropriate. I think volunteered suggestions or pressure, direct or indirect, from us to our superiors in our cases which they are called upon to review is undesirable.[102]

Frank responded:

> Since I've been on the bench, I've frequently sent copies of my opinions on diverse subjects—patents, contracts, etc.,—to Douglas, Black and Frankfurter, each of whom is an old friend. They receive all our opinions in any event, so that my sending copies of particular opinions merely calls attention to them. No one of these justices has ever thought the practice improper. I did the same with [the "harmless error" case]. Surely you don't think I was putting "pressure" on Black, whose views on harmless error are directly opposed to mine, as shown in his dissent in Bollenbach's case.[103]

Frank thought the practice of sending opinions to friends on the Supreme Court similar to any other intellectual exchange. Articles, books, and speeches were fit subjects to send to justices, and judicial opinions merely extended the interaction. While on the SEC Frank had developed the habit of sending friends on the Supreme Court those opinions that he thought would be of interest, and he continued this practice while on the Second Circuit.[104] Frank customarily forwarded copies of his opinions shortly after issuance and before the period for petitioning for certiorari had elapsed. Thus Douglas, Black, and Frankfurter might soon have been asked to vote on whether to grant review on those very opinions.

While Frank's response to Clark insisted that this practice merely "call[ed] attention" to his opinions and did not pressure the justices, the dynamics of these exchanges pose more difficult problems. When Frank sent a dissenting opinion, he clearly put himself on record as favoring reversal. In sending Bill Douglas a copy, was not Jerry Frank "calling attention" to a case that he hoped his friend would vote to review? Moreover, was not Frank expressing his position on the substantive issues and hoping, by the force of his reasoning, to persuade Douglas ultimately to adopt his views? Frank retorted that the published opinion spoke for itself, and since each justice received copies of all Second Circuit opinions, Frank's notes had little effect on the justices. Frank's mailings, however, marked those cases in which he had a strong interest. By forwarding only a select number, he automatically accented them as unusual. The cases themselves concerned topics about which Frank had firm views.

In some instances Frank did more than simply mail a copy of an opinion. In one letter he expressed to Frankfurter the fervent hope that the Court would soon address itself to an issue raised in a Frank concurrence.[105] Other letters to Douglas demonstrate poignantly how Frank sought to influence the Supreme Court. In one he commented: "Denial of certiorari in the Rubenstein case was disappointing. I enclose another in which I'm making a similar effort in what I think is a stronger case for defendant."[106] Frank thus expressed disappointment that the Court had not responded, and intimated that Douglas might amend the error by urging review in the next case. The enclosed opinion, although not identified, appears to have been *United States v. Bennett,* in which Frank dissented, once again challenging the Second Circuit's "harmless error" doctrine.[107] The Supreme Court granted certiorari and reversed in an opinion by Douglas which quoted directly from Frank's dissent.[108]

One sequence shows clearly that Frank saw himself as working in concert with the Supreme Court. He wrote to Douglas:

> I have written three dissenting opinions objecting to the manner in which my colleagues . . . use the "harmless error" doctrine so as (I think) to supersede the jury. I did so in *Keller v. Brooklyn Bus Corp.,* 128 F. (2d) 510; I did so again in *United States v. Liss,* 137 F. (2d) 995; in that case, certiorari was denied. I have again dissented on that score in *U.S. v. Mitchell,* 137 F.(2d) 1006; that dissent and my recent dissent on rehearing in that case I enclose. Judging from the failure to grant certiorari in the *Liss* case, I'm barking up the wrong tree. If so, I'll quit barking.[109]

Once again Frank exhorted his friend to push for review. Perplexed by the failure of his efforts, Frank asked Justice Douglas whether he should continue to dissent. Given the close personal relationship between the two, it is reasonable to read this letter as Jerry's request to Bill for an explanation for the Court's failure to respond. There is no indication that Justice Douglas responded to

Frank's plea. When the Supreme Court denied certiorari in *United States v. Mitchell*, Frank promptly dashed off another letter to Douglas. In a most outspoken fashion, he chastised the Supreme Court for its insensitive refusal to hear the case:

> I'm bothered that certiorari was denied yesterday as to *United States v. Mitchell*, 137 F.(2d) 1006, 138 F.(2d) 831. . . . I don't see much point in my continuing to dissent against the views of my five colleagues concerning harmless error, although I feel sure that defendants in criminal suits aren't getting fair trials and that, with the Supreme Court's indifference to the matter, innocent persons are likely to be convicted in this Circuit because of lack of such fairness.[110]

Unusual interaction between Frank and friends on the Supreme Court came in two exchanges with Douglas and Frankfurter. To Douglas he suggested a slight modification in an official Supreme Court opinion. To Frankfurter he expressed puzzlement at the meaning of a memorandum denying certiorari in a case.[111] He called upon Frankfurter to add a line to his memorandum explaining more clearly his position—an invitation Frankfurter declined. Frankfurter believed Frank was teasing him for his oblique memorandum: "If your inquiry . . . is serious and not a leg-pulling operation, I must draw on Holmes' remark while Chief Justice of the Massachusetts Supreme Judicial Court: 'May I suggest to the gentlemen of the Bar,' he said one day, 'a more extensive reading of French novels. It will cultivate in them the art of innuendo.'"[112]

Frank responded that he honestly found the memorandum obscure, as did several other lawyers with whom he had discussed the case. As for French novels, Frank commented irreverently: "I know what is popularly supposed to happen often in French novels; that's what you and I think the Court did to Leviton."[113] Again Frankfurter avoided comment. Although he thought his memorandum clear, he recognized that others did not:

> When you tell me that you and "several lawyers who are really intelligent" thought that what I wrote was meant as an intimation that certiorari was properly denied, rather than the opposite, I must act on the wisdom of the Talmud. The Talmud says that if, when you are stone sober, a man tells you that you are drunk, knock his teeth out; if

two men tell you that, laugh at them; but if three men tell you that, go to bed.[114]

In overtly pushing the Supreme Court, Frank did not simply seek to win support for his own strongly held views. To a remarkable degree he tried to divorce the ideas themselves from the fact that he espoused them. Pride of authorship did not impel him to write his friends.[115] He passed judgment on issues and cases that only remotely reinforced his own efforts. At least five Supreme Court justices received letters from Frank applauding particular opinions.[116] Commenting on Supreme Court decisions allowed Frank an opportunity to support positions he liked and perhaps to bolster the resolve of justices whose spirits might be flagging.

The correspondence between Frank and the justices reveals the extent to which mutual support and admiration are critical ingredients in judging, as in most activities. The justices exhibited no uneasiness about Jerry's practice of forwarding copies of his opinions and they actively welcomed his favorable criticism. As Justice Jackson wrote: "Your line commenting on my opinion . . . is the more appreciated because I am so lonely among my associates. It is comforting to know that in some parts there is an interest in the subject."[117] A similar theme emerged in a letter from Frankfurter:

> Naturally enough I could be confident that you would approve of Bollenbach [in which the Supreme Court finally reversed the Second Circuit's harmless error rule]. Sofar as doing his job is concerned, a judge must not give a damn about approval or disapproval but humanly it is comforting to know one is not a solipsistic fool.[118]

Frank's notes offered encouragement and support to the Supreme Court justices. As these replies reflect, waging battle may prove a lonely task. There is comfort in knowing that others—persons whom you respect—share your perspective. Encouragement may strengthen the will to persevere.

No justice sent Frank any substantive comments on his opinions.[119] Frankfurter wrote: "If I say nothing about the opinion which you were good enough to enclose, it is because, as you indicate, the case may well be brought here." Frankfurter, quite predictably, demonstrated a marked sensitivity to the boundaries placed on him by his office—a sensitivity he attributed to his "stodgy views on judicial propriety." Yet he often approved Frank's habit of forwarding opinions, and noted that they "greatly interested" him, or gave "me, as is usually true, pleasure and enhanced my knowledge." On one occasion, after Frank feared he had offended Frankfurter, Felix dismissed the fear with the explicit assurance that none of Frank's letters had ever offended him. Once an appeal ended, Frankfurter would express his opinion on the merits; during the period when an appeal might be taken, Felix's comments carefully hedged his substantive beliefs.[120]

Frank's candid criticism of Supreme Court actions won the approval of Justice Jackson. In one letter, Frank, hoping Jackson would "not take it amiss," quoted a paragraph from a recent letter to Frankfurter criticizing a Supreme Court decision.[121] Jackson responded:

Of course I do not take amiss what you wrote to Felix about Michelson. I think the most wholesome kind of results come from free and informal criticism. I said to my colleagues when the Maggio bankruptcy problem was pending that it was a strange code of ethics which will allow us to have a law clerk just out of law school advise us but would condemn so sensible a move as my going over to New York with you fellows who are working with a problem and talking it over. We move here in such an atmosphere of unreality that it is a wonder that we do as well as we do, especially since so many of us have never moved in the real atmosphere of combat in the lower courts.[122]

Frank's notions about relating to Supreme Court personnel comport with his views on other intellectual matters. He possessed an unquenchable thirst for the exchange of ideas and an indefatigable willingness to correspond and thus attempt to identify points of agreement, of conflict, and of adaptability. Just as he criticized the efforts of his superiors, he enjoyed receiving their comments on his opinions.[123] Frank did not single out Supreme Court justices. He often wrote other circuit judges praising recent opinions, and he solicited comments from his brethren on the Second Circuit on cases on which they were not sitting.[124]

Frank tactics raise squarely the legitimacy of subjecting Supreme Court justices to these pressures. As Justice Jackson pointed out, it seems highly incongruous for justices to enjoy a dialogue with neophyte law clerks, on the ground that they help hone the rough edges of judicial opinions, and yet be denied interaction with the Jerome Franks of their generation. To deny exchange with the brightest and most experienced minds is an odd way to produce the soundest opinions. This prohibition rests on the fear that personal friendship may interfere with the independence of the justice. Lower-court judges are keenly aware of how a higher court handles their opinions. At the beginning of his judicial career, Jerome Frank kept a tally of those cases in which petitions for certiorari were filed.[125] Conversely, Supreme Court justices evinced sensitivity to the feelings of the inferior courts. The Supreme Court followed the first two of Frank's opinions that reached it, and Justice Douglas penned him congratulations: "Jerry at Bat!/2 hits/2 runs/no error."[126]

Jerome Frank, in particular, displayed marked sensitivity to criticism by the Supreme Court.[127] Naturally, he was pleased when the Court sustained his position.[128] Therein lies the dilemma: upper-court sensitivity to the feelings of a friend on an inferior bench is compounded when that judge earmarks a particular decision as an important one.

Frank's tactics apparently did not jeopardize the independence of any Supreme Court justice, a result that should not seem surprising. A justice would abdicate his judicial oath if he lost his freedom of movement. This loss would occur if a justice favored Jerome Frank's sensitivity over his best judgment on the proper disposition of a case. Such a consequence demeans the character of men reared as attorneys in the adversary system and committed to a job whose essence is resolution of conflict.

On the other hand, did the justices benefit from Jerome Frank's input? By sending copies of his judicial opinions, Frank contributed little except the injection of his own personality and ideology. He labored fastidiously with opinions before issuing them; consequently, the printed version constituted as strong a legal argument as Frank could make. No private letter or memorandum elaborated the legal issues more fully that the printed opinion. In a private letter a judge may accent the importance of a case in a form that he would hesitate to include in a formal opinion. Jerome Frank, however, spoke freely and candidly in judicial opinions, and his correspondence with the justices rarely mentioned aspects not contained in the reported version. Those that did were usually confidential personal characterizations.[129]

Frank's notes approving recent opinions, urging the Court to hear a case, or commenting on the performances of other judges—on both the high and lower courts—gave support to the values and attitudes of Supreme Court justices. Waging war became less lonely when an able mind such as Frank's shared the effort. Frank broadly supported an ideological position that insisted on reexamining old concepts in order to produce a more just legal order. At a time when the Supreme Court began to develop sensitivity to issues of civil liberty, Jerome Frank expressed the inherent need to do so. He persistently urged compelling reasons for prompt judicial action in defense of basic liberty.

IV

Since this kind of correspondence between a lower-court judge and Supreme Court justices has seldom been published, one is tempted to conclude that Frank's relations with the justices were atypical.[130] Many others, however, probably had relationships similar, though not identical, to those of Judge Frank.[131] On the other hand, few people possess either the physical stamina or intellectual drive of Jerome Frank. He devoted enormous energy to the world of ideas, of which the law constituted only a part. And Frank's interaction may have been idiosyncratic for another reason: the New Deal thrust together many people who ultimately assumed high judicial positions. When Frank reached the Second Circuit, he was on a first-name basis with a majority of the Supreme Court justices. The bounds of judicial propriety make candid exchanges unlikely except between persons who had previously developed close personal bonds. Frank had forged such bonds through his prior political activities and the range of his intellectual interests.

Although few persons could interact with Supreme Court justices in Frank's dramatic style or with his persistence, many people might share friendships with justices. Gallup polls, *New York Times* editorials, and billboards reading "Impeach Earl Warren" are public reactions to Supreme Court decisions. Justices regularly receive congratulatory notes on their opinions. Friends at the bar or on the bench also forward critical appraisals of particular opinions.[132] Similarly, justices often share with each other personal reactions to draft opinions.[133] Individual friendships and ideological alignment must generate an array of informal and candid judgments on the Court's actions. In this connection, one wonders how often nose counting occurs at the Supreme Court level. To what extent do doctrinal strategies shape the dynamics of the Court's decision-making process? How often does a justice vote to deny certiorari because he fears full review would produce a decision with which he would disagree? Do justices rely on one line of reasoning rather than another because they hope to secure the critical vote of a pivotal justice?[134]

Further research is necessary to document the informal interactions that Supreme Court justices enjoy with friends and the way these interactions relate to their performances as justices. Although Frank injected his personality into the judicial process, he does not appear to have hampered performance or jeopardized independence on any given issue. In his friendships he exhorted justices to persevere, and in his letters he generally endorsed liberal positions. His support came exactly when the Supreme Court began to grapple with new issues of civil liberties. In this context, Frank's opinions and letters indicate how intelligent judges may offer protection to individual rights. There is absolutely no proof that Frank's efforts changed a single vote, but even "stodgy" Mr. Justice Frankfurter, who did not "give a damn about approval or disapproval," found it "comforting to know one is not a solipsistic fool."[135]

Chapter Five

LEGAL REALISM ON THE BENCH

> Our legal concepts often resemble the necks of the flamingos in
> Alice in Wonderland which failed to remain sufficiently rigid to
> be used effectively as mallets by the croquet-players.
>
> —Jerome Frank

I

Frank's highly refined concept of his role as intermediate court
judge—his willingness to occupy a subservient position, to adhere
faithfully to precedent, and to take legal doctrine seriously—raises
a problem. The author of *Law and the Modern Mind* proclaimed that
"all legal rules, principles, precepts, concepts, standards—all generalized statements of law—are fictions."[1] Yet Judge Frank wrote
lengthy opinions, fine-tuned legal rules, quibbled over the scope
and intended meaning of prior judicial decisions, and adumbrated
policy considerations to govern the present and future cases. Did
he repudiate his extreme legal-realist skepticism on becoming an
appeals court judge? Frank did adjust his views after criticism from
both legal positivists and sympathetic liberals and after further
reflection on the importance of legal doctrine brought on by his
own experience in the New Deal. In the Preface to the sixth printing of *Law and the Modern Mind,* as well as in *Courts on Trial,* Frank
paid at least lip service to the importance of legal rules.[2] Notwithstanding these modifications, however, Frank remained an unabashed skeptic, particularly with respect to fact-finding. In his
judicial opinions he elaborated his skepticism about both rules and
facts, which ultimately became the principal theme of *Courts on
Trial.* Thus, as a judge, he did not significantly repudiate his extreme version of legal realism.

How, then, did Philosopher Frank reconcile his beliefs with his position as Judge Frank? Why did his judicial opinions sometimes develop his legal realism yet on other occasions depart significantly from his philosophic writings? The departures stem from judicial responsibilities that required him to operate within a system whose premises he rejected. As a philosopher, Frank was free to criticize, ridicule, and challenge the legal profession's public statements about the rule of law. As a judge, however, he knew that his judicial opinions would be used by real people in the real world, perhaps to achieve results he abhored. Judicial decisions in individual cases may be as unpredictable as Frank the realist suggested. Nonetheless, once issued, they became tools for lawyers and other judges to use, manipulate, and interpret as precedent in similar cases. Even if law is only court orders backed by force, as Holmes suggested, federal and state judges routinely issue thousands of orders, injunctions, declaratory judgments, demands for specific performance, and other remedies on the basis of their understanding of relevant legal principles. As a judge, Jerome Frank found himself creating new tools for others to use in future cases.

In myriad ways the legal system constrains judges to follow norms and expectations. According to legal tradition, judges should wear judicial robes, read the briefs of counsel, and listen attentively to argument. Appellate judges must issue written opinions squaring the facts of the instant case with precedent or explaining why this case is not governed by, or should depart from, past cases. Ironically, Jerome Frank accepted institutional constraints and abided by professional expectations, thus giving credence to legal rules denied by his legal philosophy. His judicial career illustrates the parameters for reform placed on even an extreme cynic. Legal rules are not manipulable at will, even by a legal realist. Legal rules may be relatively autonomous, permitting a range of options and choices, but institutional constraints fettered the will of even Jerome Frank. Prior case law and statutes confined the possibility of legal change. In addition, judges and courts will not issue unpopular decisions without the support of political constituencies. In the 1950s, liberals, such as Frank, who accepted the constraints of their judicial positions ultimately legitimated the cold-war mentality and suppressed dissent.

Frank's legal philosophy and New Deal experience shaped his judicial performance, yet institutional constraints prompted him to write opinions that departed significantly from realist principles and the New Deal's political agenda. On the whole, Frank's judicial opinions continued his precourt legal philosophy and political orientation. His New Deal experience tempered but did not break his commitment to capitalism. While he steadfastly maintained that free competition maximized collective wealth and individual liberty, his judicial opinions supported economic liberalism. In several important cases Frank urged that an economic competitor could ruthlessly gain an unfair advantage from the work of another. In copyright, trademark, and patent law, Frank was reluctant to create a monopoly that would free a business from competition.

On the other hand, as an ardent New Dealer, he understood that unbridled competition posed serious economic problems not merely for individuals but for the nation's economy. His experience at the Agricultural Adjustment Administration, Public Works Administration, and Securities and Exchange Commission taught him that certain government regulation actually maintained the smooth functioning of a basic capitalist model. Thus Frank broadly interpreted the power of administrative agencies to regulate business. These regulations provided an adequate flow of reliable information to permit investors to make intelligent decisions. His securities law opinions particularly manifested an unshakable belief in the wisdom of and necessity for securities regulation in order to prevent fraud, mismanagement, and deception, which in turn would weaken investor confidence in the securities market and consequently weaken the country's economy.

Frank's commitment to economic competition did not blind him to the realities faced by the downtrodden and economically disadvantaged. In admiralty law, he wrote opinions allowing liberal compensation to stevedores for injuries suffered in their employment. Aware of gross disparities in bargaining power, Frank wrote a seminal opinion holding that a form contract containing a waiver was a "contract of adhesion" and not binding on the consumer. Harking back to his days at the AAA, Frank's judicial opinions evince a strong desire to protect the ultimate consumer of goods in a highly complex, technologically advanced market economy.

Litigation has expanded dramatically in twentieth-century American society. Jerome Frank's judicial opinions contributed to this growth by providing broad access to the courts and by sanctioning new causes of action for plaintiffs. This judicial activism reflects how his judicial career built on his legal realism. In *Law and the Modern Mind* Frank argued that judges should not permit legal rules and doctrine to stand in the way of just results. "Doing justice" became the key responsibility for the sensitive and enlightened judge. To a significant extent, Frank carried through on this obligation as a judge. His judicial work continued many themes first articulated in *Law and the Modern Mind* and also elaborated the fact skepticism that culminated in *Courts on Trial.*

II

Frank's antitrust opinions reflect his antimonopoly philosophy. In one case Frank upheld the issuance of a temporary injunction, thereby preventing the defendant from purchasing additional shares of a competitor's stock and thwarting its attempt to enlarge its percentage of the interstate market.[3] The case turned on Section 7 of the Clayton Act, which prohibits one corporation from acquiring the assets of another when the effect may substantially lessen competition or tend to create a monopoly. Frank similarly revealed his antimonopoly philosophy in a case challenging professional baseball's "reserve clause." This clause prohibited a player from contracting with a team other than the one that originally signed him. Despite Supreme Court precedent that found that major league baseball was not interstate commerce and thus beyond the purview of the Sherman Antitrust Act,[4] Jerome Frank interpreted the act broadly to prohibit organized baseball's attempt to monopolize the services of individual players. In light of the economic growth of baseball and doctrinal developments under the commerce clause, Frank considered this earlier ruling "an impotant zombi." The "reserve clause" greatly offended his sense of individual autonomy and dignity.[5]

Frank generally opposed judicial or administrative interference with fairly bargained contracts. In *Oldden v. Tonto Realty Corporation,* for instance, the Second Circuit construed the Bankruptcy Act to require a landlord to deduct the amount of security held under a commercial lease from the total claim allowable under the act. Frank dissented, sarcastically protesting that Congress was not

> activated by any Henry Georgian animosity to owners of land. It is difficult for me to believe that Congress has become so collectivist-minded, so opposed to the common characteristics of our profit system, that it intended that a landlord should not (to quote my colleagues) "obtain an advantage merely because he has been shrewd or economically powerful enough to have obtained a substantial deposit as security."[6]

Frank's procompetition, antileveling impulse found simultaneous expression in *Fate and Freedom,* his 1945 philosophic work that lashed out at determinism of all sorts. The essence of freedom, according to Frank, is individual action, not collective or socialistic endeavors. The legal and economic system should tolerate the full range of economic decisions whether intelligent or not, whether freely entered or made under duress or from a weak bargaining position.

Therefore, Frank opposed the judiciary's reliance on concepts of fairness to prevent a competing manufacturer from misappropriating trade secrets. When the Second Circuit enjoined a new manufacturer from competing with an established firm, Frank protested that damages would adequately compensate for the past wrong. The new manufacturer, Frank demonstrated, would shortly have entered into active competition with plaintiff even without the misappropriation. Consequently, a permanent injunction did not serve the public interest in free competition. The misappropriator's unfair tactics should not result in permanent restraint of competition.[7] Frank similarly refused, in another case, to order a corporation's board of directors to pay certain dividends to preferred shareholders. The board clearly acted within its discretion in withholding payment, and "preferred stockholders are not—like sailors or idiots or infants—wards of the judiciary."[8] Courts should not intervene and revise contracts entered into by uncoerced adults.

Frank's copyright, patent, and trademark opinions reflect his commitment to economic competition, which he believed benefited consumers. Since these three areas offer some measure of protection from competition, his reasoning requires elaboration. The patent system, designed to stimulate invention, requires that the inventor demonstrate a large measure of novelty in order to qualify for a patent. A copyright, designed simply to protect authorship, does not require great originality. Therefore, Frank's opinions sharply distinguished between a patent, whose holder may prohibit a subsequent inventor from reproducing the design even if the second inventor independently created the object, and a copyright, which protects only against actual copying with knowledge. He also treated patents and copyrights, which are statutorily recognized, differently from trademarks, which are creations of the judiciary designed to protect a business's designation of its product. His attitude in these three areas depended ultimately on his perception of the likely impact of the legal doctrine on consumers.

Frank chastized people with "monopoly-phobia" who failed to appreciate how protection from some competition might ultimately benefit the consuming public.[9] Frank thought that the patent system needed overhauling. In *Picard v. United Aircraft Corp.* he argued that modern large-scale research laboratories had completely revolutionized methods of invention.[10] The old method of invention as a creative flash of genius yielded to painstaking progress, not by single inventors but by large and elaborate research staffs. Yet the legal standard required judges to find a "flash of creative genius" and thus encouraged subjective decisions about scientific advancements.[11] This demanding legal test meant that many patents issued by the Patent Office would not be upheld if challenged in court. Nonetheless, they constituted effective monopolies because many businesses could not afford to litigate the issue of validity.

For Frank, the key economic justification for a patent monopoly was to stimulate investment rather than invention. He would prohibit, as economically undesirable, large corporations from buying patents issued to third parties for products competing with the corporation's, and then retiring the new product. Frank recognized the economic and social disutility of preventing society from enjoying the benefits of a new invention. His focus on the incentive to investments offered extremely broad patent protection. Frank believed that the possibility of obtaining a monopoly would stimulate small companies to challenge entrenched concerns. Similarly, ongoing companies, under the threat of competition, would undertake additional research to protect their position. Thus he thought that patents aimed at stimulating investment would actually foster competition and benefit the public.[12]

Frank's concern for consumers, a theme first evident during his AAA experience, produced a quite different attitude toward trademarks. He favored economic competition not as an end in itself but for its benefits to consumers. Trade name protection rests on the social policy of protecting businesses that have built up goodwill against unfair practices by competitors. The public's interest, Frank argued, includes preserving fair dealing and honesty and rewarding businessmen with a monopoly in order to induce them to bring out new products that will benefit consumers. Since the consumer's interest ultimately justifies trademark protection, courts should award a trademark monopoly to a business only on proof that a competitor's use of the mark actually confuses consumers.[13]

Triangle Publications v. Rohrlich epitomizes Jerome Frank's concern for protecting consumers. The publisher of *Seventeen* magazine sued Ms. Seventeen Foundations Co., a manufacturer of girdles which used the trademark "Ms. Seventeen." Judge Augustus Hand granted an injunction, reasoning that the word "Seventeen" had acquired a secondary meaning and the girdle manufacturers' use would be likely to cause confusion. Frank's dissent argued that the magazine and the girdles were not even potential competitors. Evidence to the contrary adduced at trial Frank considered mere surmise. Drawing on his fact skepticism, Frank, perhaps with tongue in cheek, wrote:

> As neither the trial judge or any member of this court is (or resembles) a teen-aged girl or the mother or sister of such a girl, our judicial notice apparatus will not work well unless we feed it with information directly obtained from "teen-agers" or from their female relatives accustomed to shop for them. Competently to inform ourselves, we should have a staff of investigators like those applied to administrative agencies. As we have no such staff, I have questioned some ado-

lescent girls and their mothers and sisters, persons I have chosen at random. I have been told uniformly by my questionees that no one could reasonably believe that any relation existed between plaintiff's magazine and defendant's girdles.

To buttress his economic argument, Frank significantly quoted from Brandeis: "'sharing in the goodwill of an article unprotected by patent or trade-mark is the exercise of a right possessed by all— and in the free exercise of which the consuming public is deeply interested.'"[14]

In *Standard Brands Inc. v. Smidler,* the manufacturer of V-8 canned vegetable juice sued the distributor of vitamin tablets marked "V-8" for trademark infringement and unfair competition.[15] Frank reluctantly concurred in the court's issuance of a permanent injunction, believing that prior case law left him no option, but hoped for U.S. Supreme Court reversal. He argued that trademark doctrine had become an ill-considered judicial protection of the first user of a mark or symbol rather than genuine protection for consumers. Courts assumed that consumers were harmed by the deceit of a second user of a mark. Frank challenged this assumption as utterly unverified, arguing that second users frequently sell identical products at lower costs, quite clearly benefiting consumers. He suggested that trademark plaintiffs demonstrate, as part of their cause of action, that defendant's product is actually inferior to plaintiff's. *Standard Brands* once again found Jerome Frank, the consumer advocate, seeking to reshape the judicially created trademark doctrine.[16]

III

Notwithstanding his commitment to free competition, Frank's writings, on and off the bench, expressed concern for the economically oppressed and disadvantaged. In *M. Witmark & Sons v. Fred Fisher Music Co.,* the Second Circuit construed the Copyright Act to permit an author to assign his right to an extension of a copyright. Frank dissented because authors as a group are "notoriously inexperienced in business." This author, "in desperate financial straits," sold the extension for the copyright for the song "When Irish Eyes Are Smiling" to an experienced and successful publisher for a small amount of money at a time when it was impossible to calculate the value of the copyright extension. Drawing on the history of the Copyright Act and on American economic history, Frank argued that laissez-faire was a myth in the American past which had never existed in unadulterated form. The state historically used power indirectly to enforce bargains it believed appropriate. Since "individualism, if utterly unrestrained, becomes self-devouring and has produced slums and other social evils, laissez-faire must be tempered by other concerns."[17]

Frank reserved special solicitude for seamen who were considered "wards of admiralty." In *Hume v. Moore-McCormack Lines, Inc.,* a seaman sought damages for tuberculosis developed and aggravated while working on defendant's ships, allegedly as a result of improper sleeping quarters on board the vessels. The district court granted summary judgment for defendants because the seaman had signed a "release of all rights" for $150, even though at the time he signed the release he did not know that he was suffering from tuberculosis. Frank reversed, counseling courts to make "realistic appraisals of the inability of the individual seaman to cope effectively with his employer in bargaining."[18] Judicial protection of the seaman compensates for his inability to bargain equally and for the lack of a lawyer or other competent adviser to represent him when he signed the release.[19]

Frank also refused to enforce contract provisions in other contexts. In *Siegelman v. Cunard White Star,* a passenger sued a steamship company for injuries suffered when she fell from a dining room chair that was not bolted to the floor. The steamship ticket, a sheet of paper thirteen inches by eleven inches, contained terms and conditions in small print including a one-year limitation on actions for bodily injury, a denial of liability not acknowledged in writing, and a provision that English law would govern all questions arising under the contract. These terms prompted the Second Circuit to dismiss the suit. In an influential dissent, Frank characterized the contract as a "contract of adhesion," which, as a printed form prepared by defendant, should be construed strongly against defendant. The small type on the back of the ticket did not represent terms and conditions to which both parties consciously assented. To the contrary, the passenger probably had no knowledge of those terms. This one-sided bargaining prompted Frank to interpret the terms favorably to the plaintiff. Echoing his legal realism, Frank insisted on the need for courts to "do justice in particular instances."[20]

Frank's *Siegelman* dissent was an important opinion, widely followed, which refused both to allow legal rules to stand in the way of just results and to pretend that two parties have entered fairly into a contract when in reality one side dictated the contract terms. Commercial law has recently built on these principles in recognizing that consumers rarely bargain for warranties and other terms of purchase. Form contracts reflect the powerful economic leverage of the manufacturer or supplier of goods and services who chooses to limit liability.[21]

Frank similarly protected consumers in *Lichten v. Eastern Airlines.*[22] Eastern Airlines submitted to the Civil Aeronautics Board (CAB) a tariff providing that the carrier would not be liable for jewelry carried by the passenger and lost by the airline. The Second Circuit upheld this tariff as part of the contract under which the passenger and her baggage were carried. Frank's dissent asserted that the CAB lacked power to authorize such a significant limitation on liability. Given Frank's normal predisposition to ratify broad governmental power, especially in the hands of administrative agencies, his *Lichten* dissent poignantly illustrates his effort to protect the ultimate consumer from a contract of adhesion ratified by a goverment agency.

A main theme of Frank's legal philosophy, "doing justice," found expression in his judicial opinions, often by creating new causes of action or otherwise recognizing access to courts for wronged individuals. *Haelan Laboratories v. Topps Chewing Gum,* an important Frank opinion creating a "right of publicity," epitomized his approach.[23] Plaintiff, a chewing-gum manufacturer, entered a contract with a major league baseball player granting plaintiff the exclusive right to use the ballplayer's photograph on a baseball card. Defendant, a rival chewing-gum manufacturer, induced the ballplayer to sign a contract permitting defendant to use the player's photograph. Defendant argued that plaintiff's contract with the ballplayer simply released the company from potential liability for using the player's photograph and did not grant plaintiff an exclusive right. The federal district court agreed and dismissed the case. Plaintiff appealed to the Second Circuit, where Frank wrote the country's first opinion recognizing a "right of publicity."[24] Frank wove together tidbits from earlier state court decisions that, he asserted, created this new protection for persons to authorize the use of their countenances. A seminal decision, *Haelen Laboratories* has led to the enormous growth of a cottage industry of entertainers, athletes, and other prominent persons who receive compensation for endorsing products.

A recent phenomenon contributing to the "litigation explosion" has been the willingness of courts to "imply" or "infer" causes of action from regulatory statutes that have not expressly provided for damage actions.[25] Jerome Frank played a key role in creating and encouraging this development. In *Fitzgerald v. Pan American World Airways,* Frank held that airline passengers were entitled to damages when the carrier engaged in racial discrimination.[26] The Civil Aeronautics Act prohibited carriers from giving "unreasonable preference" to any person or engaging in "any unjust discrimination." Knowing violation of this section constituted a federal crime, and the CAB was authorized to investigate any complaint and to issue "an appropriate order" to comply with the act.[27] Notably, the act did not expressly provide for a civil cause of action for damages. Nonetheless, Frank reasoned that the prohibition on discrimination was for the benefit of passengers and concluded that the act, by implication, created a civil action on behalf of any person who had been harmed by the violation.[28] Coming less than two years after the Supreme Court's historic *Brown v. Board of Education* decision ordering racial integration in public schools, *Fitzgerald* found Frank significantly expanding the scope of *Brown* in concluding that the act prohibited the airline's insistance that the black passengers ride in seats other than the first-class seats that they held. While the Supreme Court eventually ratified this course, in 1956 the scope of *Brown* remained cloudy.[29]

Frank conferred broad access to courts by creating liberal standing rules in several important decisions. When a federal agency promulgated a regulation allowing synthetic vitamins to be added to oleomargarine with the simple designation "Vitamin A added," a dealer in fish oils, a natural source of vitamin A, sought judicial review both as a producer and as a consumer. In a Frank opinion, the Second Circuit upheld the dealer's standing to sue as a consumer "adversely affected" by the regulation.[30] While the petitioner lost on the merits, Frank nonetheless cemented a broad theory of access to judicial review of administrative action.

His most comprehensive protection of access to courts came in his effort to create standing for "private attorney generals"— citizens who sue government officials in order to prevent them from violating federal statutes. The seminal case, *Associated Industries of New York State v. Ickes,* found the Second Circuit, through Judge Frank, holding that an association of coal-consuming industrial and commercial firms had standing to challenge Secretary of the Interior Ickes's decision, under the Bituminous Coal Act of 1937, to raise the minimum price for bituminous coal by 20 cents a ton. Section 6(b) of the act permits "any person aggrieved" by a regulation to seek judicial review in a U.S. Court of Appeals. Building on earlier Supreme Court precedent,[31] Frank argued that Congress can, by statute, authorize a government official to seek judicial review to prevent another government official from violating statutory powers. Frank continued, in dictum, to assert an extraordinarily broad concept of standing to sue:

> Instead of designating the Attorney General, or some other public officer, to bring such proceedings, Congress can constitutionally enact a statute conferring on any non-official person, or on a designated group of non-official persons, authority to bring a suit to prevent action by an officer in violation of his statutory powers; for then, in like manner, there is an actual controversy, and there is nothing constitutionally prohibiting Congress from empowering any person, official or not, to institute a proceeding involving such a controversy, even if the sole purpose is to vindicate the public interest. Such persons, so authorized, are, so to speak, private Attorney Generals.[32]

It was unnecessary for Frank to argue broad citizen standing because the trade group, as consumers, plainly were "persons aggrieved" within the meaning of the congressional grant of standing to challenge regulations under the Bituminous Coal Act. The central thrust of his *Associated Industries* opinion was recognition of consumer standing. Frank, harking back to his AAA days, read the Bituminous Coal Act to protect consumers. "[I]t should surely be construed, if possible, in such a way as not to block out all protection to consumers. In fact . . . Congress (recognizing that this legislation granted immunity to coal producers from provisions of the Anti-Trust laws) was bent on giving adequate off-setting protection to consumers."[33]

IV

Frank's securities regulation opinions continued his effort as former SEC commissioner and chairman to protect the small investor and to make the securities exchanges function openly and fairly. Without a full and adequate flow of information, investors, whether institutional or small, are unable to make intelligent economic decisions and capital formation is impeded. The collapse of the stock market and the nation's economy during the Great Depression convinced Frank of the need for government protection of investors and for regulation of financial markets. His securities opinions granted broad access to courts, implied causes of action on behalf of investors concerning complex regulatory statutes, and held accountable persons who undermined investor confidence by manipulating stock prices. These opinions echo Frank's consumer advocacy and demonstrate an economic liberalism tempered by an awareness that unmitigated competition in a complex market economy does not produce healthy long-term economic results, but instead tends to encourage business and financial market abuses that curtail economic growth.

In *Fischman v. Raytheon Manufacturing Co.*, stockholders who had allegedly purchased stock in reliance on a prospectus and registration statement that contained untrue statements of material facts as well as omissions of material facts sued the company and its president.[34] The federal district court dismissed the complaint but the Second Circuit, with Judge Frank writing, reversed. Frank held that the Securities Exchange Act of 1934, together with Rule 10b-5, promulgated by the SEC, permits a suit for damages by a purchaser of securities described in a prospectus and registration statement. A seminal decision, *Fischman* was the first court of appeals case to recognize a cause of action under 10b-5. It required judicial creativity to reach this result because, first, the 1934 act did *not* expressly provide for a civil cause of action for damages for violation of 10b-5 and, second, the 1933 act, in expressly authorizing a cause of action, set limits to it by a statute of limitations and other restrictions.[35] *Fischman* confronted Frank with the need to reconcile 10b-5 with the express but limited civil liability provision of the 1933 act. He finessed the problem by requiring plaintiffs to establish defendant's scienter, an element not requisite for recovery under the 1933 act. Although this test places a heavy burden on plaintiffs, Frank apparently felt it inappropriate to create judicially a cause of action whose scope would exceed a congressionally created cause of action under an analogous statute. *Fischman* became a widely cited precedent that the U.S. Supreme Court ratified in its superseding decisions.[36]

In another important 10b-5 decision, *Joseph v. Farnsworth Radio & Television Corp.*, Frank dissented from a holding that 10b-5 required "privity" between plaintiff and defendant.[37] Frank protested that this holding had the anomalous effect of immunizing from liability the issuing of admittedly false statements simply because the persons who relied on such statements purchased shares on the open market. To Frank, it should not matter whether the consumers had a contractual relationship with the persons who issued the false statements. Rule 10b-5 speaks broadly of acts that operate to defraud "any person, in connection with the purchase or sale of any security."[38] Frank saw no justification for curbing responsibility for admittedly false statements. Ultimately, securities law developed as Frank's dissent urged.[39]

In another significant securities law opinion, *Subin v. Goldsmith*, Frank's dissent encouraged the growth of shareholder derivative suits by implying a cause of action under Section 14(a) of the Securities and Exchange Act of 1934. Section 14(a) prohibits solicitation of a proxy or other authorization in violation of SEC rules, one of which prohibits false statements in proxy solicitations. The statute and the rule, Frank argued, permitted a civil action for damages.

An economy like ours, which thrives on the fact that thousands of persons of modest means invest in corporate shares, will be poorly served if our courts regard with suspicion all minority stockholders' suits, and, therefore, out of a desire to discourage such suits, apply to them unusually strict pleading rules, thus tending to thwart judicial inquiries into the conduct of wrongdoing, controlling stockholders. The unfortunate consequence will be that those in control may be immunized from effective attacks on their misdeeds, and, as a result, the small investors will lose confidence in all corporate managements, the honest as well as the dishonest.[40]

Courts play a special role in securities regulation by ensuring the integrity of the economic process. Given the separation of corporate ownership and corporate control, courts must be alert to protect the myriad small investors from those corporate managements that seek personal profit. A prescient dissent, Frank's *Subin* opinion foreshadowed the Supreme Court's important decision in *J. I. Case Co v. Borak,* which followed Frank's approach.[41]

A final important securities opinion concerned construction of Section 16(b) of the Securities Exchange Act of 1934, which allows the recapture of short-term trading profits from corporate officers, directors, or other "insiders" in order to prevent them from using confidential information to profit in the stock market.[42] In attempting to curb this practice, the 1934 act also required reports of transactions of any officer, director, or other person who is a "beneficial owner" of more than 10 percent of any class of stock of a company registered with the SEC. These provisions have spawned an enormous amount of litigation, with complicated legal questions. In *Stella v. Graham-Paige Motors Corp.,* Frank held that a person became a "beneficial owner" at the moment when a stock transaction increased that person's ownership above the 10 percent minimum required by Section 16(b), once again broadly construing a securities provision to uphold plaintiff's cause of action for damages.[43]

V

The seeds of Frank's legal realism and New Deal experience took root and flourished in his judicial opinions regarding administrative law. The AAA and SEC, pragmatic responses to problems generated by unrestrained individualism, epitomized the problem of the regulatory state: how to reconcile administrative agencies' regulation of individuals and enterprises with economic liberalism and with the hallmark of the American character—individualism.[44] Frank's rationale, typical of the New Deal generally, was that administrative agencies serve a public purpose by placing a coterie of neutral experts in authority. These government officials, armed with investigative powers and staffs, research the facts causing the problem at hand and issue rules and regulations in the public interest. The underlying premise of New Deal administrative agencies was their capacity to identify a common public interest and to render objective decisions to further that interest. In retrospect, this belief in the expertise and objectivity of government regulators seems extraordinarily naive, yet it justified the growth of the regulatory state.[45] Just as Frank's realism did not focus on conflicting economic interests or political ideologies, he assumed the good faith of administrators who, subject to due process limitations, would issue respectable judgments to which courts should defer.

Frank's administrative law decisions evince his commitment to expansive federal power, his tendency to construe New Deal legislation broadly, and his deference to the judgment and findings of fact of administrative agencies.[46] In *Guiseppi v. Walling*, plaintiff challenged the decision of the Wage and Hour administrator of the U.S. Department of Labor to issue a wage order for the embroideries industry. The wage order established a minimum wage of 40 cents an hour and prohibited embroidery work in residences except by persons who obtained special homework certificates.[47] The administrator justified the prohibition of homework because it presented an easy method of violating the minimum wage provision. The administrator found that the order "will not prohibit any type of work or occupation but will merely compel the transfer of work and occupations formerly carried on in the homes to the factory." Frank upheld the wage order, even though the act prohibited wage orders that "substantially curtail employment in the industry." He recognized that the Fair Labor Standards Act would be otherwise unenforceable. The administrator remarkably found that the order complied with the act and Frank was not inclined to look closely at the facts. Brushing aside equal protection and due process challenges, Frank narrowed the theory of unlawful delegation of legislative power from Congress to administrative agencies. Arguing for a flexible concept of separation of powers, Frank observed that legislatures have always delegated authority to administrative officials. Persons who opposed the exercise of power by administrative agencies reminded Frank of "the child who was horrified when his attention was called to the fact that his tongue was wet and his shoes full of feet." A complex industrial society often requires administrative agencies, and the task should be to seek "the selection of well-trained, honest, able men, conscientiously obeying the laws, and imbued with the spirit of democracy, to serve as administrators."[48] Frank did not envision administrative officials as engaging in political decision making and he accepted the prohibition on homework as not "substantially curtailing employment."

In *Queensboro Farm Products v. Wickard,* Frank sustained the power of the Secretary of Agriculture under the Agricultural Adjustment Act to classify milk for price-fixing purposes according to the form of the milk (for example, fluid milk, cream, frozen desserts, butter, cheese). Perhaps recalling his turbulent years at the AAA, Frank observed that "[t]he city-dweller or poet who regards the cow as symbol of bucolic serenity is indeed naive. From the udders of that placid animal flows a bland liquid indispensible to human health but often provoking as much human strife and nastiness as strong alcoholic beverages." Although the secretary's power to set milk prices was unclear, Frank wove together pieces of legislative history and Supreme Court dicta to uphold the regulation. He urged courts not to intrude on administrative discretion, particularly since they are inadequately staffed to undertake the administration of AAA programs. Courts should give "considerable weight" to an interpretation of a statute by officials who "act in administering it as specialists advised by experts."[49]

Frank sought to protect the work of administrative agencies by deferring both to their fact-finding and to their interpretation of the enabling legislation.[50] Given the critical role of contested facts and the number of occasions in which more than one reasonable interpretation of a statute is possible, this process minimized the occasions when courts would overturn administrative agency decisions.

On the other hand, Frank's New Deal orientation did not blind him to arbitrary agency rulings. When the New Haven Railroad went into bankruptcy reorganization, an issue arose as to the value of certain property appraised by the Interstate Commerce Commission (ICC). Frank refused to accept the ICC's judgment because the commission had merely rubber-stamped the judgment of others. To Frank, the only reason to defer to administrative agencies was their assumed expertise. "When they openly abdicate their judgment, they make a mockery of the administrative process." Administrative agencies must publicize the reasons for their actions because "no aspect of a democratic government should be mysterious." Frank thought the ICC arbitrarily placed a value on the property, and thus the term "value" misleadingly connoted an objective rational conclusion. He suggested substituting for "value" the term "woosh-woosh," sarcastically urging that the rule of law would then become "'when the I.C.C. has ceremonially woosh-wooshed, judicial scrutiny is barred.'"[51]

Frank's willingness to defer to administration officials did not extend to decisions involving the deportation of aliens or to questions of criminal procedure.

> [O]ne can say that it does not pay to take too seriously the possibility that one man, more or less, may be unjustly imprisoned, considering the fact that, in the recent war, millions have died and that the Atomic Age just begun may end any minute in the destruction of all this planet's inhabitants. Yet (perhaps because I am growing old or because, despite my years, I have not yet fully matured) it seems to me that if America's part in the war was meaningful and if mankind's development has any significance against the background of eternity, then the dignity of each individual man is not an empty phrase. If it is not, then we judges, part of a human arrangement called the government, should proceed with great caution when we determine whether a man is to be forcibly deprived of his liberty.[52]

Arbitrary governmental action bothered Frank, especially action that impinged on individual freedom or shrouded the government in mystery. Some of his most influential opinions concerned the deportation of aliens and criminal procedure. American law has traditionally considered deportation an administrative process, so that the person affected is not entitled to the range of procedural safeguards associated with a criminal charge. But the impact on liberty, particularly confinement and then literal banishment from the United States, can be enormous—far worse than most criminal sanctions. Frank railed against lax deportation procedures that unfairly subjected many immigrants to great hardship.

In *Repouille v. United States,* Frank dissented from a ruling that a father who committed euthanasia of his seriously brain-damaged, blind, mute, and malformed son lacked "good moral character" for purposes of becoming a naturalized citizen.[53] Frank considered the standard extremely subjective, calling for judges to guess, under the guise of taking "judicial notice," about the public's moral standards. In *United States v. Watkins,* Frank protested against a distinction between an exclusion order, not subject to judicial review of the jurisdictional fact of alienage, and deportation, as applied to a United Sates resident who had temporarily left the country.[54] Frank considered the distinction silly and artificial, with enormous adverse consequences for the individual involved.

Frank's unwillingness to defer to Board of Immigration Appeals decisions is quite evident in *United States ex rel. Accardi v. Shaughnessy.* The Second Circuit refused to go behind the administrative record to assess the allegation that the U.S. attorney general had improperly influenced the board to deny an alien's application for suspension of his deportation. Petitioner alleged that the board's "review" of the Immigration and Naturalization Service's decision was a sham. Frank protested:

Having served for a considerable period as an administrative officer, I am fairly callous to the cries of men who denounce all such officers as power-hungry bureaucrats, and I am perhaps unusually aware of the danger to the workings of government if any administrative officer could be dragged into court, to stand trial, on a mere suspicion of impropriety behind the scenes. However, there would be greater danger to democratic government in judicial acceptance of every administrative record as final and invulnerable, no matter how grave and serious the charges against the official.[55]

Thus the board should have listened to, and the court should have reviewed, allegations going beyond the fact of the administrative record.

In *United States ex rel. Fong Foo v. Shaughnessy,* Frank granted a summer recess stay of a deportation order. The petitioner was admittedly deportable, but stated that he had supported the Nationalist government of China, and were he deported to the mainland, the Communist government would execute him. Frank took judicial notice of "the notorious and virtually indisputable fact . . . of the ruthless behavior of the Communist Governments in China and Russia" which would lead to petitioner's torture and death. "Illegal entry into this country should not be punished by death."[56] An earlier Second Circuit case had limited Frank's ability to aid the petitioner. Frank argued, however, that stare decisis should not control when a person's life is at stake. This theme, echoing his legal realism, showed his willingness to upset settled doctrine in order to reach results he considered just.

Finally, in *United States ex rel. Lee Kum Hoy v. Shaughnessy,* Frank protested against a Board of Immigration Appeals decision to deny citizenship status because blood tests proved nonpaternity.[57] The immigration service used these tests only for Chinese applicants, not for white applicants. From earlier Supreme Court rulings Frank pieced together a theory that this practice constituted unconstitutional administration of an otherwise valid law.[58]

VI

Frank's legal philosophy found direct expression in his criminal procedure opinions. First, he repeatedly insisted that judges should "do justice" regardless of the particular legal doctrine. Second, his fact skepticism shaped important opinions on harmless error, third-degree police practices, and other procedures that raised questions about the accuracy of jury verdicts. His criminal law and procedure opinions attempted to erect rules against oppressive governmental action and police practices. In *United States v. Parrino,* Frank protested against affirming a conviction of a defendant who pleaded guilty after his counsel advised him that a conviction would not subject him to deportation. Frank voted to permit him to withdraw his guilty plea and considered counsel's gross incompetence "manifest injustice" within the statute. Writing candidly about his aspirations as a judge, Frank observed:

> [S]ometimes a statute inescapably commands judges to conform to a legal ritual indifferent to justice. Then, regret it as we may, we judges must administer "injustice according to law." But we should regard such instances as exceptional, deplorable, and should not, generalizing from them, conclude that doing justice is not our role, that the "administration of justice" is an empty phrase not to be taken literally. When, therefore, a Rule tells us in the plainest words to avoid manifest injustice, I believe we should eagerly embrace the opportunity, not extend earlier decisions to escape it.[59]

Similarly, in *United States v. Johnson*, Frank's dissent argued for a narrow construction of a statute permitting federal district judges to deny leave to indigents to file *in forma pauperis* appeals if the judge concludes that the appeal is not undertaken in good faith. Frank urged that indigents be permitted to appeal, even though many will present frivolous issues. Unimpressed by arguments regarding the congestion of court dockets, Frank thought that the rare valid appeal required courts to grant appeals in all cases. "I, for one, cannot sleep well if I think that, due to any judicial decisions in which I have joined, innocent destitute men may be behind bars solely because it would cost the government something to have their appeals considered."[60]

In *United States v. Leviton*, the trial judge rebuked defendant's counsel and two jurors applauded. The Second Circuit characterized the trial judge's action as human error, during a long and difficult trial, which did not require reversal of the conviction. Frank acknowledged that judges, as human, make mistakes, but this error may have seriously prejudiced the jury, and therefore there should be a new trial. "We should be humane as well as human. And since the defendants are languishing in jail and the trial judge is not, they should be the object of our humaneness."[61]

Frank's criminal procedure decisions reflect his skepticism about the accuracy of the fact-finding process. Judicial fact-finding "is a job of history-writing, and, like all history-writing, inescapably involves 'subjective' factors and encounters other obstacles sometimes insurmountable."[62] His appellate court experience allowed him to develop his fact skepticism. In a series of important opinions, usually dissents, he articulated the criticism of the fact-finding process which he later published for general audiences in *Courts on Trial* and *Not Guilty*.

In *In re Fried*, Frank criticized the distinction between procedural and substantive rules, arguing that a substantive rule has no practical value if the court misapprehends what actually happened and therefore applies the substantive rule to "facts" that never existed.[63] He urged, in *United States v. Liss*, that courts recognize that juries consist of ordinary citizens, not expert fact-finders, and therefore judges must exercise care to ensure that juries are not confused. Foreshadowing an argument he developed in *Courts on Trial*, Frank observed that the "contentious method" of trial accents the lawyer's skill rather than enhances the accuracy of the fact-finding process. Therefore, judges should refuse to be "mere umpires," and instead should assume responsibility lest the accused suffer from the mistakes of his or her attorney.[64]

United States v. Murphy, Frank's most passionate attack on prolonged interrogation and other third-degree police practices, granted a writ of habeas corpus to a petitioner who had been held incommunicado for more than forty hours and subjected to prolonged and repeated interrogations. The net effect, Frank thought, brutalized the police: " '[T]he horrible thing about all legal officials, even the best, about all judges, magistrates, detectives, and policemen, is not that they are wicked (some of them are good), not that they are stupid (several of them are quite intelligent); it is simply that they have got used to it.' " Frank had concern for "humble inconspicuous men" because "repeated and unredressed attacks on the constitutional liberties of the humble will tend to destroy the foundation supporting the constitutional liberties of everyone. The test of the moral quality of the civilization is its treatment of the weak and powerless."[65] Third-degree police practices smack of totalitarianism and undercut the fabric of a democratic society. They undermine respect for police and generate public cynicism about the ideals of the Constitution. Confessions tainted by torture are notoriously unreliable, casting doubt on any finding of guilt. Frank's antipathy to police interrogation led him to permit a pre-indictment suppression of an allegedly coerced confession.[66] Prior case law did not support him, and the subsequent course of the law has not developed as Frank argued.[67]

VII

Frank elaborated important themes from his legal philosophy in his judicial opinions. As a judge, he remained concerned with "doing justice," frequently disregarded stare decisis, and bent legal rules to achieve desirable results. He insisted that the government must operate openly because a democratic society cannot tolerate mysterious government. He was enormously skeptical about civil juries, general verdicts, and, generally, the accuracy of the fact-finding process. *United States v. Forness (Salamanca Trust Co.)* vividly illustrates the embodiment of realist principles in a judicial opinion. Frank refused to follow an ancient property doctrine that would have unfairly prevented the Seneca Nation of Indians from canceling leases. Despite an annual rent of only $4 per plot, the lessees repeatedly defaulted. They tried to avoid cancellation because the Indians had not made a proper "demand," as required by the common law. Frank simply refused to apply mechanically an old rule of the common law which served no contemporary purpose.[68]

In *Ricketts v. Pennsylvania Railroad Co.,* the court considered the validity of a release signed by an injured railroad employee who was covered by the Federal Employers' Liability Act. Contract law theory had long debated whether a contract represented a "meeting of the minds" of two parties (a subjective theory reflecting the actual state of mind of the particular persons entering the contract) or a "reasonable" standard to which all persons were held, regardless of their "actual intent" (an objective theory). Frank attacked the effort of contract theorists to impose a single model on the legal universe. "Fortunately, most judges are too commonsensible to allow, for long, a passion for esthetic elegance, or for the appearance of an abstract consistency, to bring about obviously unjust results."[69]

He demonstrated how courts, while purporting to use an objective theory, actually examined the subjective state of mind of the parties. Frank repudiated the objective test in favor of a maleable doctrine that would protect ignorant persons from unscrupulous parties. He suggested not only that courts reach a just result, but also that they articulate this shift in legal doctrine. His flexible attitude toward contracts would not produce legal chaos, Frank thought, but instead would actually promote greater certainty because legal doctrine would finally be compatible with the way courts in fact behave. Piercing legal verbiage to determine "what the courts will do in fact" is, of course, a mainstay of legal realism. Frank the jurist demonstrated a yearning to make judicial behavior consistent with articulated legal doctrine, just as did Frank the legal realist.

As a judge Frank continued his realist critique of judges who hid behind the facade of legal doctrine. One dissent commented starkly, "A legal system is not what it says but what it does."[70] Another dissent protested that:

> the conventions of judicial opinion-writing—the uncolloquial vocabulary, the use of phrases carrying with them an air of finality, the parade of precedents, the display of seemingly rigorous logic bedecked with "therefores" and "must-be-trues"—give an impression of certainty (which often hypnotizes the opinion writer) concealing the uncertainties inherent in the judging process. On close examination, our legal concepts often resemble the necks of the flamingos in Alice in Wonderland which failed to remain sufficiently rigid to be used effectively as mallets by the croquet-players.[71]

Frank sought to "do justice" by repudiating the doctrine of stare decisis in criminal cases. Since a person's liberty was at stake, an established rule of law should be discarded if it was no longer reasonable or just.[72] In another example of "doing justice," Frank addressed an issue not briefed or argued by counsel, an action that normally would have been foreclosed. "A Court striving to do justice between the parties, should not put on blinders and ignore matters which counsel overlook."[73] Frank's disdainful attitude toward rules exposed him to the criticism that he engaged in ad hoc decision making. Consider, for instance, *Ochs v. Commissioner of In-*

ternal Revenue. Frank voted to allow, as a medical expense, private school tuition for children of a family of modest means when the mother developed cancer and her physician recommended boarding school. The Second Circuit opted for a rigid rule rather than face an array of potentially fraudulent medical expense claims. Frank, recognizing the humane consideration undergirding this case, voted to allow the deduction, even though he acknowledged the "spectacle of opening the flood gates" to expenses claimed for cooks, governesses, and other conveniences.[74]

Legal realism characteristically and cynically perceived legal concepts as not possessing any inherent content or creating bright-line boundaries of legal rights, but simply as masks for judges' ultimate preference for one position over another. Yet one case, *Addison v. Huron Stevedoring Corp.,* had an odd twist, with Frank arguing for protecting "vested rights" and Learned Hand for openly balancing the competing interests.[75] Before *Addison,* the U.S. Supreme Court had construed "work week" within the Fair Labor Standards Act (FLSA) of 1938 to include the time workers took to dress and undress and to travel to and from their work stations.[76] A subsequent congressional investigation concluded that the Supreme Court's construction was a wholly unexpected interpretation of the act which would generate windfall payments to workers, threaten financial ruin for many companies, and saddle the U.S government with retroactive liabilities of over 81 billion for cost-plus wartime contracts. These facts prompted Congress, in 1947, to enact the Portal-to-Portal Act, repudiating the Supreme Court's construction. In subsequent litigation, the Second Circuit rejected an argument that the Portal-to-Portal Act retroactively destroyed vested rights.[77] In a parallel development in 1948, in *Bay Bridge Operating Co. v. Aaron,* the Supreme Court held that the FLSA entitled employees to overtime pay for work performed during the years 1943–45 because, while the collective bargaining agreement treated certain working shifts as regular time, the act required overtime pay.[78] This decision prompted another round of statutory amendments in 1949 and 1950. The constitutionality of these amendments reached the Second Circuit in *Addison,* where Learned Hand upheld their constitutionality, rejecting a rigid concept of "vested rights," which, by making compensable even slight changes in the enjoyment of property, would seriously restrict Congress' ability to act in the public interest. Frank's dissent, full of "vested rights" rhetoric, seems to repudiate the New Deal canon that judges not interfere with social legislation enacted by Congress and seems inconsistent with his realist skepticism about bright-line legal concepts.

A prominent theme in Frank's books, articles, and judicial opinions insists, however, that the government act openly, obey its own rules, and be humane. In *Addison,* Frank reasoned that the new amendments, unlike the Portal-to-Portal Act, were not responses to an emergency. First, *Bay Bridge* was unlikely to affect more than a few industries. Second, the Supreme Court's construction did not create a truly unexpected liability. Third, the construction did not threaten employers with financial havoc because the government would ultimately bear the burden of these cost-plus contracts. Indeed, the U.S. attorney general litigated the case on behalf of the employers. Frank found it unseemly for the Congress to overturn the Supreme Court's reasonable construction of the FLSA simply to avoid paying compensation to workers. Learned Hand argued that these congressional amendments would occasion no great harm because the employees, during the years in question, received the wages that "had sufficed to keep them on their jobs throughout the period."[79] Frank protested that longshoremen had been woefully underpaid for years and that the prime purpose of the FLSA was to increase the wages of workers who lacked the bargaining power to command a decent wage. To Frank, a true emergency, such as the justification for the Portal-to-Portal Act, was different from a simple change of heart by a Congress concerned with limiting the cost of government contracts.[80] Frank's *Addison* protest reflected his belief in government accountability, which also manifested itself in repeated objections to the government's interposition of sovereign immunity to bar legal claims.[81]

VIII

Frank's cynical attitude toward legal doctrine, his dismissal of judicial opinions as "emasculated explanations of decisions . . . of limited assistance to the practicing lawyers," softened, we have seen, under criticism he received during the 1930s.[82] His judicial opinions reflect this shift, especially the incredible length at which Frank would quibble over the shape or content of a legal rule. The typical Frank opinion approached legal doctrine with a surgeon's scalpel, ready to fine-tune, recast, affirm, distinguish, or perhaps repudiate, but in all cases to take legal doctrine very seriously. In *In re Barnett,* for example, Frank insisted that courts should be reluctant to alter precedent on which people have significantly relied.[83] Another example of Frank's change in attitude toward legal doctrine is *Repouille v. United States.* Although the Second Circuit's decision had no practical significance to petitioner, an alien seeking citizenship, because the expiration of time during appeal meant that he was now eligible for citizenship, Frank dissented because "this case may, as a precedent, have a very serious significance for many another future petitioner."[84] Frank came to recognize that past judicial decisions may substantially affect the future interests of real people. This force of precedent encouraged him, as a judge, to be careful in erecting legal rules. In one opinion, he backed away from his extreme rhetoric in *Law and the Modern Mind.* "A few years ago there was much talk adverse to legal 'conceptualism.' Some of the talkers seemingly went so far as to decry all concepts. Others, more sagely, objected to the logical application of the wording of the legal concept unless adequate attention is given to the policy the words are designed to express."[85]

These opinions illustrate the principal explanation for the seeming inconsistency between the cynical realist and the doctrinal judge: the institutional differences between philosophers and judges. Authors of books or articles may criticize sharply, provoke by overstatement, or even be completely disingenuous. Essayists are unaccountable; their ideas carry no consequences other than inherent merit or persuasiveness. A poor idea, weakly reasoned, generally does no harm. A judicial decision, on the other hand, has immediate, often profound consequences for the litigants. Court judgments deeply affect liberty, property, personal reputation, and other important values. A glib judicial pen may injure real people. A new judge quickly finds out how litigants put judicial opinions to uses never dreamed of by, and perhaps horrifying to, the author.[86]

Once issued, a judicial opinion becomes ammunition available for use by all lawyers. As a shrewd litigator with thirty years' experience in private practice and government, Jerome Frank needed no introduction, on ascending the bench, to the distinction between essays and judicial opinions.

The American legal system places institutional constraints on judges. Frank's concept of his role as intermediate appellate court judge perfectly illustrates both the occasions for the exercise of judicial power and the principles that restrict judicial activism. The legal profession's traditions, as well as society's expectations, encourage judges to conform to certain canons. Judges must not take bribes, permit personal friendships or financial consequences to affect decisions, or allow the race, creed, religion, or political affiliation of parties, witnesses, or counsel to influence decisions. More narrowly, standards have developed for when and how to overrule opinions, for which decisions of which courts must be followed by which judges, for distinguishing holding from dictum, for interpreting statutes, and for deferring to the judgment of other decision makers—legislators, executives, administrators, magistrates, and police officers. These rules help define what a judge is and how a judge operates as part of the entire legal system. These institutional constraints curbed Jerome Frank's realist impulses and led to a variety of results that Frank, if unfettered, would not have reached. On becoming a judge, Frank accepted unequivocally the rules, traditions, and constraints under which he was expected to operate.

Judge Frank acknowledged that some legal doctrines are so well entrenched that the judiciary cannot significantly alter them.[87] Judges may criticize constitutional provisions, either on or off the bench, but they are not free, given their judicial oath, to refuse to enforce provisions they deem undesirable.[88] "[J]udges, owe an obligation to do their job, as prescribed by statute, in a manner, which, within practical limits, publicizes the rational bases of their performance."[89]

Frank's legal philosophy and his acceptance of constraints coalesced in cases reviewing summary judgments. Federal Rule of Civil Procedure (FRCP) 56 permits a trial judge to grant summary judgment in civil cases if "there is no genuine issue as to any material fact."[90] In jury cases, this procedure results in the judge, not the jury, making the final decision. Borrowing from his fact skepticism, Frank regularly voted to reverse grants of summary judgment, reasoning that the fact-finding process is so unpredictable that the trial judge should rarely abridge the right of the parties to have the assigned fact-finder—the jury—determine the facts.[91] From another vantage point, these decisions conflict with his legal philosophy. *Courts on Trial* castigated the civil jury as lawless, unpredictable, and biased, and therefore urged its abolition. Philosopher Frank might not like civil juries, but Judge Frank felt duty-bound to preserve the right to a jury trial. A celebrated example is *Arnstein v. Porter.* Ira B. Arnstein, an unknown composer, brought a *pro se* copyright infringement action against Cole Porter, alleging that defendant's "Begin the Beguine" was plagiarized from his "The Lord Is My Shepherd" and "A Mother's Prayer." Arnstein made similar allegations concerning Porter's "Night and Day," "I Love You," "You'd Be So Nice to Come Home To," and "Don't Fence Me In." Arnstein had previously filed five similar cases and Judge Clark's dissent convincingly demonstrated how utterly frivolous Arnstein's allegations were. Nonetheless, Frank reversed because, while Arnstein's allegations might be "fantastic," he was entitled to have these improbabilities, inescapably raising questions of credibility, decided by a jury.[92] Judge Frank steadfastly protected access to an institution he personally thought should be abolished.

In contrast, Frank reversed the facts found by the trial court as "clearly erroneous" in *Orvis v. Higgins.* Supreme Court precedent insulated jury verdicts from scrutiny but permitted greater review of facts found at a bench trial, particularly if the findings were based on documentary evidence, the inferences from which may be equally assessed by an appellate court. Frank accepted these varying standards for judicial review but sarcastically observed:

> [A] wag might say that a verdict is entitled to high respect because the jurors are inexperienced in finding facts, an administrative finding is given high respect because the administrative officers are specialists (guided by experts) in finding a particular class of facts, but, paradoxically, a trial judge's finding has far less respect because he is blessed neither with jurors' inexperience nor administrative officers' expertness.[93]

A similar attitude led Frank, in *Skidmore v. Baltimore & Ohio Railroad Co.*, to uphold a judge's denial of defendant's request for a special jury verdict.[94] Federal Rule of Civil Procedure 49(a) and (b) authorize the trial judge to instruct the jury to return a written finding on each factual issue, thus permitting greater scrutiny of the jury's actions. While FRCP 49 permits special verdicts, it does not compel them. Frank could have sustained the judge's discretion in a brief opinion. Instead, he wrote an extended essay analyzing the problems with civil juries. A general verdict allows juries to disregard the judicial instructions on rules of law, either by mistake or on purpose. The legal system pretends that a jury of lay persons fully understands a judge's precise explanation of complicated legal rules, and appellate courts will reverse for technical errors in jury instructions. Frank attacked this assumption as highly unlikely, yet he felt compelled to follow this legal fiction "while acting in our judicial capacity."[95] Despite his deep mistrust of civil juries, Frank notably upheld the trial judge's refusal to order a special verdict. Judge Frank reached a conclusion at war with Philosopher Frank's realism.

This tension can be seen also in *Dyer v. MacDougall*, where Frank distinguished between a motion for a new trial and a motion for a directed verdict.[96] A motion for a new trial, coming after a jury verdict, permits the judge to assess independently a witness's credibility. In a motion for a directed verdict, which truncates the trial and deprives the jury of an opportunity to decide, the judge must consider the evidence in the light most favorable to the nonmoving party. "[W]hatever may be the views of judges about the jury system, it is their duty to maintain the function of the jury in all jury trials, until the jury is abolished by legislation and constitutional amendment."[97]

Sometimes during trial, a witness will blurt out a prejudicial or inflammatory comment in front of the jury. Rather than begin a new trial with a different jury, a legal rule has developed which has the trial judge instruct the jury to disregard the offensive remark. Frank considered this rule horrible, likely not to produce a just result but rather to intensify the impact of the prejudicial statement on the jury by focusing attention on it.[98] Yet in one case Frank reversed precisely because the trial judge had failed to instruct the jury to disregard certain testimony.[99] Philosopher Frank thought these instructions a waste of time and perhaps actually harmful, but Judge Frank carefully applied this accepted rule of law.

Frank's willingness to accept institutional constraints is seen again in *Commissioner of Internal Revenue v. Bagley & Sewall Co.*, where Frank chastised the majority for ignoring an established principle of statutory construction in order to "do justice."[100] Since "doing justice" exemplifies Frank's realism, one might have expected him to join the majority. Nonetheless, Congress established a list of exceptions in the Internal Revenue Code and judges should not rewrite the statute. Once again he accepted a recognized limit on his institutional role.

As the wave of anticommunist sentiment swept the United States in the late 1940s and early 1950s, it did not exempt federal judges. Jerome Frank detested communism. From his work at the AAA through his antideterminist tract, *Fate and Freedom*, Frank placed himself solidly in the camp of American liberalism. After Julius and Ethel Rosenberg were convicted of conspiring to commit espionage by passing atomic information to the Soviet Union, they appealed to the U.S. Court of Appeals for the Second Circuit. Arising in the midst of the cold war, the case generated enormous publicity and controversy over their guilt or innocence, a debate that still rages.[101] The case also claimed the world's attention because Judge Irving Kaufman sentenced the Rosenbergs to death. When Kaufman pronounced the Rosenbergs' crime "worse than murder," he condemned them for giving Russia the atomic bomb, for causing the Communist aggression in Korea, and for costing thousands, perhaps millions, of lives by their treason.[102] While many people applauded the death sentences as deserved retribution, others protested its severity. Assuming the Rosenbergs' guilt, they passed relatively insignificant information to the Soviet Union in 1944–45, when Russia was a wartime ally. Pleas for leniency came from around the country and from around the world—even from Pope Pius XII.

Jerome Frank sat on the Second Circuit panel with Thomas Swan and Harrie Chase to hear the Rosenbergs' appeal. The legal issues included whether conviction under the Espionage Act required the testimony of two witnesses, as required by the Constitution in

treason cases; whether Judge Kaufman's in-court hostility prejudiced the jury; whether perjured testimony compromised a fair
trial; whether the death sentences violated the Eighth Amendment's prohibition against "cruel and unusual" punishment; and
whether the death sentences should be reduced because they constituted an abuse of Judge Kaufman's discretion. Although Judge
Swan was scheduled to write the opinion, Jerome Frank relieved
him of the duty.[103] In a carefully crafted and detailed opinion,
Frank upheld the convictions, finding the evidence persuasive, the
trial judge's active role legitimate, a free speech argument contrived, and a vagueness argument unconvincing.[104] Frank parted
company from Swan and Chase, however, in voting to reverse the
conviction of codefendant Morton Sobell, because the evidence did
not establish a single, unified conspiracy. Frank also wrote only for
himself in urging the Supreme Court to review the death sentences. As an intermediate appeals judge, he felt bound to follow
an undeviating line of precedent which prohibited appellate courts
from modifying criminal sentences. Frank, however, opposed
capital punishment, thought its application to the Rosenbergs unduly harsh and disproportionate, and believed that appellate
courts should be able to reduce excessive sentences. Accordingly,
he mustered arguments to persuade the Supreme Court to grant
certiorari and reduce the death sentences.[105] On the merits, the
evidence convinced Frank that the Rosenbergs were guilty.[106] Notwithstanding Frank's efforts, the Supreme Court denied certiorari.[107]

Frank's participation in the *Rosenberg* legal proceedings continued as counsel for the Rosenbergs petitioned the U.S. District
Court to vacate the sentence, alleging that there had been perjured
testimony and prosecutorial misconduct.[108] The District Court denied the petition, the Second Circuit once more affirmed in a Swan
opinion which Frank joined, and the Supreme Court again denied
certiorari.[109] Next, lawyers for the Rosenbergs sought a new trial on
the basis of the discovery of "new evidence," a plea rejected by
District Judge Kaufman, the Second Circuit (including Frank), and
the Supreme Court.[110] Defense efforts continued and Justice Douglas issued a last-minute stay of execution, precipitating an extraordinary special session of the Supreme Court which dissolved the

stay.[111] Frank's final connection with the *Rosenberg* case came on the scheduled day of execution. Arthur Kinoy, counsel for the Rosenbergs, had first approached Chief Judge Swan, using a variation of the argument on which Douglas had based his stay. After hearing Kinoy's argument, Swan agreed to convene a panel of the court and to vote for a stay, provided Kinoy could convince another Second Circuit judge to hear the case. Kinoy confidently expected Jerome Frank, the court's leading liberal, to agree to a hearing. Kinoy went to Frank's New Haven home and argued his case. After an extended argument, Frank refused to grant the stay. "If I were as young as you are, I would be sitting where you are now and saying and arguing what you are arguing. You are right to do so. But when you are as old as I am, you will understand why I . . . why I cannot do what you ask. I cannot do it."[112] That evening the Rosenbergs died in the electric chair.

The *Rosenberg* case posed to Frank, and to an entire generation, the crisis of the liberal conscience. How could Frank uphold death sentences imposed by a vindictive judge for giving information of dubious value to a wartime ally? Did the judicial activism of a liberal judge dissipate because the defendants were Communists and the case arose at the height of the cold war? Did the fear of anti-Semitism prompt the Jewish trial judge and Jewish prosecutor, perhaps also Jewish appeals judges, to treat the Jewish defendants with special severity? Why did the United States condemn the Rosenbergs to death when Britain and Canada gave traitors modest prison sentences?[113] Frank's role in the *Rosenberg* case evinces his fidelity to, not departure from, liberal principles. Given Frank's acceptance of the institutional constraints on his role as an intermediate appeals judge, he felt obliged to uphold the trial judge's sentences. If the trial judge committed error, then Frank, believing that error is rarely harmless, would have voted to reverse. Frank has been criticized for not finding error in Judge Kaufman's aggressive role during the Rosenbergs' trial.[114] But Frank opposed the notion that trial judges should act merely as referees at a boxing match; passivity, he thought, obstructed the search for truth.[115] Frank did not consider Judge Kaufman's behavior reversible error. Nor did the other novel and complicated legal issues convince Jerome Frank, the cynical commentator on judicial discretion, that the Rosenbergs had been unfairly convicted. While Frank opposed capital punishment and considered the trial judge's sentences excessive, he also believed that the evidence established the Rosenbergs' guilt.

Assuming the Rosenbergs were guilty, which is a reasonable position, what message did Frank intend by his "when you are as old as I am" comment to Kinoy? Did he fear how his position would be construed if he interfered with the execution of atomic spies? Did he think that liberalism would be hurt by a progressive judge's defense of Communist spies? Was he concerned, as a Jew, about encouraging anti-Semitism if a Jewish judge stayed the execution of Jewish spies? These serious questions cannot be satisfactorily answered. His comment probably meant that in his youth Frank would have defended the Rosenbergs even though they were guilty or even though their case seemed hopeless. The outrage of the *Rosenberg* case is not trumped-up evidence or false charges, but that the government made scapegoats of puny spies in order to discredit the political left by identifying communism with atomic espionage. As a lawyer, Frank could have protested this political use of the criminal process by defending the Rosenbergs. But as a judge, accepting the limitations on his position, he reviewed convictions supported by abundant evidence for violation of a valid law.

Frank's performance confirms the institutional limits on his intermediate-court position. The argument presented to him on the final afternoon tracked the argument the full Supreme Court found unpersuasive. Justice Douglas later recalled that Frank said that he would have found the imposition of the death sentences improper if the Supreme Court had not vacated Douglas' stay and the case had returned to the Second Circuit for plenary consideration.[116] In refusing to intervene, Frank commented to Kinoy, "How can I overrule my bosses?"[117] It would have been highly uncharacteristic of Frank to ignore the clear mandate of the Supreme Court. Nothing in his judicial bones made him lawless. He unequivocally accepted the rules of law and the canons and traditions of his chosen profession.

At the same time, how can one explain Judge Swan's apparent willingness to grant the stay? If Judge Swan had a clear conscience and a viable legal theory, why did Jerome Frank reach the opposite conclusion? Frank's position, though consistent and defensible, did not reflect great moral courage. Jerome Frank, who eloquently protested injustice against sharecroppers, tenant farmers, consumers, indigent defendants, and even Nazis and other unpopular defendants, turned a deaf ear to the Rosenbergs' plea.[118] During the cold war, Frank was not alone among liberals, Jews, or judges in running for cover.

Frank's timidity was seen earlier in *United States v. Sacher.* In 1950, after a long and tumultuous trial, eleven Communist leaders were convicted of violating the Smith Act.[119] At the end of the trial, Judge Harold Medina cited Harry Sacher, George Crockett (now U.S. representative), and other defense counsel in the *Dennis* case for contempt, summarily found them guilty, and sentenced them to jail. The Second Circuit affirmed, with Frank the pivotal concurring judge.[120] *Sacher* was not Frank's finest hour.[121] The disruptive in-court behavior of defense counsel horrified Jerome Frank, who saw orderly legal proceedings as the imperative bedrock of government under law. Courageous advocacy could never justify what he considered the intolerable behavior of the *Dennis* defense counsel. Unfortunately, Frank failed to distinguish between the propriety of counsel's actions and the procedural legitimacy of summary contempt. Judge Clark's stirring dissent argued that due process required notice to counsel of the contempt charges and a hearing before a different, less personally involved judge. Frank did not reach very far to protect the rights of counsel for Communists. Although he initially voted to reverse and remand for a hearing before a judge other than the trial judge, in the end he joined Augustus Hand's opinion.[122] The Supreme Court obviously found the Frank and Augustus Hand opinions persuasive, for it followed their reasoning and quoted a passage from Frank's concurrence.[123] It was nearly two decades before calmer times and defendants other than counsel defending Communists convinced the Supreme Court of the need for more careful procedures in contempt cases.[124]

Chapter Six

The Influence of a Circuit Judge
in Shaping Constitutional Law

> If ye win through an African Jungle,
> Unmentioned at home in the press,
> Heed it not: no man seeth the piston,
> But it driveth the ship none the less.
> —Ronald Hopwood

I

American legal historians traditionally have ignored not only the piston that drives the ship of law but even the possibility that such a piston exists. For decades these scholars were preoccupied with narrow doctrinal accounts of legal issues, missing an understanding of the law as a social institution and isolating legal doctrine from the broader cultural mix. Only recently have American legal historians, led by Willard Hurst, turned to writing the social history of the law.[1] This new movement in legal writing recognizes that various factors, including many outside the traditional legal community, have shaped the growth of the law, and legal historians who take part in the movement are increasingly concerned with placing legal development in a larger context.[2]

Literature on the U.S. Supreme Court is only now beginning to break away from the traditional narrow view of the law. Constitutional history too often has detailed only how doctrine changes from one Supreme Court decision to the next or how a position captures the vote of a critical swing justice on the Court. Deficiencies necessarily arise, because this concentration on the nuance of doctrine is effectively an attempt to analyze the Supreme

164

Court in a vacuum. Most constitutional historians have failed to describe the interaction between different levels of the federal judicial system or to assess the influence of one level upon another. Thus most legal histories produce a rather skewed vision of nine Supreme Court justices doing battle with the states or Congress.

Literature on the Vinson and Warren Courts is particularly devoid of an understanding of the larger context within which the Court operated. Several excellent books describe the legal revolution wrought by the Warren Court, but there is hardly a suggestion that the Supreme Court relied on more than "nine men."[3] Constitutional historians have too often ignored the external forces affecting the Supreme Court.[4]

As an appellate judge, Jerome Frank displayed energy and persistence in successfully pushing the Supreme Court toward law reform. During the time he served on the Second Circuit, the Supreme Court developed an increasing sensitivity to issues of civil liberties.[5] The advances made by the High Court depended in part on the work of intelligent and active lower-court judges who served to focus issues, document needs, and lend support to positions. Jerome Frank brilliantly performed these roles. Enormous changes occurred in the recognition of civil liberties, procedural protection for criminal defendants, school desegregation, and legislative reapportionment. No doubt the Supreme Court, as the nation's supreme legal authority, pointed the way for lower courts in these developments; at the same time, however, it received guidance from those courts. An intellectual movement in the law, with a broader basis than Supreme Court personnel alone, forged the contributions of the Vinson and Warren courts. Second Circuit Judge Jerome Frank participated in this movement and helped influence the Supreme Court to accord legal respect to individual dignity.

II

The failure of historians to address questions of influence in the law may be attributable to difficulties in the effort. There is no single, defined method by which to measure influence. Indeed, there is no single method by which to define it. Certain problems of measurement are inherent in the task of examining the possible influence of a circuit court judge on the U.S. Supreme Court and thereby on the development of the law in this country. One must consider questions unique to the individual whose influence is to be measured. To ascertain Frank's influence, one might focus on his judicial opinions, his books and articles, his jurisprudence, or his personal relations. Each may have influenced the Supreme Court.

Frank's position as a federal appeals court judge makes the measurement more difficult. Unlike the highest courts of the nation and states, a federal circuit court of appeals lacks final judgment power. Any contribution to legal thought is likely to be only temporary, until the highest tribunal reviews and settles the issue.[6] In addition, common law adjudication, because of its accretive nature, moves slowly. Consequently, it is difficult to pick out one case or expression of doctrine and attribute creativity to its author. Stare decisis encourages in all members of the legal profession, including judges, backward-looking habits that link even progressive decisions to dusty antecedents.[7]

Other problems arise in measuring influence on a particular entity. For instance, by "the Court" does one mean the institution of the Supreme Court, particular justices sitting on it, or perhaps an ideological grouping of justices? Further, is influence on the Court confined to a single case or a discrete category of doctrine, or does it extend to long-term trends and broad philosophic attitudes?

Finally, when one attempts to measure the influence of a particular individual on a particular institution, problems are compounded. The Supreme Court naturally prefers to rely on its own cases and analyses as opposed to those of another, necessarily inferior court. Where possible, High Court precedent bolsters new decisions. The work product of a lower court may emerge only in camouflaged form in the *United States Reports*. The Supreme Court thus avoids the appearance of reliance on other courts in reaching its decision.

Further difficulty in assessing Frank's influence on the Supreme Court stems from the disparate array of forces that converge upon it. Many factors, extending beyond the work of lower courts, may influence the Court. A partial list would include the performance of counsel, the research of law clerks, stimulating articles and books, Supreme Court precedent, other court opinions, a justice's ideology and past decisions, current public opinions, the structure of legal thought, and technological developments.[8] Legal historians lack empirical techniques to isolate a single force from the many and measure its strength. This analysis makes no contrary claim. Its conclusion that Judge Frank did exert influence on the Supreme Court does not argue exclusivity; on the contrary, other forces certainly contributed to Supreme Court action even when that action clearly followed the urgings of Frank. Further, this analysis rejects facile reliance on instances when the Court itself identified Frank as an influence. High Court opinions that rely on Frank's efforts, perhaps even quoting him by name, cannot alone be used to show his influence on the Court. A formidable body of jurisprudence precludes any such analysis. Frank himself would have been quick to point out that a justice's references to him in a decision may indicate no more than the justice's use of Frank's writing as a convenient tool for fashioning his own opinion. Citations and quotations may merely mask the fact that the justice had previously and independently determined to reach the same result.

These problems have encouraged a search for new methods by which to study judicial behavior.[9] Political scientists have pioneered the search, developing behavioralist techniques that rely almost exclusively on the quantification of data.[10] Using sophisticated computer programs and elaborate charts and graphs, these studies assess judicial performance solely on the basis of justices' votes in cases before them.[11] Behavioralist methodology grounds Marvin Schick's *Learned Hand's Court*—the only study that attempts to relate the performance of a court of appeals to the Supreme Court. Within narrow limits, Schick's approach has some utility. For a ten-year period it confirms what has been widely believed, that Supreme Court reversals of Second Circuit cases fell far below the average for federal courts of appeals.[12] Statistics of this sort led Schick to conclude that the Supreme Court admired and respected the Second Circuit and was influenced by it. Quantification enabled Schick to draw similar conclusions about individual judges. Jerome Frank, he found, enjoyed more success in the Supreme Court than any other member of the Second Circuit. A higher percentage of justices agreed with Frank than with any other judge—including Learned Hand.[13]

Statistics may offer some indicia of a judge's influence. Jerome Frank wrote 725 opinions for the court, in concurrence, or in dissent.[14] In these cases, counsel petitioned for certiorari 292 times, or in 40.2 percent of his cases. This figure contrasts sharply with the percentage of cases (23.9 percent) in which petitions for certiorari were sought for the entire Second Circuit.[15] An explanation may lie in Frank's propensity to write dissents and concurrences as well as to turn garden-variety cases into causes célèbres.[16] Frank had an uncanny knack for unearthing tricky legal issues from routine appeals, often to the surprise of counsel. His literate style on occasion would reveal, where others could not, the importance of issues in the record but not pursued on appeal. Once Frank dusted them off, the losing party had incentive to petition for certiorari. In addition, Frank's keen awareness of the Supreme Court sometimes led him to plead explicitly for Supreme Court review—a hint not lost on counsel.[17] This is particularly evident when Frank wrote separately. Of the 128 cases in which he dissented, counsel filed for Supreme Court review on 76 occasions, or 59.3 percent. When Frank concurred, as he did in 61 cases, counsel petitioned for certiorari on 27 occasions, or 44.2 percent.

The Supreme Court was apparently receptive to the pleas of either Frank or counsel in such cases. The High Court granted certiorari in 74 cases in which Frank had written a separate opinion, which translates into 25.3 percent of the cases in which certiorari was sought. Again, this figure is substantially higher than the Second Circuit average of 15.2 percent.[18] Of the 74 Frank cases in which the Supreme Court granted review, Frank dissented in 29 and concurred separately in 7, for a total of 36 or 48.6 percent of the cases, a percentage indicating that concurrence or dissent enhanced the likelihood of High Court review.[19]

Ultimate disposition by the Supreme Court cuts in the same direction. When the Supreme Court reached the merits, it supported Frank in 48 of 68 cases, or 70.6 percent.[20] Unfortunately, data that would permit precise comparisons with other Second Circuit personnel are not currently available. Schick tabulated interaction between each Supreme Court justice and each Second Circuit judge.

His results indicate that Frank received the highest degree of support from the Supreme Court. He also calculated that the Supreme Court reversed the Second Circuit in approximately 45 percent of the cases on which it heard argument.[21] Frank's role in these cases, however, is unknown.

Pointing to these statistics as conclusive proof of Frank's influence poses problems: they may demonstrate a correlation rather than a cause-and-effect relationship. That the High Court often reached the same conclusion as Frank does not necessarily prove that Frank influenced the Court toward that end. And the crude statistical techniques raise another hurdle; an exclusive focus on the votes of the justices ignores other variables that may confirm or refute the thesis that Frank was influential. It would be relevant, for example, to compare precise statistics for other members of the Second Circuit. The presence of Learned Hand, alone or in combination with Jerome Frank, possibly persuaded the Supreme Court to grant an unusually large number of reviews.

Schick made no effort to determine whether the Supreme Court rested its decision on the same grounds as did Frank. He analyzed only the outcome. But the Supreme Court may have decided a case on a procedural ground—such as mootness—which relates in no way to the merits. In these instances, an identical conclusion manifests neither support nor rejection of Frank's position. Even on the substantive issues, the Court might use a completely different rationale to reach the same result. Behavioralist models offer no way to account for varying degrees of support or rejection.

Frank's judicial style reveals yet another weakness in the use of quantification to assess influence. In a number of cases, he pleaded for the Supreme Court to reverse him, and the Court often obligingly did so.[22] A tally sheet would record that the Supreme Court reversed Frank; this record, while correct, masks the true character of Supreme Court support for Frank's position. One approach to these statistical problems seeks to improve the mathematics to make computations more accurate, thereby increasing statistical validity.[23] These improved statistics offer some additional utility in assessing influence, and sophisticated mathematics would make the data more reliable.

The raw statistics offer support for the thesis that Jerome Frank had a marked influence on the Supreme Court. His opinions encouraged an unusually large number of petitions for certiorari, and the Court granted hearings in a disproportionately large number of cases. Frank's separate opinions spurred frequent appeals and, on the merits, the Supreme Court sustained Frank's position in a much larger percentage of instances than it did for the whole Second Circuit. Frank's separate opinions bore special fruit: in twenty-five cases the Supreme Court reversed or modified Second Circuit decisions in which Frank found himself unable to join the majority opinion.

Ultimately, quantification has only limited value, even assuming that advanced mathematics produces statistically valid data. The tragic flaw in efforts to quantify judicial decisions is the implicit assumption that one case equals any other case. No decision can receive greater weight or credence than another. That method obviously slights the importance of seminal decisions, such as Learned Hand's Second Circuit opinion in *United States v. Dennis* and Jerome Frank's in *United States v. Roth*.[24] Similarly, the numbers fail to recognize that a series of lower-court decisions may receive instant vindication through one Supreme Court case. In the area of "harmless error," for instance, Frank wrote at least six dissenting opinions that fell on deaf ears before *Kotteakos v. United States*.[25] Concentration on vote tallies completely ignores quality. It converts the art and craft of judging into a result-oriented practice with the character of political lobbying. What matters is tallying the result reached; reasoning becomes irrelevant. Quantitative analysis fails to distinguish between the significance of arguments advanced in a case and the final result.

III

Guideposts to Frank's influence range from primitive notches in trees to light-emitting-diode arrows. A number of facts hint at Frank's influence in rather oblique ways. As a principal formulator of legal realism, he made a substantial contribution to legal philosophy. Although no one has documented its impact, the ideas of legal realism probably affected the Supreme Court.[26] The recognition of the enormous discretion wielded by judges, on which Frank focused attention,[27] now serves as a vital premise in the debate over judicial activism versus self-restraint. Both modern positions assume as basic what legal realism pointed out earlier: that judges have real discretion in making decisions. As a prominent legal realist, Frank probably had an impact on the Supreme Court, but the intellectual heritage is blurred since Frank shared leadership of the realist movement. Further, while philosophic ideas underpin Supreme Court decisions, no tools exist by which to measure how these ideas altered specific Supreme Court opinions.

Another problem in measuring influence exists in regard to Frank's opinions that did not reach the Supreme Court. Frank often sprinkled his opinions with gratuitous comments about current legal issues. As he was one of the most literate judges of his time, his opinions were widely read by the legal community, including Supreme Court justices.[28] No doubt these opinions awakened or prodded justices, judges, and lawyers alike, but no formal influence can be traced. Since the High Court did not review these cases, one can only speculate as to their persuasive character. That speculation would inevitably lead to an assessment of possible *indirect* influence of Frank on the Court. Federal and state judges cited and relied on his decisions in a huge number of instances.[29] These decisions, in turn, might be persuasive to the Supreme Court, yet it would be hazardous to attribute influence to Frank on this basis.

Frank may also have swayed the Supreme Court by following the opinion of another judge. Because Frank lent his judgment and prestige to such an opinion, the Supreme Court might pause before deciding to grant certiorari, or might follow the reasoning and affirm. *Johansen v. United States* illustrates this dilemma.[30] Frank wrote a dissent that relied heavily on a Fourth Circuit decision holding that seamen had a right to sue the United States under the Public Vessels Act. On appeal to the Supreme Court, four dissenting justices accepted that position, relying on the same Fourth Circuit opinion. By adding his weight of authority to the decision of the Fourth Circuit, Frank affirmed the reasonableness of the opinion and its capacity to persuade.[31] Yet surely the justices could have reached that result without Frank's dissent. On the other hand, his dissent drew attention to a split between the circuits, and this stressing of inconsistent appellate court decisions could have prompted the High Court to grant certiorari. Even though a majority of five justices specifically rejected Frank's position, his dissent may have persuaded them to resolve the conflict. While the Supreme Court's actions create suspicion that Frank at least persuaded the Court to accept *Johansen* for review, no evidence exists to segregate Frank's role from that of other influences.[32]

Other minor indications support the position that Frank was influential. A plethora of Supreme Court citations refer to Frank opinions. As noted above, these general references may indicate that the cited case was influential, that the authority supports a preordained judicial position, or only that the cited case describes one way in which a legal proposition has been decided. The bulk of these Supreme Court citations lack import, except to note Frank's general contribution to the growth of the law. Nonetheless, some High Court references endorse, sometimes enthusiastically, Frank's position.[33] This mark of recognition seems most obvious on those occasions when the citation refers to a Frank dissent.[34] There is another, indirect hint that the Supreme Court had a special respect for Frank's opinions. The Supreme Court might cite a string of decisions. Before *A Uniform System of Citation* outlined the proper sequence in which to cite cases, the Supreme Court often tipped its hat to Frank by placing his opinion first in line, although it was neither the most recent nor the earliest decision.[35] Deference can speak in subtle fashion.

Finally, one suspects that when the Supreme Court denies certiorari or affirms per curiam, the strength of the lower-court opinion has encouraged a summary procedure.[36] While Supreme Court justices have insisted that denial of certiorari implies no position on the substantive issues, lower-court judges frequently conclude that denial means either approval of their decisions or a belief that the issues lack sufficient import to warrant High Court review.[37] For the opinions of a select number of judges, denial of certiorari surely reflects the Supreme Court's position on the merits. The clearest evidence comes from Justice Harlan, who told Learned Hand, in a session designed to honor Hand's service on the federal bench, "May I say that when you read in Monday's *New York Times* 'Certiorari Denied' to one of your cases, then despite the usual teachings, what the notation really means is 'Judgment Affirmed.'"[38] As for Jerome Frank, it appears the High Court often refused review because his opinion persuaded the Court the result he reached was the correct one.

Citations to cases and denials of certiorari do not establish that it was Frank, as opposed to any other influence, that persuaded the Court to act in a particular manner. Nonetheless, each is reasonably subject to that interpretation; collectively, they suggest Frank's broad role. That skeletal thesis needs filling in by more substantive evidence.

IV

Supreme Court justices held Frank in high regard. As noted earlier, Justices Black, Douglas, Frankfurter, and Jackson enjoyed close personal relations with Frank, while Justices Reed and Harlan were on a first-name basis with him. Their extensive correspondence with Frank abounds in mutual respect. Hugo Black once described him as "one of the great judges."[39] In seeking a law clerk, Stanley Reed apparently wrote to three judges: Learned Hand, Augustus Hand, and Jerome Frank.[40] That Reed initiated the search by writing Frank indicates a measure of his respect for Frank; that he wrote only to the two Hands plus Frank confirms Reed's selectivity. Frankfurter called Frank "a much-cherished friend, and ardent seeker after truth and justice;" Douglas acknowledged that the Supreme Court followed Frank's "great dissent" in *United States ex rel. Leyra v. Denno.*[41]

Supreme Court justices did not confine their warm appreciation of Frank to private correspondence and off-the-record writings. The pages of the *United States Reports* reiterate their esteem for him. The Supreme Court tends to rely on its own opinions. It seldom quotes from the opinion of a lower-court case on appeal; even more rarely does it refer to the lower judge by name. When a citation is followed by "(Cardozo, J.)," it informs readers that the cited case was not written by a pedestrian judge. The parenthesis signals readers to consider the earlier case carefully. In practice, literate judges wish more information about a case than its holding, for an opinion by "a distinguished court" receives greater credence.[42] Not all judges are equal, and few attain the stature reflected by" (_____, J.)"[43] Jerome Frank received such recognition from judges on a host of courts. The Supreme Court alone singled him out by name on at least thirty-nine occasions, in opinions authored by no fewer than eleven justices.

The most direct evidence of Frank's influence occurs in his cases in which the Supreme Court heard argument and wrote full opinions, for one may compare those opinions with Frank's earlier opinions to gauge his influence. Jerome Frank's sixteen-year tenure on the Second Circuit, together with his proclivity to dissent or concur, ensured a large body of decisions on which the Supreme Court wrote opinions: 68, to be exact. As is to be expected, Supreme Court reactions to Frank's opinions vary in their tendency to show his influence. At a simplistic level of analysis, one can simply find whether the Supreme Court reached the conclusion Frank desired. It did so in an unusually high proportion of cases. The Supreme Court majority agreed with Frank on 48 occasions, or in 70.6 percent of his 68 cases.[44] Even in times of disagreement, Frank might be influential. Felix Frankfurter, who despite his personal friendship with Frank often disagreed with him,[45] described this type of impact:

> Contributions to thought are not to be determined by the actual increase to the body of knowledge. Men may greatly further the thinking of others even though their own ideas be rejected. There can be no doubt that Judge Frank served as a powerful ferment in formulating more searchingly the problems that are put to law and in discouraging distortion of such problems by question-begging and parochial answers.[46]

Justices might look to Frank's opinions not necessarily for the result he reached but for the reasoning process he used to get there. Justice Douglas acknowledged his debt. "We [Supreme Court justices] can only be grateful that Judge Frank explored a problem ahead of us. For this search usually left the clues to the answer we seek."[47]

A brilliant judge may exert influence even in a losing battle.

Frank's literate and fluent writing could set the terms of debate within which the Supreme Court would consider the case. Frank framed the legal issues and structured the various arguments. Appellate counsel necessarily must respond to the circuit opinion, for it is that opinion which he or she seeks to reverse. All Supreme Court justices, regardless of ideological inclinations, might look to Frank to outline the issues. Even when rejecting his substantive position, the Court normally operated within the parameters set by Frank.[48]

More often the Court adopted Frank's position, though not always by following his path.[49] In these instances, assessment of Frank's influence is speculative, for the Court tacitly may have rejected his reasoning. But it also may simply have found another rationale that appealed to a large number of justices, or was narrower, or presented fewer procedural hurdles. The embracing of a different rationale does not necessarily imply rejection of Frank's reasoning. Most often the Court followed Frank's reasoning.[50] Because the Supreme Court is reluctant to rely on lower-court opinions, it is hazardous to argue that Frank's opinion influenced the Court to follow his reasoning to reach his conclusion. Yet on certain occasions, striking parallels increase the likelihood that it did.[51]

Even stronger proof of influence arises in those cases where the Supreme Court reached the result urged by Frank, followed his argument, and indicated its reliance on him. The Court might refer to Frank by name or quote from his Second Circuit opinion. A simple reference generally would reflect respect and esteem for Frank, but a quotation would admit that the Court could not improve upon Frank's formulation. To quote a passage is to recognize that the particular phrasing incisively captures a position. At the very least, a Supreme Court quotation indicates that the Court would not otherwise have adopted that precise language. As mentioned above, at least eleven justices referred to Frank by name on thirty-nine occasions. Usually quotations buttressed points in the Court's argument, so the Court selectively quoted from Frank's opinions. Nonetheless, Frank's role seems crucial on those occasions when the remainder of the High Court opinion accepted Frank's reasoning and reached his conclusion.[52]

Three cases illustrate the acme of Frank's influence.[53] In each case, three or four justices opted to rely solely on Frank's opinion rather than to prepare their own dissents. The full dissent in one Supreme Court case reads: "Mr. Justice Black, Mr. Justice Douglas, and Mr. Justice Rutledge would affirm the judgment for reasons stated by Judge Frank, writing for the court of appeals. See 166 F. 2d 778."[54] One might argue that time pressures on Supreme Court justices are so severe[55] that these justices opted to rely in dissent on Frank's opnion, even though the dissent would look quite different had they written for themselves. This argument slights the overwhelming fact that the justices did, on balance, decide to adopt Frank's opinion. A freshly written opinion would certainly vary from Frank's, but the fact remains that the justices found Frank's opinion an adequate statement of their own position.

This observation suggests a second possible retort. The mere fact that the justices agree with Frank does not establish that it was Frank that coaxed them to that position; no cause-and-effect relationship has been demonstrated. These justices may simply have found Frank's opinion a convenient shortcut to express conclusions they reached independently. This possibility exists, but it minimizes the probable impact of a well-reasoned opinion in a specific case. Since many legal issues revolve around narrow, often technical points, the probability is slight that justices harbor preconceived, reasoned positions on such issues. Instead, current research and reflection persuade justices to join one side or another. Further, even assuming a justice has firm and well-established views, how likely is it that a legal opinion drafted by another judge would accurately reflect his precise view? It is more likely that adoption of an opinion exactly reflects the influence of that opinion.

Judge Frank's dissents vividly illustrate his influence. Dissents encourage a high percentage of appeals and often spur the Supreme Court to grant certiorari.[56] As noted above, Frank's dissents frequently resulted in Supreme Court review. More important, in nineteen cases in which Jerome Frank dissented, the Supreme Court reversed on the merits. These occasions vindicated Frank's dissents and thereby upheld the single voice of Frank over the court of appeals majority. Over a ten-year period, the Supreme Court reversed approximately 1.5 percent of the cases decided by courts of appeals.[57] If Frank dissented, the percentage rose to 14.8, and this figure would increase sharply if one looked not to the immediate outcome on appeal but to ultimate vindication.[58] Frank wrote six dissents challenging the Second Circuit's "harmless error" doctrine, for example, yet it took but one Supreme Court decision to agree with Frank that the doctrine operated unjustly.[59] Frank's dissents might awaken the High Court's interest in an area previously considered settled. In the *Roth* case, for instance, the circuit court upheld the constitutionality of the federal obscenity law on the basis of repeated Supreme Court decisions assuming the law's validity. Judge Frank, however, pieced together a mosaic of doctrine that cast grave doubt on the law's constitutionality. His opinion impelled the Supreme Court to review an issue previously believed to be settled.[60]

V

Frank's notion of the proper role of an appellate judge allowed him great leeway to coax and persuade the High Court to reform the law. He welcomed, rather than shirked, opportunities to revamp old doctrine. To this end, he developed a rather sophisticated set of principles and tactics allowing him to exert pressure on the Supreme Court. And so Jerome Frank's disposition and judicial philosophy enabled him to help guide the Supreme Court.

Judge Frank's judicial philosophy could not alone influence the Supreme Court; it depended as well on a receptive Court. Frank shared basic attitudes with the Vinson and early Warren Courts. He enjoyed a higher incidence of success than, for instance, Learned Hand because Frank adhered more closely to the Court's emerging attitude of judicial activism in defense of civil liberties. Unlike Hand, he endorsed a strong judiciary prepared to protect "preferred freedoms."[61] He eagerly accepted the challenge to be vigilant in the protection of civil liberties.

Conventional wisdom regards Learned Hand as the greater judge, yet Jerome Frank had more influence because he was more attuned to the prevailing mood of the Supreme Court. The Vinson and early Warren Courts paid increasing attention to civil rights and civil liberties.[62] Jerome Frank mirrored this perspective—with all the limits attached to it. Like the Supreme Court during the late 1940s and 1950s, Frank defended the procedural claims of criminal defendants more quickly than he did such pure issues of civil liberties as free speech.[63] Like the Supreme Court, Frank did not decry the harassment of purported members of the Communist Party.[64]

The defense of civil liberties is a most persistent theme in Frank's judicial opinions. He based one book of philosophy on the premise that individuals control their own destinies.[65] He believed that republican government maximizes free choice and affirms the dignity of the individual. His judicial opinions struggled to protect this vision. He tried valiantly, for instance, to bring humaneness to immigration and deportation law, which perennially accorded aliens less protection than citizens because deportation was labeled "civil" rather than "criminal."[66] Frank fought against summary procedures and loose rules of evidence because "[d]eportation, while not literally constituting punishment may have far more dire effects."[67]

To Frank, any limitation on the free will of the citizens signaled danger to liberty in general. This attitude can be seen in his opinion in *United States v. Roth*.[68] While obscenity hardly seemed worth a fight, the real issue, to Frank, was the ability of the government to control the minds of its citizens. If the government can dictate what citizens shall read, then it has power to stifle noxious ideas.

Frank's *Roth* opinion illustrates how his tactics as circuit judge sometimes prompted the Supreme Court to hear and resolve an issue even though its resolution differed widely from the one proposed by Frank. Frank concurred in finding the challenged obscenity statute constitutional under prior Supreme Court rulings, but, in a judicial tour de force, his opinion outlined major constitutional problems in federal regulation of obscenity and clearly argued for reversal. While the High Court had never expressly determined the constitutionality of federal obscenity statutes, Frank felt duty-bound to follow clear intimations of constitutionality in prior Supreme Court doctrine. That left him the alternative of writing a concurring opinion outlining troublesome issues that he expressly called on the Supreme Court to address. While he pushed the Court to handle the vagueness problem inherent in obscenity, on review the Supreme Court sidestepped the issue. Hindsight confirms that this problem did not go away, as cases from *Roth* through *Miller v. California* have demonstrated.[69] Frank similarly pushed the Court to distinguish adults from children, thus anticipating the Supreme Court's handiwork in *Ginsberg v. New York*.[70] He also identified legal process issues in obscenity cases which still pose vexing difficulties—that juries exercise enormous discretion and that courts are asked to determine the value of a piece of work.[71] While Jerome Frank contributed enormously, his intellectual lineage in obscenity law is difficult to discern. Frank borrowed analyses from law review articles as well as from the social sciences, especially sociology and psychology, so he was not the first intellectual to address the problems he pinpointed in *Roth*. But he was the first federal judge to call on the Supreme Court to clarify and change the law with an eye toward reconciling First Amendment interests with the permissible interests of government regulation.

In *Roth*, Frank made the link between obscenity and free speech by canvassing prior Supreme Court decisions on free speech and identifying the presence of the same issues in obscenity regulation. Thus, although earlier commentators had focused on obscenity, Frank's opinion was a strikingly original statement of the problems inherent in attempts to regulate obscenity. Although the Supreme Court on review in *Roth* was not prepared to follow Frank's lead, subsequent developments have demonstrated Frank's prescience and two succeeding Supreme Court opinions have relied on his lower-court concurrence, even though the Court in *Roth* followed a different route.[72] Such reliance is a most unusual occurrence once a circuit opinion has been replaced on review by a Supreme Court opinion. While Jerome Frank's *Roth* opinion had no direct effect on the Supreme Court, through it he contributed to a climate of opinion that recognized dangers to free speech in the regulation of the sordid obscenity business.

Although Frank contributed significantly to the defense of civil liberties, he occasionally had a narrow view of them. One of his first dissents, *Chrestensen v. Valentine*, concerned an ordinance regulating the distribution of handbills.[73] Frank distinguished between commercial and protected speech and hesitated to extend First Amendment protection to commercial speech. The Supreme

Court reversed the Second Circuit and sustained Frank, relying on this distinction. Streets are not a proper forum for commercial speech, absent approval by the legislature, which was expressly denied by the ordinance.

Frank's opinion unquestionably influenced the Supreme Court. Not only did it reverse and uphold the position of a single dissenting judge, but it injected a commercial/noncommercial distinction into First Amendment law. Apparently no case had previously made such a distinction, and so the Supreme Court accepted Frank's unique argument made in the court below. Counsel in *Chrestensen* relied heavily on Frank's dissent and quoted extensively from it, both in the petition for certiorari and in the brief. Furthermore, Justice Douglas penned a note to Frank after the Supreme Court decision, indicating that Frank had performed well and that the Supreme Court had followed his lead.[74]

Chrestensen found Frank niggardly in the protection of free speech and his influence created a doctrine that has not withstood the test of time. The Supreme Court gradually recognized its analytical weakness and has since retreated from it. Such cases as *New York Times v. Sullivan* demonstrated its infirmity, and while *Chrestensen* has never been expressly overruled, subsequent cases have undermined it.[75] Frank created the commercial/noncommercial distinction despite the fact that the other two members of the panel described it as "shadowy." In conference memoranda, Judges Clark and Swan attacked the distinction as unworkable and affording inadequate protection to freedom of speech.[76] These judges articulated other views, but Judge Frank saw merit in treating commercial speech differently, and he succeeded in convincing the Supreme Court.

In other cases, Frank also affected the Supreme Court in ways that lacked fervor for protection of civil liberties. After the turbulent trial of high-ranking members of the Communist Party which produced *Dennis v. United States,* the trial judge cited defense counsel for multiple contempts and imposed punishment that included jail terms. On appeal, a divided Second Circuit, with Judge Frank the pivotal concurring vote, sustained all but one count of contempt. To Frank, counsel's methods were an outrageous interference with the orderly processes of law. Both Frank and the Supreme Court agreed that disruptive tactics had no place in an American courtroom.[77]

In *United States v. Sacher*, Frank failed to sever the merits of the contempt citations from issues of procedural regularity. Egregious behavior does not excuse a lack of due process. *Sacher* is another example of a Frank position embraced by the Supreme Court, only later to be repudiated. More recent decisions would require notice to the accused, an opportunity to be heard in defense, and perhaps a trial before a different judge.[78] Once again, an alternative was available to Frank. In a conference memorandum Judge Clark argued that "denying them a chance to offer anything in rebuttal— not even an apology for acts happening months before—seems not a picture of American courts we can afford to publicize."[79] In *Chrestensen* and *Sacher*, Frank's influence actually retarded the course the law ultimately took. He customarily anticipated Supreme Court advances in civil liberties, sometimes to an extent the Supreme Court has yet to fulfill.[80] Frank normally challenged the Supreme Court to extend its protection of civil liberties.

An electronics surveillance case provided the occasion for Frank to articulate notions of privacy that ultimately were embodied in Supreme Court doctrine. In *United States v. On Lee*, the Second Circuit rejected a claim of unlawful search and seizure and accepted the conventional rule that the Fourth Amendment considerations came into play only upon physical penetration or physical removal.[81] Relying on Supreme Court precedent in *Olmstead v. United States* and *Goldman v. United States*, the Second Circuit refused to chart new law.[82] In dissent, Jerome Frank likened the government practice to "lurid gangster movies," arguing that the failure to seize something tangible is not conclusive: ears and eyes may seize intangible conversations. A microphone used without permission effectively ensured the government agent's presence. Thus Frank employed a functional approach to the Fourth Amendment. He examined the practical effect of this particular conduct: it infringed privacy, smacked of totalitarianism, and realistically was more insidious and stultifying than an open encounter. Places such as the home should be sacred and free from this type of intrusion.

Frank was not the first to argue that the seizure of something intangible was nonetheless seizure within the purview of the Fourth

Amendment. Justice Brandeis expressed that position in his famous dissenting opinion in *Olmstead v. United States,* but the argument was not fully developed.[83] Frank articulated more fully than
anyone else the view that the Fourth Amendment should protect
against seizure of a conversation. Reaching this position required
judicial creativity. For one thing, he was faced with Supreme Court
precedent that tended to cut against him, and Frank never ignored
relevant Supreme Court decisions. In *On Lee* he argued that intervening events, including an opinion written by Chief Justice Vinson as a circuit judge, had weakened both *Olmstead* and *Goldman.* As
Frank noted, the Supreme Court had later cited that Vinson circuit
opinion. Further, he argued that the earlier position was mere dictum and did not oblige him to follow it.

The influence of Frank in *On Lee* was not felt immediately. On
the contrary, the Supreme Court majority rejected his arguments
on review. A dissent by Justice Harold Burton joined by Justice
Frankfurter, however, specifically relied on Frank's dissent. In a
new and forceful manner his circuit opinion served to crystallize
the issue of seizing intangibles. After *On Lee,* Frank's opinion was
used by Justice Potter Stewart for a Court majority in *Silverman v.
United States.*[84] Justice Stewart held that a so-called spike mike inserted into a wall was sufficient physical intrusion to warrant the
protection of the Fourth Amendment. Justice Stewart quoted from
Judge Frank's circuit opinion and refused to extend *Goldman* "by
even a fraction of an inch."[85] Justice Brennan's dissent in *Lopez v.
United States* next picked up Frank's analysis and quoted him in an
effort to show why *Olmstead* should be overruled.[86] Justice Brennan's opinion, in turn, became a mainstay of the Court's analysis in
Katz v. United States.[87] In *Katz,* the Court finally abandoned the
analysis of *Olmstead* and *Goldman,* concluding instead that the physical trespass notion had been eroded and a conversation could be
seized.

Judge Frank wrote his most passionate opinions in the field of
criminal law and procedure. His skepticism about the accuracy of
the law's fact-finding processes led him to believe that courts convicted many innocent persons.[88] In his last book, *Not Guilty,* he
chronicled cases of many persons wrongly convicted of crime. This
sensitivity made Frank a stalwart defender of careful procedures in

criminal cases. He deplored third-degree tactics and carefully scrutinized confessions obtained after extensive police interrogation.[89] Typical Jerome Frank opinions ensured adequate representation by counsel, advocated that counsel receive transcripts and other necessary tools for a careful defense, lambasted conspiracy charges that risked the conviction of one person for the actions of another, and protested excessive sentences imposed by trial judges.[90]

Throughout the Vinson and Warren Court eras, the Supreme Court moved to control offensive police practices. The Supreme Court sharply curbed prolonged interrogation with physical threats or promises of leniency, and gradually moved from a case-by-case elaboration of the "totality of the circumstances" to impose more rigid and comprehensive rules.[91] In *United States ex rel. Leyra v. Denno,* the Second Circuit denied a petition for a writ of habeas corpus.[92] In dissent, Judge Frank argued that prolonged interrogation with promises of leniency and use of a psychiatrist to elicit statements had effectively induced the defendant to confess. His opinion masterfully analyzed the record in an effort to demonstrate that a series of interrogations was part of a single ongoing process. A prior Supreme Court decision, *Lisenba v. California,* stood in his way.[93] Frank avoided the thrust of *Lisenba* by seizing on a portion of the opinion which indicated that inducements to confess may vitiate a confession's voluntary nature.[94]

On review, the Supreme Court reversed, following in Frank's footsteps. In a Hugo Black opinion, the Court found that due process had been denied. Frank's prominent role in producing this Supreme Court reversal is evident from his correspondence with Justices Black and Douglas. Frank wrote to Justice Black, "Your splendid opinion in *Leyra* raises hope that a majority of your Court will more frequently follow you, especially in civil liberties cases." Black responded, "I was happy to be able to follow your lead in the *Leyra* case."[95]

Such decisions as *Leyra* caused bitterness among state judges and spurred efforts in Congress to overturn several Supreme Court decisions dealing with habeas corpus cases. One bill in particular concerned Frank, and he urged several justices to take a public stand against the legislation, but judicial propriety cautioned them otherwise.[96] Frank met with Chief Justice Warren at the suggestion of Justice Douglas: "I suggest you come down to see the Chief. You will find him very happy and eager to talk, and I think that you as the writer of the great dissent in Leiyra [sic] which we followed, can make a great dent on him."[97] Frank, however, found Warren embarrassed by the Judicial Conference's approval of the bill.[98]

In *United States v. Murphy* Frank again encouraged the Supreme Court to curb certain police practices in procuring confessions. Frank granted a writ of habeas corpus because of police practices that denied "the barest minimum of civilized principles of justice." Petitioner had been held incommunicado in an unheated cell for twenty-seven hours. Using a totality-of-the-circumstances approach and citing *Leyra v. Denno,* Frank found that due process had been violated because of the continuous interrogation, effective kidnapping by holding the accused incommunicado, unlawful detention, and elements of deceit. "All decent Americans soundly condemn satanic practices like those described above."[99] Several Supreme Court opinions subsequently cited Frank's opinion.[100]

Another confession case, *United States v. Delli Paoli,* vividly illustrates Frank's cumulative impact on the Supreme Court.[101] In *Paoli,* Learned Hand upheld the admission of evidence against one defendant which was inadmissible against others. His caveat was that a judicial instruction be given to the jury not to consider the evidence against the other defendants. In dissent, Frank argued that either the evidence ought to be inadmissible or the trials should be severed. On review, the Supreme Court accepted and affirmed Learned Hand's position. The Court assumed that juries follow judicial instructions. To the four dissenters, speaking through Felix Frankfurter, Jerome Frank's arguments were persuasive; indeed, Frankfurter explicitly relied on them.[102] Ultimately the Supreme Court vindicated Frank by overruling *Paoli* in *Bruton v. United States,* an opinion that relied on a number of Frank's contributions.[103]

To begin with, Frankfurter's dissenting opinion in *Paoli* had borrowed Frank's reasoning and concluded, "In substance, I agree with the dissenting opinion of Judge Frank . . . and would therefore reverse."[104] The *Bruton* opinion showed that time had demonstrated the wisdom of his dissent. The *Bruton* opinion also quoted from an opinion by Justice Jackson in *Krulewitch v. United States,* to the effect that "[t]he naive assumption that prejudicial effects can be overcome by instructions to the jury . . . all practicing lawyers know to be unmitigated fiction."[105] As noted below, that language was derived from another Jerome Frank opinion. The *Bruton* Court also referred to and quoted from Jerome Frank's Second Circuit dissent in *Delli Paoli* as well as his opinion in *United States v. Grunewald*.[106]

In *Grunewald* Frank blended case analysis with persuasive argument to encourage the Court to extend greater protection against possible self-incrimination. To avoid the need to ignore Supreme Court precedent to reach his desired goal, he argued that the precedent had, in effect, been overruled by subsequent doctrinal developments.[107] The Supreme Court granted certiorari and reversed, following the reasoning used by Judge Frank and referring to him at several key points. Several other Supreme Court decisions have used Frank's *Grunewald* opinion. In *Murphy v. Waterfront Commission,* Justice Arthur Goldberg, writing for the majority, quoted Frank's lower-court dissent.[108] But intervening Supreme Court doctrine sometimes blunts the impact of lower judges. A later High Court case on self-incrimination quoted Justice Goldberg's opinion in *Murphy,* even though the language came from Jerome Frank's *Grunewald* opinion.[109]

Sometimes Frank's opinions contributed to a climate of thought. In *Griffin v. Illinois* the Supreme Court took a strong stand in favor of ensuring indigent defendants the right to appeal from convictions.[110] The next year, in *United States v. Johnson,* Frank seized on the *Griffin* opinion and attempted to flesh out its implications for equal justice for indigents. In dissent, he urged that an *in forma pauperis* petition be granted despite possible encouragement of frivolous appeals. "[H]ow can the existence of such a meritorious appeal be shown unless the defendant has access to a transcript of the events at the trial?"[111] Frank enthusiastically embraced *Griffin* and urged a broad interpretation of it. Not fearful of change, indeed welcoming it, Frank sought to extend Chief Justice Warren's message in *Griffin*.[112] On review, the Supreme Court accepted Frank's reasoning and reversed.[113]

Frank had earlier contributed to the climate of thought in *United States v. Ebeling*.[114] Discovery in criminal cases traditionally had been quite narrow, but in *Ebeling* Frank argued that the district court should have examined an FBI report to determine whether anything in it was favorable to the defendant. Frank based his opinion on the belief that justice required a criminal defendant to have access to any information that might enable him or her to establish innocence. Ultimately the Supreme Court vindicated Frank's position in *Jencks v. United States,* where the Court substantially increased the defendant's access to information.[115] When the government puts forward a claim of privilege as a reason that defendant ought not to receive relevant information, then the criminal action must be dismissed. While the Court did not explicitly rely on Frank's *Ebeling* dissent, the spirit is very much in harmony with the position urged by Frank.

A final area of criminal procedure, the doctrine of "harmless error," vividly reveals Frank's influence. His dogged persistence, personal relations, and forceful dissents in such cases ultimately propelled the Supreme Court to revamp Second Circuit doctrine. The Federal Rules of Civil and of Criminal Procedure contain a provision designed to prevent slight technical errors from voiding an entire trial. Unless the error affects "the substantive rights of the parties," that error will not support reversal.[116] An attempt to determine when substantive rights have been affected led to a sharp split among the judges of the Second Circuit. Frank steadfastly insisted that the Second Circuit's approach unduly slighted the rights of litigants, particularly criminal defendants, and permitted harmful errors to go unredressed. In a series of dissents Frank decried the Second Circuit's approach, complaining that the court would affirm, notwithstanding serious trial court errors, if it was convinced from a reading of the entire record that the trial court decision was in fact correct or that the defendant was in fact guilty.[117] In his view, this involved the appellate court sitting as a substitute fact-finder relying only on the printed record. He urged that the harmless-error doctrine should carry a heavy burden before an appellate court could conclude that real error was nonetheless "harmless."[118]

The "harmless error" dispute nettled Jerome Frank. Ordinarily, he would acquiesce in doctrine that he disliked if a majority of the Second Circuit had adopted it. In this area, however, he adamantly refused to acquiesce. Frank dissented six times because in criminal cases the "harmless error" doctrine concerned a person's liberty and because a Supreme Court precedent arguably sanctioned his approach.[119] The Supreme Court responded slowly to Frank's dissents, denying certiorari in several pertinent cases.[120] Finally, however, his efforts succeeded: the Supreme Court granted certiorari. Justice Douglas wrote an opinion for the Court which followed Frank's reasoning and quoted directly from his dissent.[121] While the opinion did not adopt Frank's exact phrasing, it clearly rejected the Second Circuit's approach and moved closer to that urged by Frank.[122] An apparently unbroken line of Second Circuit decisions, in all of which certiorari had been denied, came to a halt as a result of Frank's persistent efforts to change the law. What began as a quest of a single circuit judge turned into national law formulated by a majority of the Supreme Court.

Jerome Frank also contributed an original idea in the area of standing to sue. In *Associated Industries of New York State v. Ickes*, coal consumers challenged orders of the Secretary of the Interior which increased the price of coal. An appeal focused on whether the consumer groups had standing to challenge the secretary's orders. Writing for the court, Frank urged that Congress had power to confer authority to sue on any person who sought to prevent a government officer from violating his statutory powers. The objective would be to vindicate the public interest, and accordingly he denominated these plaintiffs "private Attorney Generals."[123]

Justices Douglas and Harlan each attributed the phrase "private Attorney General" to Jerome Frank, and the notion embodied in the phrase has surfaced in a number of Supreme Court decisions.[124] While the Court has never adopted the idea, individual justices have come very close. Consider the dissenting opinions of Justices Blackmun and Douglas in *Sierra Club v. Morton*.[125] Each justice wished to allow the Sierra Club standing to challenge the decision of the Secretary of the Interior permitting construction of a ski resort in a wilderness section of the Sierra Nevada. Under traditional law of standing, the Sierra Club lacked sufficient interest to have standing to sue. While not expressly adopting Judge Frank's phrase, each justice sought to expand traditional standing requirements in order to permit a private organization to litigate this important public issue. And in *Flast v. Cohen,* the Court permitted a taxpayer to challenge aid to religious schools under the Elementary and Secondary Education Act of 1965. Again the majority did not use Frank's terminology, but Justice Harlans's dissent devastatingly exposed weaknesses in the majority opinion. According to Harlan, no other basis existed for standing except the notion of private attorneys general.[126]

Two tax cases reveal how Frank combined critical analysis and marked persistence to prod the Supreme Court to overrule one of its earlier decisions. *Helvering v. Proctor* concerned the relationship between two Supreme Court decisions, and Learned Hand argued that nothing in the latter decision either explicitly or implicitly overruled the former.[127] Frank believed that circuit judges should follow "a pronounced new doctrinal trend" in Supreme Court decisions, and a close reading of the two Supreme Court cases led him to conclude that the earlier decision had been implicitly overruled. He therefore dissented from Hand's opinion. Normally such a dissent was a signal to petition for certiorari, but in *Proctor* the government chose not to seek review.[128] Having expressed his view in dissent, Frank ordinarily would have acquiesced in subsequent decisions on the same issue, but when an identical case arose, Frank dissented once more.[129] This time he seized on the fact that in an intervening concurrence Justice Douglas had stated that it was an open question whether the earlier decision survived the latter. Frank grabbed this comment by a single justice as another available technique to use to push the Supreme Court to reform its own doctrine.

In these cases, Frank's attitudes prevailed. By his sharp criticism he encouraged the Court to review and clarify its decisional law. The occasion for the Court's overruling of its earlier decision came on review of a decision from the Third Circuit which had followed the Court's earlier decision. Citing criticism that included Frank's dissent, the Supreme Court overruled. One measure of Frank's influence comes from Justice Frankfurter, who wished to follow Learned Hand's approach instead. According to Frankfurter, Frank was the only circuit judge who had thought the second opinion overruled the first.[130] Though neither of Frank's dissents on this issue led directly to reversal by the Supreme Court, the ultimate course of the law affirmed Frank. His opinions lucidly demonstrated the inconsistency between the Supreme Court decisions, and the subsequent change toward consistency offers solid evidence of the importance of his role.

Frank's contributions to a climate of opinion can be seen as well in *Skidmore v. Baltimore and Ohio Railroad Co.* In this opinion and in numerous other writings, Jerome Frank castigated the jury as a lawless institution.[131] General verdicts, he declared, insulated the jury's actions as to what the law was, what the facts were, and how the law was to be applied to the facts. Such verdicts assume that the jury understands legal rules, yet appellate courts require trial judges to state the rules with technical precision. Frank described as naive the traditional theory that the judge conclusively determines the substantive rules while a jury confines itself to finding the facts.[132]

Justice Jackson later picked up Frank's ideas in a Supreme Court concurring opinion. "The naive assumption that prejudicial effects can be overcome by instructions to the jury, all practicing lawyers know to be unmitigated fiction."[133] While Jackson did not need Frank to tell him that juries often ignore judges' instructions of law, Frank's *Skidmore* opinion was most influential. At the time, it was an unprecedented exposure of the myths on which our jury system rests. Because it concerned the currently debated topic of special verdicts, it received wide circulation. Frank and Justice Black even carried on correspondence about special verdicts. Thus Jerome Frank probably influenced Justice Jackson. Other justices have, in turn, frequently quoted analogous language in Jackson's *Krulewitch* opinion.[134]

In re Luma Camera Service, Inc. confirms not only Frank's influence but also the limits of quantitative methods in the study of judicial behavior. As discussed earlier, *Luma Camera* involved a "turnover order" under federal bankruptcy law. Even if the individual was not in actual possession of assets, he was commanded to turn them over to the trustee. Failure to comply might result in imprisonment for contempt. Frank thought that this fiction operated unjustly, but he felt obliged to follow unwavering precedent. At the same time, he expressed his strong disapproval by ridiculing the very result reached and imploring the Supreme Court to accept the case for review and overturn these precedents.[135]

As expected, the Supreme Court granted certiorari and reversed the Second Circuit. On the surface, the Court reversed Judge Frank; Frank, however, hoped to be reversed and the Supreme Court obliged. Quantitative methods crudely focus simply on appellate affirmance or reversal and register such cases as *Luma Camera* as reflecting disagreement with its opinion's author. Thus they misrepresent reality.

On one level, *Luma Camera* employed elements of legal realism that may have derived somewhat from Jerome Frank's jurisprudential writings. Justice Jackson, writing for the Court, spoke of a "fiction" and noted that "generalities do little to solve concrete issues."[136] On another level, *Luma Camera* illustrates how a circuit court opinion frames the legal issues and sets the terms of debate. Counsel appeals from that decision and calls on the Supreme Court to rule differently on the issues resolved by the circuit court. Justice Jackson practically acknowledged that Jerome Frank's sarcasm led the Supreme Court to grant certiorari in *Luma Camera:*

> Whether [Frank's comment] is to be read literally as its [the Second Circuit's] deliberate judgment of the law of the case or something of a decoy intended to attract our attention to the problem, the declaration is one which this Court, in view of its supervisory power over courts of bankruptcy, cannot ignore.[137]

While Frank prompted Supreme Court review, the majority rationale did not exactly follow the route he urged. Judge Frank had construed a Supreme Court decision in *Oriel v. Russell* as holding that findings of fact made in connection with a turnover order are res judicata in subsequent contempt proceedings.[138] The *Maggio* majority refined the thrust of *Oriel* by allowing additional evidence to be introduced in the contempt proceeding in order to rebut the prima facie case made by the turnover order. In giving *Oriel* this interpretation, the Supreme Court traveled a route different from Judge Frank although its response was within the framework set by Frank's opinion.

The concurring opinion of Justice Black, joined by Justice Wiley

Rutledge, exhibits more obvious Frank influence.[139] Justice Black
followed Frank's reasoning closely, quoted from his opinion, and
agreed that the turnover order should not act as a substitute for a
criminal fraud prosecution. Even the dissent by Frankfurter
operated within the parameters set by Frank. Indeed, the entire
thrust of Frankfurter's dissent is directed toward Judge Frank's
interpretation of *Oriel*.[140] Thus all three Supreme Court opinions
reflect the influence of a brilliant circuit judge. The dissent, in
particular, is most unusual: Frankfurter chose not to respond to the
majority opinion, but to concentrate instead on the route taken by
the circuit court. All three opinions manifest to differing degrees
the impact that a circuit judge can have on ultimate Supreme Court
resolution of federal law.

VI

From his corporate practice in Chicago during the 1920s to his
role as a legal braintruster in the New Deal during the social and
economic crises of the 1930s, from his challenging and controversial forays into the relationships between law and the social sciences
to his role as circuit court judge and self-appointed adviser to the
highest court in the nation, Jerome Frank's legal career provides a
fascinating chronicle. A close examination of his impact as a circuit
court judge, however, suggests the limited value of the use of quantitative methods to investigate modern judicial behavior. Frank's
judicial style and strategy vividly demonstrate how mere
quantification of data slights subtlety and nuance and begs questions of quality and importance. Still, a flexible historical inquiry
employing empirical data, problematic and speculative reflection,
and direct and concrete evidence establishes beyond any doubt the
importance of Second Circuit Judge Jerome Frank in directing the
Supreme Court and shaping constitutional adjudication.

Frank's legal career was dominated by his drive to expand
governmental respect for the rights and liberties of individuals.
From seeking protection for southern sharecroppers during the
Depression through calling for a more realistic jurisprudence that
would render law more humane, or at least more mature, Frank

passionately sought legal reform that promised to maximize individual dignity. He took seriously the notion of "innocent until proved guilty." Characteristically, he saw the cutting edge of liberty in the confrontation between the state, with its extraordinary power, and the accused, standing alone. His career on the bench reflected these ideals, and, to the extent that these ideals are embraced in law today, it would be difficult to deny Judge Frank's contributions. The progressive constitutionalization of American criminal process secured by the Vinson and Warren Courts reflected not merely the judgment of a majority of the Supreme Court, but a broader legal movement to restrict egregious police practices and accord legal respect to the rights of the accused. From his forum on the Second Circuit, Judge Frank was a leader in that movement.

Appendix A

Judge Frank's Opinions
Reprinted in Casebooks

Arnstein v. Porter, 154 F. 2d 464 (2d Cir. 1946) (on the propriety of summary judgment)

    Reprinted in P. Carrington and B. Babcock, *Civil Procedure* 551 (2d ed. 1977).

    Reprinted in M. Rosenberg, J. Weinstein, and H. Smit, *Elements of Civil Procedure* 613 (2d ed. 1970).

    Reprinted in E. Kitch and H. Perlman, *Legal Regulation of the Competitive Process* 699 (2d ed. 1979).

    Reprinted in B. Kaplan and R. Brown, Jr., *Cases on Copyright* 283 (1960).

Fischman v. Raytheon Mfg. Co., 188 F. 2d 783 (2d Cir. 1951) (permitting cause of action for damages under the Securities Exchange Act of 1934 and SEC Rule 10b-5)

    Noted in R. Jennings and H. Marsh, Jr., *Securities Regulation, Cases and Materials* 866–68 (2d ed. 1968)

Guttman v. Illinois Central R.R. Co., 189 F. 2d 297 (2d Cir. 1951) (on the meaning of noncumulative preferred shares)

    Reprinted in V. Brudney and M. Chirelstein, *Cases and Materials on Corporate Finance* 161 (1972).

    Reprinted in N. Lattin, R. Jennings, and R. Buxbaum, *Corporations* 1193 (4th ed. 1968).

    Quoted in W. Cary and M. Eisenberg, *Cases and Materials on Corporations* 1199 (5th ed. unabridged 1969).

Heim v. Universal Pictures Co., 154 F. 2d 480 (2d Cir. 1946) (on copyright formalities)

    Reprinted in M. Nimmer, *Cases and Materials on Copyright* 161 (2d ed. 1979).

    Noted in E. Kitch and H. Perlman, *Legal Regulation of the Competitive Process* 706 (2d ed. 1979).

Reprinted in B. Kaplan and R. Brown, Jr., *Cases on Copyright* 298, 862 (1960).

Hunter v. United States, 219 F. 2d 69 (2d Cir. 1955) (on attorney's fees in alimony dispute)

Reprinted in W. Andrews, *Basic Federal Income Taxation* 391 (2d ed. 1979).

In re Barnett, 124 F. 2d 1005 (2d Cir. 1942) (on who may appeal)

Reprinted in M. Rosenberg, J. Weinstein, and H. Smit, *Elements of Civil Procedure* 1014 (2d ed. 1970).

In re Fried, 161 F. 2d 453, 458–59, 465 (2d Cir. 1947) (dissenting) (on the inadequacy of postindictment relief to protect a person's reputation)

Quoted and cited in Y. Kamisar, W. LaFave, and J. Israel, *Modern Criminal Procedure* 730–31 (4th ed. 1974).

McAllister v. Commissioner, 157 F. 2d 235 (2d Cir. 1946), *cert. denied*, 330 U.S. 826 (1947) (dissenting) (on taxation of substitutes for future ordinary income)

Reprinted in W. Andrews, *Basic Federal Income Taxation* 892 (2d ed. 1979).

NLRB v. Universal Camera Corp., 190 F. 2d 429, 431 (2d Cir. 1950) (concurring) (on reviewing facts found by an administrative agency)

Noted in W. Gelhorn, C. Byse, and P. Strauss, *Administrative Law* 794–95, 802 (7th ed. 1979).

Ochs v. Commissioner, 195 F. 2d 692, 695 (2d Cir. 1952) (dissenting) (on extraordinary medical expenses)

Reprinted in B. Bittker and L. Stone, *Federal Income Taxation* 215 (5th ed. 1980).

Reprinted in S. Surrey, W. Warren, P. McDaniel, and H. Ault, *Federal Income Taxation*, vol. 1, 622 (1972).

Reprinted in W. Andrews, *Basic Federal Income Taxation* 424 (2d ed. 1979).

Oldden v. Tonto Realty Corp., 143 F. 2d 916 (2d Cir. 1944) (dissenting in part) (on a landlord's claim under the Bankruptcy Act)

Reprinted in W. Warren and W. Hogan, *Cases and Materials on Debtor-Credit Law* 689 (2d ed. 1981).

Picard v. United Aircraft Corp., 128 F. 2d 632 (2d Cir. 1942) (concurring) (test of patentability)

Reprinted in A. Smith, *Patent Law* 40 and 455 (1964).

Ricketts v. Penn. R.R. Co., 153 F. 2d 757, 760 (2d Cir. 1946) (concurring) (on the theory of contracts)

Quoted in E. Farnsworth and W. Young, *Cases and Materials on Contracts* 171 (3d ed. 1980).

Siegelman v. Cunard White Star Ltd., 221 F. 2d 189, 199 (2d Cir. 1955) (dissenting) (on contracts of adhesion)

> Reprinted in R. Crampton, D. Currie, and H. Kay, *Conflict of Laws* 146, 150 (2d ed. 1975).

> Reprinted in W. Reese and M. Rosenberg, *Cases and Materials on the Conflict of Laws* 612 (6th ed. 1971).

United States v. Grunewald, 233 F. 2d 556 (2d Cir. 1956), *rev'd*, 353 U.S. 391 (1957) (dissenting) (on comparative law)

> Noted in R. Schlesinger, *Comparative Law* 43n8a (4th ed. 1980).

United States v. Johnson, 238 F. 2d 565, 572 (2d Cir. 1956) (dissenting) (on services needed by impoverished criminal defendants in addition to legal counsel if equal justice is to be a reality)

> Quoted in Y. Kamisar, W. LaFave, and J. Israel, *Modern Criminal Procedure* 121n7 (4th ed. 1974).

Usatorre v. The Victoria, 172 F. 2d 434 (2d Cir. 1949) (on interpretation of civil-law codes)

> Reprinted in R. Schlesinger, *Comparative Law* 443 (3d ed. 1970).

Walter v. Arabian American Oil Co., 233 F. 2d 541 (2d Cir. 1956) (on the application of foreign law)

> Reprinted in R. Crampton, D. Currie, and H. Kay, *Conflict of Laws* 51 (2d ed. 1975).

> Reprinted in A. Von Mehren and D. Trautman, *The Law of Multistate Problems* 91 (1965).

Williams v. McGowan, 152 F. 2d 570 (2d Cir. 1945) (dissenting) (on taxing the sale of a business)

> Reprinted in W. Andrews, *Basic Federal Income Taxation* 874 (2d ed. 1979).

Appendix B

JUDGE FRANK'S LAW CLERKS

1941–1942   Boris I. Bittker
Sterling Professor of Law, Emeritus
Yale University

1942–1943   Sidney M. Davis, Esquire
Shanks, Davis & Remer
New York City

1943–1944   Richard Donnelly, Esquire
Professor of Law
Yale University

1944–1945   Philip B. Kurland
William R. Kenan, Jr., Distinguished Service Professor
University of Chicago

1945–1947   Carmel Prashker Ebb, Esquire
Poletti, Freidin, Prashker & Gartner
New York City

1947–1948   Richard H. Paul, Esquire
Paul, Weiss, Rifkind, Wharton & Garrison
New York City

1948–1949   Daniel W. West
Debevoise, Plimpton & McLean
New York City

1949–1950   Jay Topkis, Esquire
Paul, Weiss, Rifkind, Wharton & Garrison
New York City

1950–1951   Stuart H. Johnson, Jr., Esquire
Breed, Abbott & Morgan
New York City

1951–1952   Honorable Patricia A. Wald
United States Circuit Judge
for the District of Columbia Circuit
Washington, D.C.

1952–1953   Martin Carmichael, Esquire
             New York City
1953–1954   Sondra K. Slade, Esquire
             Pitt, Agulnick, Supplee, Johnson & Slade
             West Chester, Pennsylvania
1954–1955   Gerald G. Schulsinger
             Klagsbrunn, Hanes & Irwin
             Washington, D.C.
1955–1956   George C. Zachary, Esquire
             Rosenfeld, Meyer & Susman
             Beverly Hills, California
1956–1957   Walter E. Shuttleworth, Esquire
             Townley, Updike, Carter & Rodgers
             New York City

NOTES

Unless otherwise noted, all letters and memoranda are in the Jerome Frank Papers, Yale University Library, and are used by permission. Material from the Columbia Oral History Collection is copyrighted by the Trustees of Columbia University in the City of New York and is used by permission; Rexford G. Tugwell, © 1972; Jerome N. Frank and Lee Pressman, © 1975; Henry A. Wallace, © 1976.

1. "A Charmingly Disporting Gazelle"

1. Florence Kiper Frank (hereinafter cited as FKF) to Walter Volkomer, Feb. 12, 1961.

2. Matthew Josephson suggested that Herman was disbarred, but he practiced in Chicago until the end of his life (*see* M. Josephson, *Infidel in the Temple* 281 [1967]); interview with FKF, New Haven, June 26, 1975 (all interviews with Mrs. Frank were conducted in New Haven); interview with Marie B. Sturman and Frank C. Bernard, Chicago, July 20, 1983. Mrs. Sturman and Mr. Bernard are Jerome's niece and nephew, children of his sisters.

3. Interview with FKF, Aug. 8, 1974.

4. Interview with Marie B. Sturman, Chicago, July 20, 1983.

5. *See* E. Purcell, Jr., *The Crisis of Democratic Theory* 17–18 (1973); B. Karl, *Charles E. Merriam and the Study of Politics* (1974); S. Diner, *A City and Its Universities* 154–75 (1980).

6. *See* Frank memoir, Columbia Oral History Collection, at 2 (hereinafter cited as COHC).

7. *See* Frank COHC at 4.

8. *See* FKF to Richard H. Rovere, Feb. 19, 1974.

9. Frank actually entered practice in 1913 with the firm of Newman, Northrup, Levinson & Becker. Newman and Northrup separated in 1914 and ultimately founded the prominent Chicago firm of Jenner & Block. Also in 1914, Levinson and Becker added Cleveland and Schwartz as named partners; Jerome Frank remained as an associate.

10. Interviews with FKF, Aug. 6, Aug. 8, Aug. 12, 1974; June 26, 1975.

11. *See* Frank, COHC at 5, 7, 11.

12. *See* Frank, COHC at 5; Ulysses S. Schwartz to Rovere, Dec. 20, 1947.

13. Schwartz to Rovere, Dec. 20, 1947.

14. *See* W. Volkomer, *The Passionate Liberal* 4–6 (1970); Wrigley, "The Jerome N. Frank Papers," 48 *Yale U. Lib. Gazette* 163, 165 (1974).

15. *See* Benjamin V. Becker to Rovere (memorandum), Dec. 27, 1946.

16. *See* Francis X. Busch to Rovere, Jan. 10, 1947.

17. *See* Partnership Dissolution Agreement of Salmon O. Levinson, Benjamin V. Becker, Jerome N. Frank, and Otis F. Glenn, Dec. 31, 1929.

18. For background on bankruptcy reorganization, *see* T. Finletter, *The Law of Bankruptcy Reorganization* 1–35 (1939); H. Black, *Handbook of the Law and Practice in Bankruptcy* 101–17 (2d ed. 1930); G. Glenn, *The Law Governing Liquidation* 66–72, 250–89 (1935).

19. Information on Frank's Chicago law practice comes from interviews with Florence Kiper Frank, Frank C. Bernard, Marie B. Sturman, Max F. Goldberg, William J. Friedman, and John J. Abt. Also useful were letters written to Richard H. Rovere by friends and associates of Frank for a planned "profile" in *The New Yorker* which Rovere never completed. *See* "Selected Documents from the Papers of Richard Rovere Concerning Jerome Frank," Franklin D. Roosevelt Library, Hyde Park, N.Y. Goldberg, Friedman, and Abt practiced law with Jerome in Chicago.

20. *See* Busch to Rovere, Jan. 10, 1974; Becker to Rovere (letter and memorandum), Dec. 27, 1946.

21. Interviews with William J. Friedman and Max F. Goldberg, Chicago, July 19, 1983.

22. Interviews with Frank C. Bernard and Marie B. Sturman, Chicago, July 20, 1983.

23. *See* Partnership Dissolution Agreement, *supra* n. 15; interview with William J. Friedman, Chicago, July 19, 1983.

24. *See* Barbara Frank to Rovere, Dec. 7, 1946.

25. Interview with William J. Friedman, Chicago, July 19, 1983.

26. On the Leopold-Loeb case, see the splendid account in K. Tierney, *Darrow* 320–51 (1979). *See also* N. Leopold, *Life Plus 99 Years* (1958).

27. *See* Becker to Rovere (memorandum), Dec. 27, 1946.

28. Interview with FKF, Aug. 6, 1974.

29. *See* FKF to Herbert L. Packer, Dec. 5, 1972; Rovere, "Jerome N. Frank: 1889–1957," *Memorial of the Ass'n of the Bar of the City of New York and the New York County Lawyers' Ass'n* 18, 23 (1957).

30. Telephone conversations with Marie B. Sturman, Dec. 1, 1980; Ethel Stein, Dec. 2, 1980; and Max F. Goldberg, Dec. 4, 1980.

31. *See* Frank, COHC at 2, 11.

32. Rovere, *supra* n. 29, at 19.

33. Frank, COHC at 12, 63.

34. J. Frank, *Law and the Modern Mind* 19 (1930) (hereinafter cited as *L&MM*).

35. *See* Frank, COHC at 12.

36. *See* Jerome N. Frank (hereinafter cited as JNF) to Morris R. Cohen, June 4, 1931; Cohen to JNF, July 3, 1931.

37. On Cohen, see D. Hollinger, *Morris R. Cohen and the Scientific Ideal* 69–96 (1975). For a sensitive evaluation of Cohen's thought and personality, see JNF to

Edmond Cahn, May 4, 1950, reprinted in Newman, book review, 18 *Duquesne L. Rev.* 387, 395–400 (1980) (D. Hollinger, *Morris R. Cohen and the Scientific Ideal*).

38. *See* Cohen to JNF, July 3, July 7, and July 9, 1931; JNF to Cohen, July 7 and July 9, 1931.

39. Cohen to JNF, Nov. 7, 1931.

40. JNF to Cohen, Sept. 8, 1931.

41. Cohen to JNF, Sept. 18, 1931.

42. *See, e.g.,* JNF to Felix Frankfurter and Thomas Reed Powell, Sept. 2, 1931.

43. JNF to Cohen, Oct. 7, 1931.

44. JNF to Cohen, Dec. 8, 1931.

45. JNF to Frankfurter, Oct. 26, 1931.

46. Interview with Marie B. Sturman and Frank C. Bernard, Chicago, July 20, 1983.

47. Frankfurter to JNF, April 29, 1943.

48. After Frank's death, Frankfurter recalled:

To have known Jerome Frank only through his writings was not to have known him. On paper he appeared prickly and pugilistic; in personal relations he was warm-hearted and generous. His combative curiosity gave battle at the drop of a word, so that those who encountered him only on paper were apt to be surprised when they found in him a devoted, uncritical friend and a compassionate observer of the human scene. [Frankfurter, "Jerome N. Frank," in *Of Law and Life* 100 (P. Kurland, ed., 1967)]

The devotion of Frank's friends is evident in Edmond Cahn's dedication of *The Moral Decision* (1955) to "Judge Jerome Frank, Champion of Enlightenment and of Humane Justice."

49. "My friends and neighbors always seemed to be more brilliant when they were with him than at any other time. I certainly felt that way myself" (Elisabeth Ballard to Rovere, Dec. 20, 1946).

50. Rodell, "Jerome N. Frank: In Remembrance," 3 *Yale L. Report* 3 (1957).

51. Barbara Frank to Rovere, Dec. 7, 1946.

52. Interview with Boris I. Bittker, Aug. 7, 1974.

53. *See* JNF to Frankfurter, Nov. 30, 1932; Frank, COHC at 13.

54. Initially Rexford Tugwell offered Frank the position of solicitor for the Department of Agriculture, but James Farley, Roosevelt's patronage boss, blocked the appointment after hearing the erroneous story that Frank's father-in-law had been a member of Tammany Hall. The AAA post proved more interesting and important.

55. *See* Frank, COHC at 14, 65–67, 72.

56. *See* Frank, "Experimental Jurisprudence and the New Deal," *Cong. Record* 78, pt. 2, 73d Cong., 2d Sess., 12412 (1934).

57. *See* Alabama Power Co. v. Ickes, 302 U.S. 464 (1938), and Duke Power Co. v. Greenwood County, 302 U.S. 485 (1938).

58. *See* J. Auerbach, *Unequal Justice* 198–99 (1976).

59. *See* JNF to John Gutknecht, May 31, 1940. On the early history of the National Lawyers Guild, *see* Auerbach, *supra* n. 58, at 198–209 (1976).

60. *See* W. Douglas, *Go East Young Man* 264 (1974); William O. Douglas to Rovere, Nov. 14, 1946.

61. *See* JNF to Harry Hopkins, Aug. 19, 1940; interview with FKF, Aug. 12, 1974.

62. *See* Douglas, *supra* n. 60, at 254–93 (1974).

63. *See* J. Frank, *Save America First* 264–67, 278–310 (1938); *Time*, Mar. 11, 1940, at 75; J. Seligman, *The Transformation of Wall Street* 217–22, 231–37 (1982); M. Parrish, *Securities Regulation and the New Deal* 179–80 (1970); Volkomer, *supra* n. 14, at 147–86.

64. *Newsweek*, April 1, 1940, at 52.

65. *See* Parrish, *supra* n. 63, at 227.

66. *See id.* at 219–21, 227, 230–31.

67. J. Frank, *Save America First* xii (1938).

68. *See id.* at 109–49, 170.

69. *See id.* at 185–222, 235–50, 350–422.

70. *Id.* at 400 (italics omitted).

71. Franklin D. Roosevelt to JNF, April 24, 1941, quoted in Wrigley, *supra* n. 14, at 174.

72. *See* Wrigley, *supra* n. 14, at 172; Box 156, Folders 431 and 432, Jerome Frank Papers; "Red-White-and-Blue-Herring," *Sat. Evening Post*, Dec. 6, 1941, at 9.

73. *See* JNF to Thomas G. Corcoran, Mar. 17, 1939; JNF to Hopkins, Aug. 19, 1940.

74. *See* JNF to Corcoran, Mar. 17, 1939.

75. *See* JNF to Hopkins, Aug. 19, 1940.

76. Interviews with FKF, Aug. 6 and Aug. 8, 1974.

77. *See* Frank, "Red-White-and-Blue Herring," *Sat. Evening Post*, Dec. 6, 1941, at 84.

78. *Id.* at 10.

79. Interview with FKF, Aug. 6, 1974; *see* Wrigley, *supra* n. 14, at 177.

80. Simon H. Rifkind to Robert Jerome Glennon, Nov. 16, 1983.

81. Brooks, "Profile: Simon H. Rifkind," *New Yorker*, May 23, 1983, at 68.

82. *See* Max Rodin to Rovere, Dec. 3, 1946.

83. *See* M. Schick, *Learned Hand's Court* 124–29, 143–44, 219–304 (1970). Frank held a dinner party for the Clarks before one term of court opened. The friendship remained intact, for after Frank's death Clark graciously presided over a memorial service, made glowing remarks about Frank, and worked hard to get an annuity for his widow (interview with FKF, Aug. 6, 1974).

84. "If men were angels, no government would be necessary" (*The Federalist Papers*, no. 51).

85. *See* J. Frank, *If Men Were Angels* 22–32 (1942).

86. *See* J. Frank, *Fate and Freedom* 89 (1945).

87. *Id.* at 16.

88. Interview with Mary Strickland, Aug. 15, 1974.

89. Interview with FKF, Aug. 15, 1974. In addition to his published books and his unpublished novel, Frank partially completed biographies of Charles Evans Hughes, Theodore Roosevelt, and Julius Rosenwald, the president of Sears, Roebuck & Co. *See* Boxes 147–53, Jerome Frank Papers.

90. Interview with Boris I. Bittker, Aug. 7, 1974.

91. Interview with FKF, Aug. 6, 1974.

92. Douglas remembered that at an SEC conference held to consider a voluminous staff report, "the rest of us would have barely started when he would have finished thumbing through the pages and have put the document down in front of

him. At first I did not believe he had read and digested and understood what was in the document. But I found out that he would take in a page at a glance. Moreover, he retained what he had read" (Douglas to Rovere, Nov. 14, 1946).

93. Sidney Davis, quoted in Rovere, *supra* n. 29, at 25.

94. Interview with FKF, Aug. 15, 1974.

95. *Time*, Mar. 11, 1940, at 72–73.

96. Interview with Mary Strickland, Aug. 15, 1974.

97. *See* Rovere, *supra* n. 29, at 26.

98. Rodell, *supra* n. 50, at 4.

99. *Id.*

100. *See id.* at 5.

101. *See* Volkomer, *supra* n. 14, at 18.

102. In the preface to *Courts on Trial* (p. viii), Frank wrote:

Since my position in this book is somewhat novel, I have deliberately used a technique which, as I said in the preface to an earlier book, is reminiscent of the following: Mr. Smith of Denver was introduced to Mr. Jones at a dinner party in Chicago. "Oh," said Jones, "do you know my friend, Mr. Schnicklefritz, who lives in Denver?" "No," answered Smith. Later in the evening, when Smith referred to Denver, Jones again asked whether Smith was acquainted with Schnicklefritz, and again received a negative reply. As the dinner party broke up, Smith remarked that he was leaving that night for Denver, and Jones once more inquired whether Smith knew Schnicklefritz. "Really," came the answer, "his name sounds quite familiar."

103. JNF to Frankfurter, Jan. 6, 1932. Indeed, Frank once parodied Frankfurter's turgid writing style by rewriting Lincoln's Gettysburg Address as a Frankfurter judicial opinion.

Mr. Justice Frankfurter delivered the opinion of the Court.

A semi-centennial, three decades and seven winter solstices preceding the present, our paternal progenitors gestated and regurgitated upon the western hemisphere (49° longitude 38° latitude) a pristine commonwealth, political, social, and economic, of our glorious and heterogeneous population proclaiming the universal hypothesis, proposition and thesis, that all male issue are politically and economically liberated and equal, pari-passu per capita and not per stirpes. Engaged now we are in a collosal bellis civilis (cf. Slaughter House Cases 9 Wall—construing "civil war" to mean "War Between the States" in Alabama) for the purpose of determining qualitatively and quantitatively in perpetuity the tensile strength and viscosity of a government, including its interstices and lacunae, with this ontogeny. In convention assembled, we are congregated on a stupendous panoramic scene of that conflict. We have been transported here to deify a circumscribed area of that territory as a situs of ultimate collectivistic internment of those individuals who here alienated their existence in space and time as creative beings to raise a presumption that this governmental authority will continue in a conscious state. Conformity to accepted tenets makes it necessary that we perform this requirement so universally accepted. But in a broader viewpoint, on a higher plane, exaltation and apotheosis of this terra firma is ultra vires and beyond our mortal capacity. The male human beings of courage, in esse or deceased, who participated jointly and severally in combat on this locus have given it a theistic attribute tremendously superior to our impecunious capability to augment, diminish, multiply, divide or partition either in law or in equity. This cosmos will make no memoranda of what is declaimed here but its memorizing and associative processes will in future eternally record the accomplishments performed on this terrain. It is the obligation of those in being, perforce, to be here anointed and consecrated to the immense duties envisaged for the future, that from these sanctified decedents we partake of enhanced reverence to that shibboleth or fetish for which they ceded the penultimate in obeisance, that we here supremely asseverate that those who have left this mortal coil shall not have performed a futile and unproductive activity, and that this political authority of the vox populi shall not be obliterated from this planetary sphere. The opinion of A. Lincoln at Gettysburg, November 19, 1863, is reversed and he is directed to take further proceedings in accordance with this opinion. Mr. Justice Reynolds concurs in the result.

Although it seems likely that Frank wrote this parody, found in his papers and with his handwriting on it, the original is typed and it is possible that Frank only contributed to the final spoof. At any rate it beautifully captures Frankfurter's impenetrable prose and Frank's sense of humor. I am grateful to Laura Kalman for bringing this parody to my attention.

104. Bernard D. Meltzer to Robert Jerome Glennon, Oct. 17, 1980. *See* In re Consumers Power Co., 6 SEC 444 (1939).

105. *See* A. Weinstein, *Perjury* 40–41, 133, 135 (1978).

106. *See* Frank, COHC at 136–38, 187–88.

107. *See* Weinstein, *supra* n. 105, at 168.

108. 182 F. 2d 416 (1950).

109. Interview with FKF, June 26, 1975.

110. Learned Hand to FKF, Jan. 20, 1957. Frank dedicated *Courts on Trial* to "Learned Hand Our Wisest Judge," and expressed his admiration in "Some Reflections on Judge Learned Hand," 24 *U. Chi. L. Rev.* 666 (1957). Florence Frank confirmed Jerome's devotion to Learned Hand (interview with FKF, Aug. 6, 1974). Frank had a similar fawning attitude toward Oliver Wendell Holmes, Jr., whom he described as "the completely adult jurist" (*see* L&MM 270).

111. *See, e.g.,* "Symposium: Jerome N. Frank," 66 *Yale L.J.* 817 (1957); and "Symposium: Jerome N. Frank," 24 *U. Chi. L. Rev.* 625 (1957).

112. *See* FKF to Walter Volkomer, Feb. 12, 1961.

113. Interview with FKF, Aug. 6, 1974.

114. Clark, "Jerome N. Frank," 66 *Yale L.J.* 817, 818 (1957).

115. Interview with Mary Strickland, Aug. 15, 1974.

116. *See* JNF to Henry Porter Chandler, Aug. 27, 1956.

117. Cahn wrote Frank on March 10, 1954:

Perhaps you do not know that you are the only visitor I have not endeavored to keep away during these months of trial. Do you know that, despite your being in New York only one week a month, you have been my most frequent—because most welcome—visitor? Do you now, embarrassed as you may be, realize how much good you've done? All of these things are as obvious as they are precious—to me at least; you will not let me talk them out, and so I have written them here.

Devotedly,
Edmond

118. FKF to Herbert L. Packer, Dec. 5, 1972. One taxi driver described Jerome as "such a regular guy, you wouldn't know he was a judge" (interview with FKF, Aug. 6, 1974). Frank's housekeeper for many years, Mary Strickland, when asked about him (Aug. 6, 1974), responded, "I have nothing to say about him. He never gave me any trouble."

2. Judicial Power and the Legitimacy of Law

1. W. Blackstone, *Commentaries on the Laws of England* (Oxford 1765–69) 38–43, 69, 71, 73.

2. M. Horwitz, *The Transformation of American Law, 1780–1860* at 4–9.

3. See *id.* at 257–58; M. Bloomfield, *American Lawyers in a Changing Society, 1776–1876* at 59–90 (1976).

4. See Swift v. Tyson, 16 Peters (41 U.S.) 1, 18 (1842); Horwitz, *supra* n. 2, at 245–52.

5. Simpson, "The Rise and Fall of the Legal Treatise: Legal Principles and the Forms of Legal Literature," 48 *U. Chi. L. Rev.* 632, 668–79 (1981).

6. J. Bishop, *The First Book of the Law* 127 (Boston 1868), quoted in Simpson, *supra* n. 5, at 674.

7. Quoted in Dickinson, "The Law behind Law," 29 *Colum. L. Rev.* 113, 142 (1929).

8. See L. Friedman, *A History of American Law* 531–32 (1973); R. Stevens, *Law School* (1983); Stevens, "Two Cheers for 1870: The American Law School," in *Law in American History* 405 (D. Fleming and B. Bailyn, eds., 1971); G. Gilmore, *The Ages of American Law* 42–48 (1977); A. Sutherland, *The Law at Harvard* 162–205 (1967); Chase, "The Birth of the Modern Law School," 23 *Am. J. Leg. Hist.* 329 (1979).

9. The conventional assumption that Langdell developed the idea of law as a science has recently been challenged. See Chase, "Origins of Modern Professional Education: The Harvard Case Method Conceived as Clinical Instruction in Law," 5 *Nova L.J.* 323 (1981).

10. Thomas Reed Powell to JNF, Nov. 5, 1930.

11. See M. Keller, *Affairs of State* 404–7 (1977); F. Frankfurter and N. Greene, *The Labor Injunction* (1930); L. Boudin, *Government by Judiciary* (1932). At the same time, Morton Keller has cautioned against exaggerating the degree of judicial hostility to labor. Judicial activism could not ignore public opinion over a long period of time. By the turn of the century New York, Massachusetts, and Washington courts displayed a greater willingness to uphold pro-labor legislation. See M. Keller, *Affairs of State* 407–8 (1977); Tripp, "Progressive Legislation in the West: The Washington Supreme Court, Labor Law, and the Problem of Industrial Accidents," 24 *Labor History* 342 (1983).

12. Pollock v. Farmers' Loan and Trust Co. (Rehearing), 158 U.S. 601 (1895); In re Debs, 158 U.S. 564 (1895); United States v. E. C. Knight, Co., 156 U.S. 1 (1895).

13. See A. Paul, *Conservative Crisis and the Rule of Law* (1969). See also Lochner v. New York, 198 U.S. 45 (1905), and Allgeyer v. Louisiana, 165 U.S. 578 (1897) (using substantive due process to protect liberty to contract); Coppage v. Kansas, 236 U.S. 1 (1915) (holding unconstitutional a state statute prohibiting "yellow dog" contracts); and Adair v. United States, 208 U.S. 161 (1908) (striking down a federal prohibition on "yellow dog" contracts).

14. *See* Stagner, "The Recall of Judicial Decisions and the Due Process Debate," 24 *Am. J. Leg. Hist.* 257 (1980); G. Kolko, *The Triumph of Conservatism* 198 (1963).

15. *See* Gilmore, "Legal Realism: Its Cause and Cure," 70 *Yale L.J.* 1037, 1040–44 (1960).

16. *See* Friedman, *supra* n. 8, at 541–44. Nineteenth-century treatises were used as pedagogic tools for students, but after Langdell introduced the case system, treatises were used more by practicing attorneys.

17. *See id.* at 580–83; G. Gilmore, *The Death of Contract* 57–60 (1974); Gilmore, *supra* n. 15, at 1044–45; G. Gilmore, *supra* n. 8, at 72–74; Crystal, "Codification and the Rise of the Restatement Movement," 54 *Wash. L. Rev.* 239 (1979).

18. *See* M. White, *Social Thought in America* (1947); *cf.* H. Hughes, *Consciousness and Society* (1958).

19. W. James, *Pragmatism* 201 (1914).

20. *See* White, "The Integrity of Holmes' Jurisprudence," 10 *Hofstra L. Rev.* 633 (1982); Touster, "Holmes a Hundred Years Ago: *The Common Law* and Legal Theory," 10 *Hofstra L. Rev.* 673 (1982); Gordon, "Holmes' *Common Law* as Legal and Social Science," 10 *Hofstra L. Rev.* 719 (1982); M. Horwitz, "The Place of Justice Holmes in American Legal Thought" (forthcoming); M. Howe, *Justice Oliver Wendell Holmes,* 2 vols. (1957, 1963); Tushnet, "The Logic of Experience: Oliver Wendell Holmes on the Supreme Judicial Court," 63 *Va. L. Rev.* 975 (1977); Rogat, "Mr. Justice Holmes: A Dissenting Opinion," pts. 1 and 2, 15 *Stan. L. Rev.* 3, 254 (1962–63); Kaplan, "Encounters with O. W. Holmes, Jr.," 96 *Harv. L. Rev.* 1828 (1983).

21. *See* Holmes, "The Path of the Law, 10 *Harv. L. Rev.* 457, 465–66 (1897). Contemporary philosophy has a different conception of "formal logic." *See generally,* R. Jeffrey, *Formal Logic* (1967).

22. New York Trust Co. v. Eisner, 256 U.S. 345, 349 (1921).

23. O. Holmes, *The Common Law* 5 (1881). Holmes always thought that logic has a role in judicial decisions. *See id.* at 173; *Collected Legal Papers* 197–98 (1920).

24. *See* Holmes, "Law in Science and Science in Law," in *Collected Legal Papers* 238–39 (1920).

25. Holmes, *supra* n. 21, at 239, 469.

26. *Id.* at 459. *See* White, *supra* n. 18, at 64–68.

27. *See* Howe, "Introduction to *The Common Law*" xiv, xviii–xix (1963); 2 M. Howe, *Justice Oliver Wendell Holmes* 74–82 (1963); Gilmore, *supra* n. 8, at 48–56.

28. Lochner v. New York, 198 U.S. 45, 75 (1905) (Holmes, J., dissenting).

29. Holmes, *supra* n. 2, at 460–61.

30. Abrams v. United States, 250 U.S. 616, 630 (1919) (Holmes, J., dissenting).

31. Quoted in *L&MM* 275.

32. *See* Pound, "The Causes of Popular Dissatisfaction with the Administration of Justice," 40 *Am. L. Rev.* 729 (1906); Pound, "Liberty of Contract," 18 *Yale L.J.* 487 (1907); Pound, "Mechanical Jurisprudence," 8 *Colum. L. Rev.* 605 (1908); Pound, "The Scope and Purpose of Sociological Jurisprudence," 24 *Harv. L. Rev.* 591 (1911), 25 *Harv. L. Rev.* 140, and 25 *Harv. L. Rev.* 489 (1912). For an analysis of Pound's philosophy, see D. Wigdor, *Roscoe Pound* (1974).

33. Pound, "Mechanical Jurisprudence," 8 *Colum. L. Rev.* 605–10 (1908).

34. Pound, "Liberty of Contract," 18 *Yale L.J.* 462 (1908).

35. *See* Wigdor, *supra* n. 32, at 164, 187, 199–200, 208–9, 218–19, 230.

36. For accounts of American legal realism, see W. Rumble, *American Legal Realism* (1968); W. Twining, *Karl Llewellyn and the Realist Movement* (1973); Gilmore, *supra*

n. 8, at 78–81; Gilmore, *supra* n. 15; White, "From Sociological Jurisprudence to Realism: Jurisprudence and Social Change in Early Twentieth-Century America," 58 *Va. L. Rev.* 999 (1972); Woodard, "The Limits of Legal Realism: An Historical Perspective," 54 *Va. L. Rev.* 689 (1968); Verdun-Jones, "The Jurisprudence of Jerome N. Frank: A Study in American Legal Realism," 7 *Sydney L. Rev.* 180 (1974); Verdun-Jones, "Cook, Oliphant and Yntema: The Scientist Wing of American Legal Realism," 5 *Dalhousie L.J.* 3 (1979); Schlegel, "American Legal Realism and Empirical Social Science: From the Yale Experience," 28 *Buff. L. Rev.* 459 (1979); Schlegel, "American Legal Realism and Empirical Social Science: The Singular Case of Underhill Moore," 29 *Buff. L. Rev.* 195 (1980); Linde, "Judges, Critics, and the Realist Tradition" 82 *Yale L.J.* 227 (1972); Yntema, "American Legal Realism in Retrospect," 14 *Vand. L. Rev.* 317 (1960); Jones, "Law and Morality in the Perspective of Legal Realism," 61 *Colum. L. Rev.* 799 (1961); Lucey, "Natural Law and American Legal Realism: Their Respective Contributions to a Theory of Law in a Democratic Society," 30 *Geo. L.J.* 493 (1942); Rostow, "American Legal Realism and the Sense of the Profession," in E. Rostow, *The Sovereign Prerogative* 3 (1962); K. Llewellyn, *The Common Law Tradition* 508–20 (1960); J. Johnson, *American Legal Culture, 1908–1940* (1981); J. Paul, *The Legal Realism of Jerome N. Frank* (1959); W. Volkomer, *The Passionate Liberal* 1–47 (1970); Savarese, "American Legal Realism," 3 *Houston L. Rev.* 180 (1965); Burrus, "American Legal Realism," 8 *How. L.J.* 36 (1962); Mensch, "The History of Mainstream Legal Thought," in D. Kairys, ed., *The Politics of Law* 18 (1982); R. Summers, *Instrumentalism and American Legal Theory* (1983).

Figuring out who is a realist and what constitutes legal realism has plagued participants and observers alike for fifty years. The term appears to have been used first, but independently, by Jerome Frank and Karl Llewellyn. *See L&MM* 23n8, 46–52 (1930), and Llewellyn, "A Realist Jurisprudence—The Next Step," 30 *Colum. L. Rev.* 431 (1930).

37. *L&MM* 103–5, 24, 70, 72.

38. *See id.* at 111, 113–14, 120, 124. The idea came from Judge Joseph Hutcheson of the U.S. Court of Appeals for the Eighth Circuit. *See* Hutcheson, "The Judgment Intuitive: The Function of the 'Hunch' in Judicial Decisions," 14 *Cornell L.Q.* 274 (1929).

39. *L&MM* 125.

40. *Id.* at 159. Frank urged the abandonment of "the Santa Claus story of complete legal certainty; the fairy tale of a pot of golden law which is already in existence and which the good lawyer can find, if only he is sufficiently diligent" (*id.* at 260).

41. *See id.* at 50–51, 127–48.

42. *Id.* at 130, 148–58, 165–71, 179 (emphasis omitted).

43. *Id.* at 191, 194–95.

44. *See id.* at 221–31.

45. Quoted in *id.* at 255.

46. *See, e.g.,* MacPherson v. Buick Motor Co., 217 N.Y. 382 (1916); Palsgraf v. Long Island R.R., 248 N.Y. 339 (1928); G. White, *The American Judicial Tradition* 276–84 (1976).

47. *See L&MM* 252–55. Anon Y. Mous [Jerome N. Frank], "The Speech of Judges: A Dissenting Opinion," 29 *Va. L. Rev.* 625 (1943).

48. *See L&MM* 14–23.

49. *Id.* at 19.

50. *Id.* at 268 (emphasis omitted).

51. JNF to Thurman W. Arnold, Mar. 23, 1931; JNF to James Hart, Oct. 28, 1930.

52. *See* JNF to Thomas Reed Powell, Jan. 29, 1931; JNF to Chester Rohrlich, Dec. 11, 1930; *see* JNF to Editor of *Nation*, Sept. 9, 1931.

53. *See* Llewellyn, "Legal Illusion," 31 *Colum. L. Rev.* 82, 84, 86 (1931); Hessel E. Yntema to JNF, Oct. 28, 1930; Powell to JNF, Nov. 4, 1930. As for Holmes, Powell commented that "your completely adult jurist happens to be one of the most slavish followers of ancient doctrines in the field of common law" (Powell to JNF, Nov. 26, 1930).

54. *See, e.g., L&MM*, Preface to 6th Printing (1948) and Appendix X, Addenda to 2d Printing, 391–99 (1931).

55. *See id.* at 12, 14–23, 45n5, 82n3, 210–18. In an appendix he listed fourteen additional reasons for the basic myth; *see id.* at 281–82.

56. *See id.* at 210–18.

57. *See, e.g., id.* at 23n8.

58. *See L&MM* 95, 126, 177, 216n2, 355n1.

59. *See id.* at 16, 18, 63, 69, 83, 91–94, 100, 119, 141, 145, 161n2, 263.

60. JNF to Joseph Beale, April 6, 1931; *see* Frank, "Are Judges Human?" 80 *U. Pa. L. Rev.* 243–48 (1931); Frank, "What Courts Do in Fact," 26 *Ill. L. Rev.* 761, 767–70 (1932).

61. *See* Verdun-Jones, "The Jurisprudence of Jerome N. Frank: A Study in American Legal Realism," 7 *Sydney L. Rev.* 180 (1974); Chase, "Jerome Frank and American Psychoanalytic Jurisprudence," 2 *Int'l J. of Law and Psychiatry* 19, 27 (1978); Schlegel, "American Legal Realism and Empirical Social Science: From the Yale Experience," 28 *Buff. L. Rev.* 459 (1979); Schlegel, "American Legal Realism and Empirical Social Science: The Singular Case of Underhill Moore," 29 *Buff. L. Rev.* 195 (1980); Verdun-Jones, "Cook, Oliphant, and Yntema: The Scientist Wing of American Legal Realism," 5 *Dalhousie L.J.* 3 (1979).

62. For recent efforts to integrate law and the social sciences, see Chase, "Jerome Frank and American Psychoanalytic Jurisprudence," 2 *Int'l J. of Law and Psychiatry* 29 (1979); L. Friedman and S. Macaulay, *Law and the Behavioral Sciences* (2d ed. 1977); and R. Slovenko, *Psychiatry and Law* (1973).

63.

Despite your engaging promises of reform, and the hope that you arouse in me that you will treat in detail the concrete differences resulting from the application of your point of view, contrasted with that of the "pseudo-realists," the "crypto-fundamentalists" and the "100% Bealists" when applied to specific problems of the law, you go off and proliferate in the same old way. [Frankfurter to JNF, Jan. 9, 1932]

64. JNF to Rohrlich, Dec. 11, 1930.

65. *See L&MM* 100–107, 307–11.

66. *See* Wise, "Legal Tradition as a Limitation on Law Reform," 26 *Am. J. Comp. Law* 1 (1978); B. Bledstein, *The Culture of Professionalism* (1976); M. Larson, *The Rise of Professionalism* (1977); D. Calhoun, *Professional Lives in America* (1965); and Chase, "Harvard Law School and the Structure of Modern Professionalism," (Harvard LL.M. paper, 1979).

67. JNF to Felix S. Cohen, Feb. 18, 1921.

68. *See* JNF to Harold Laski, April 15, 1931. For other criticisms by Frank of

economic determinism, *see* J. Frank, *Save America First* 185–231 (1938), *Fate and Freedom* 45–53, 64–75, 78–80, 223–56, 271–72 (1945), and *Courts on Trial* 344–45 (1949).

69. *See* R. Hofstadter, *The Progressive Historians* (1968).

70. *See* H. Hart, *The Concept of Law* 121–50 (1961); D'Amato, "The Limits of Legal Realism," 87 *Yale L.J.* 468 (1978).

71. *See L&MM* 24–29, 46–50, 54–58.

72. This analysis led realists to place great weight on legal remedies as measuring the protection afforded by courts: a right without a remedy is no right at all. Under the realist influence, it became customary for casebooks in contracts to begin with a chapter on remedies and only later to turn to the formal elements of a contract. *See, e.g.,* L. Fuller and R. Braucher, *Basic Contract Law* (1964). For a thesis contrary to the realist position, *see* R. Dworkin, *Taking Rights Seriously* 14–130 (1977).

73. *See* JNF to Powell, Nov. 30, 1930.

74. Thurman Arnold to JNF, Sept. 25, 1931; *see* JNF to Arnold, Oct. 3, 1931.

75. Cardozo to JNF, Oct. 5, 1930.

76. *See* Danzig, "A Comment on the Jurisprudence of the Uniform Commercial Code," 27 *Stan. L. Rev.* 621 (1975).

77. For a provocative analysis tying the radical implications of Frank's thought to the psychoanalytic dimension of his jurisprudence, see Chase, "Jerome Frank and American Psychoanalytic Jurisprudence," 2 *Int'l J. of Law and Psychiatry* 29, 41–54 (1979).

78. *L&MM* 120.

79. Frankfurter to JNF, Jan. 23, 1931. Frankfurter wrote Frank: "You probably heard what Holmes once said about discussions at conference regarding due process cases: 'When the boys begin to talk about "liberty of contract," I try to compose my mind, and try to think of all the beautiful women I have known.'"

80. JNF to Frankfurter, Jan. 26, 1931.

81. *See* JNF to Jerome Hall, Feb. 27, 1947; Frank, "Are Judges Human?" 80 *U. Pa. L. Rev.* 233, 254–59 (1931); J. Frank, *Save America First* 8–18, 42, 171, 410–13 (1938); J. Frank, *Fate and Freedom* 40–41 (1945).

82. *See* JNF to Powell, Nov. 30, 1930.

83. I am indebted to Morton Horwitz for encouraging me to approach legal realism along these lines. On the autonomy of law, see Horwitz, book review, 86 *Yale L.J.* 561 (1977) (D. Hay et al., *Albion's Fatal Tree* [1975] and E. Thompson, *Whigs and Hunters* [1975]); E. Thompson, *Whigs and Hunters* 258–59 (1975); Gordon, "Introduction: J. Willard Hurst and the Common Law Tradition in American Legal Historiography," 10 *Law & Soc'y Rev.* 9 (1975); E. Genovese, *Roll, Jordon, Roll* 25–49 (1976); Balbus, "Commodity Form and Legal Form: An Essay on the 'Relative Autonomy' of the Law," 11 *Law & Soc'y Rev.* 571 (1977); P. Nouet, and P. Selznick, *Law and Society in Transition* 53–72 (1978); Tushnet, "Perspectives on the Development of American Law: A Critical Review of Friedman's 'A History of American Law,'" 1977 *Wis. L. Rev.* 81, 87–94.

84. *See L&MM* 7–8, 100–107, 307–11; J. Frank, *Fate and Freedom* 3–63 (1945).

85. *See* Schlegel, "American Legal Realism and Empirical Social Science: From the Yale Experience," 28 *Buff. L. Rev.* 459 (1979); Schlegel, "American Legal Realism and Empirical Social Science: The Singular Case of Underhill Moore," 29 *Buff. L. Rev.* 195 (1980); Verdun-Jones, "Cook, Oliphant, and Yntema," 5 *Dalhousie L.J.* 3 (1979).

86. *See* Horwitz, book review, 27 *Buff. L. Rev.* 47–50 (1978) (G. Gilmore, *The Ages of American Law* [1977]).

87. *See, e.g.,* Gilmore, *supra* n. 15, at 1038 (1961); Fuller, "American Legal Realism," 82 *U. Pa. L. Rev.* 429 (1934); Ackerman, book review, 103 *Daedalus* 119 (1974) *(L&MM)*.

88. Charles Clark remembered that *Law and the Modern Mind* "fell like a bomb on the legal world" ("Jerome N. Frank," 66 *Yale L.J.* 817 [1957]).

89. Pound, "The Call for a Realist Jurisprudence," 44 *Harv. L. Rev.* 697 (1931).

90. Llewellyn, "Some Realism about Realism—Responding to Dean Pound," 44 *Harv. L. Rev.* 1222, 1228–33 (1931). The article was published under Llewellyn's name when Frank declined to have his name appear as joint author. Llewellyn had just published "A Realistic Jurisprudence—The Next Step," 30 *Colum. L. Rev.* 431 (1930), which appeared at about the same time as *Law and the Modern Mind.* Both Llewellyn and Frank considered Pound's piece an attack on realism generally and on themselves in particular. Grant Gilmore has recently suggested that Pound apparently had no particular opponent in mind when he wrote his brief and general article as a tribute to Holmes on his ninetieth birthday. *See* Gilmore, *supra* n. 8, at 136–37. But Llewellyn and Frank had each dubbed the new jurisprudence realism, and Pound attacked it by name. Further, much of Pound's critique applies to Llewellyn but especially to Frank. And Frank, of course, had accused Pound of childish thinking. *See L&MM* 312–26. *See also* Twining, *supra* n. 36, at 72–73.

91. The dean warned against realists' substituting "a psychological must for an ethical or political or historical must," against relying exclusively on one methodological approach to understanding law, against a dogmatic insistence on a "psychological starting point," against slighting the logical element in deciding cases, and against insisting that every case is unique. *See* Pound, "The Call for a Realist Jurisprudence," 44 *Harv. L. Rev.* 697, 700, 702, 705–7 (1931).

92. *See* Gilmore, *supra* n. 8, at 78–79, 136–37.

93. *See* Llewellyn, "Legal Illusion"; Cook, "Legal Logic"; and Adler, "Legal Certainty," all in 31 *Colum. L. Rev.* (1931).

94. On Adler, see E. Purcell, *The Crisis of Democratic Theory,* 3–4, 145, 218–19 (1973).

95. For other criticisms of Frank and the realists as nominalists, see Cohen, "Justice Holmes and the Nature of Law," 31 *Colum. L. Rev.* 352, 360–64 (1931). For a last-gasp effort to rehabilitate formalism, see Dickinson, "Legal Rules: Their Function in the Process of Decision," 79 *U. Pa. L. Rev.* 833 (1931); Dickinson, "Legal Rules: Their Application and Elaboration," 79 *U. Pa. L. Rev.* 1052 (1931).

96. JNF to Frankfurter, April 17, 1931.

97. Cohen to JNF, Oct. 24, 1930.

98. *See* R. Hollinger, *Morris R. Cohen and the Scientific Ideal* 99–107, 111–27 (1975).

99. *Id.* at 110.

100. *Id.* at 111, 176–78, 181–83.

101. *See id.* at 85–89; JNF to Cohen, June 4, 1931.

102. JNF to Cohen, June 4, 1931.

103. *See* Cohen to JNF, July 3, 1931; JNF to Cohen, July 11, 1931.

104. The following three paragraphs draw heavily on Purcell's excellent study, *The Crisis of Democratic Theory* (1973). *See also* Purcell, "American Jurisprudence between the Wars: Legal Realism and the Crisis of Democratic Theory," 75 *Amer. Hist. Rev.* 424 (1969).

105. *See Purcell, The Crisis of Democratic Theory* 11, 41, 42 (1973).

106. *See id.* at 94, 117–38, 172.

107. Quoted in *id.* at 147; *see id.* at 139–58.

108. *See id.* at 156, 164–71.

109. *See id.* at 161–62; *Wigdor, supra* n. 32, at 266–81.

110. Fuller, "American Legal Realism," 82 *U. Pa. L. Rev.* 429, 443, 461–62 (1934); *see also* Kantorowicz, "Some Rationalism about Realism," 43 *Yale L.J.* 1240, 1243, 1249–50 (1934).

111. L. Fuller, *The Law in Quest of Itself* 125 (1940); *see id.* at 52–67.

112. *See Purcell, supra* n. 105, at 163.

113. *See* JNF to Jerome Hall, Feb. 27, 1947.

114. *L&MM* 168.

115. *See* JNF to Hall, Feb. 27, 1947. Frank was responding to Hall, "Integrative Jurisprudence," in *Interpretations of Modern Legal Philosophies* 313 (P. Sayre, ed., 1947). Because of the refusal of Frank and the legal realists to equate law and morals, they have often been labeled "legal positivists." Actually the story is more complicated. According to H. L. A. Hart, legal positivism has stood for at least five different doctrines: (1) laws are commands of the sovereign; (2) moral judgments cannot be proved by reasoning; (3) there is no necessary connection between law and morals; (4) there is a moral obligation to obey the law, regardless of what the law is; and (5) judicial decisions are deducible by logic and involve no discretion by the judge. *See* Hart, "Positivism and the Separation of Law and Morals," 71 *Harv. L. Rev.* 593, 601n25 (1958); Hart, "Legal Positivism," in *The Encyclopedia of Philosophy,* vol. 4, 418 (P. Edwards, ed., 1967); *see also* R. Dias, *Jurisprudence* 451–87 (4th ed. 1976). Hart cautioned against assuming that any given positivist adheres to all five strands of doctrine. That is particularly good advice in approaching Jerome Frank. He placed himself in the positivist camp by refusing to equate law and morals, yet he ridiculed the idea that laws are commands of the sovereign as well as the concept that logic produces judicial decisions.

116. *See* JNF to Hall, Feb. 27, 1947.

117. JNF to Felix S. Cohen, Feb. 3, 1931.

118. *See* Cohen to JNF, Feb. 12, 1931.

119. *See* Cohen, "Transcendental Nonsense and the Functional Approach," 35 *Colum. L. Rev.* 809, 839–41 (1935).

120. *Id.* at 844. Cohen argued that predictability had ethical value, but Frank thought it idle to talk about the ethical value of predictability if predictability is unattainable. *See* JNF to Cohen, Feb. 18, 1931.

121. Cohen, *supra* n. 119, at 842–45.

122. *Id.* at 847, 849.

123. Frank, "Mr. Justice Holmes and Non-Euclidean Legal Thinking," 17 *Cornell L.Q.* 568, 568n2 (1932); J. Frank, *If Men Were Angels* 294 (1942).

124. *See* JNF to Cohen, Jan. 9, 1946.

125. *See L&MM* at 118–19; JNF to Francis H. Bohlen, Oct. 7, 1931; JNF to Karl N. Llewellyn, Oct. 21, 1930.

126. *See* Frank, "Are Judges Human?" 80 *U. Pa. L. Rev.* 233 (1931); Frank, "What Courts Do in Fact," 26 *Ill. L. Rev.* 645, 761 (1932); Frank, "Mr. Justice Holmes and Non-Euclidean Legal Thinking," 17 *Cornell L.Q.* 568 (1932); JNF to Felix Cohen, July 11, 1950.

127. J. Frank, *Courts on Trial* (1949) (hereinafter cited as *COT*); *see, e.g.,* the following works by Frank: "Are Judges Human?" 80 *U. Pa. L. Rev.* 17, 233 (1931); "What

Courts Do in Fact," 26 *Ill. L. Rev.* 645, 761 (1932); "Mr. Justice Holmes and Non-Euclidean Legal Thinking," 17 *Cornell L.Q.* 568 (1932); "Why Not a Clinical Lawyers' School?" 81 *U. Pa. L. Rev.* 907 (1933); "What Constitutes a Good Legal Education?" 19 *A.B.A.J.* 723 (1933); *Save America First* (1938); *If Men Were Angels* (1942); book review, 54 *Harv. L. Rev.* 905 (1941) (W. Douglas, *Democracy and Finance*); "White Collar Justice," *Sat. Evening Post,* July 17, 1943; book review, 52 *Yale L.J.* 934 (1943) (R. Pound, *Outline of Lectures on Jurisprudence*); book review, 57 *Harv. L. Rev.* 1120 (1943) (G. Calhoun, *Introduction to Greek Legal Science*); "The Cult of the Robe," 28 *Sat. Rev. of Lit.* 12 (1945); *Fate and Freedom* (1945); book review, 59 *Harv. L. Rev.* 1004 (1946) (W. Friedman, *Legal Theory*); book review, 56 *Yale L.J.* 589 (1947) (M. Pirsig, *Cases on Judicial Administration*); "A Plea for Lawyer-Schools," 56 *Yale L.J.* 1303 (1947); "A Sketch of an Influence," in *Interpretations of Modern Legal Philosophies* 189 (P. Sayre, ed., 1947); "Words and Music," 47 *Colum. L. Rev.* 1259 (1947); "Say It with Music," 61 *Harv. L. Rev.* 921 *(1948); book review, 15 U. Chi. L. Rev.* 462 (1948) (H. Morgenthau, *Scientific Man vs. Power Politics*); "Cardozo and the Upper-Court Myth," 13 *Law & Cont. Prob.* 369 (1948).

128. *See COT* 14–23.

129. *See COT* 14, 25n15, 33, 80–102, 108–46, 151, 178.

130. *COT* 225.

131. *See* Frank, "Why Not a Clinical Lawyer-School?" 81 *U. Pa. L. Rev.* 907 (1933); *see also* Frank, "What Constitutes a Good Legal Education?" 19 *A.B.A.J.* 723 (1933); Frank, "A Plea for Lawyer-Schools," 56 *Yale L.J.* 1303 (1947).

132. *COT* 235. Frank's plea for clinical education did not begin to take hold until 1968, when the Ford Foundation created the Council on Legal Education for Professional Responsibility (CLEPR). Recently clinical programs have proliferated but legal education has fallen short of the overhaul first advocated by Frank almost fifty years ago. The ghost of Christopher Columbus Langdell reigns in the halls and classrooms of most law schools in the United States. On clinical legal education, see Stevens, *supra* n. 8, at 521–25; Chase, *supra* n. 8; E. Kitch, ed., *Clinical Education and the Law School of the Future* (1969); Kinoy, "The Crisis in American Legal Education," 24 *Rutgers L. Rev.* 1 (1969).

133. *See COT* viii, 254–61. As a judge, Frank deferred to tradition and wore a judicial robe.

134. *See id.* at 73–77, 160. Frank was quoting Bertrand Russell.

135. *See* Lasswell and McDougal, "Legal Education and Public Policy: Professional Training in the Public Interest," 52 *Yale L.J.* 203 (1943); *COT* 201–6, 209–21.

136. *L&MM* xx.

137. *COT* 264, 363.

138. *See id.* at 246–73, 350, 353–56, 367.

139. *See id.* at 5, 37–40, 42, 71–72, 83, 90, 164, 172, 174, 218, 292, 358.

140. *See* "Are Judges Human?" 80 *U. Pa. L. Rev.* 17, 233 (1931); "What Courts Do in Fact," 26 *Ill. L. Rev.* 645, 761 (1932); "Mr. Justice Holmes and Non-Euclidean Legal Thinking," 17 *Cornell L.Q.* 568 (1932). Indeed, Frank conceded that *Courts on Trial* said nothing he had not already said in these earlier writings. *See* JNF to Felix S. Cohen, July 11, 1950.

141. *See* Laswell and McDougal, *supra* n. 135.

142. *See* White, "The Evolution of Reasoned Elaboration: Jurisprudential Criticism and Social Change, 59 *Va. L. Rev.* 279 (1973); H. Hart and A. Sacks, *The Legal Process* (1958); Wechsler, "Toward Neutral Principles of Constitutional Law," 79 *Harv. L. Rev.* 1 (1959); L. Hand, *The Bill of Rights* (1958); A. Bickel, *The Least*

Dangerous Branch (1962); Purcell, "Alexander M. Bickel and the Post-Realist Constitution," 11 *Harv. C.R.-C.L. L. Rev.* 521 (1976).

143. *See* J. Rawls, *A Theory of Justice* (1973); R. Nozick, *Anarchy, State, and Utopia* (1974); R. Dworkin, *Taking Rights Seriously* (1976); Richards, "*Taking Rights Seriously:* Reflections on Dworkin and the American Revival of Natural Law," 52 *N.Y.U.L. Rev.* 1265 (1977).

144. 410 U.S. 113 (1973); Ely, "The Wages of Crying Wolf: A Comment on Roe v. Wade," 82 *Yale L.J.* 920 (1973).

145. *See* J. Ely, *Democracy and Distrust* (1979); M. Perry, *The Constitution, the Courts, and Human Rights* (1982); Sedler, "The Legitimacy Debate in Constitutional Adjudication: An Assessment and a Different Perspective," 44 *Ohio St. L.J.* 93 (1983); Grano, "Judicial Review and a Written Constitution in a Democratic Society," 27 *Wayne L. Rev.* 1 (1981); Tushnet, "Following the Rules Laid Down: A Critique of Interpretivism and Neutral Principles," 96 *Harv. L. Rev.* 781 (1983); Brest, "The Fundamental Rights Controversy: The Essential Contradictions of Normative Constitutional Scholarship," 90 *Yale L.J.* 1063 (1981); Brest, "The Misconceived Quest for the Original Understanding," 60 *B.U.L. Rev.* 204 (1980); Sandalow, "Constitutional Interpretation," 79 *Mich. L. Rev.* 1033 (1981); Munzer and Nickel, "Does the Constitution Mean What It Always Meant?" 77 *Colum. L. Rev.* 1029 (1977); Grey, "Do We Have an Unwritten Constitution?" 27 *Stan. L. Rev.* 703 (1975). *See also* Blasi, "The Rootless Activism of the Burger Court," in *The Burger Court* 198 (V. Blasi, ed., 1983).

146. *See* R. Posner, *Economic Analysis of Law* (2d ed. 1977); R. Coase, "The Problem of Social Cost," 3 *J. Law & Econ.* 1, 19–28 (1960); Dworkin, "Is Wealth a Value?" 9 *J. Leg. Stud.* 191, 220–25 (1980); Rubin, "Predictability and the Economic Approach to Law: A Comment on Rizzo," 9 *J. Leg. Stud.* 319 (1980); Priest, "Selective Characteristics of Litigation," 9 *J. Leg. Stud.* 399 (1980); Posner, "The Ethical and Political Basis of the Efficiency Norm in Common Law Adjudication," 8 *Hofstra L. Rev.* 487, 502–7 (1980); Kornhauser, "A Guide to the Perplexed Claims of Efficiency in the Law," 8 *Hofstra L. Rev.* 591, 610–39 (1980); Horwitz, "Law and Economics: Science or Politics?" 8 *Hofstra L. Rev.* 905 (1980); Baker, "The Ideology of the Economic Analysis of Law," 5 Philosophy & Pub. Aff. 3 (1975).

147. D. Kairys, ed., *The Politics of Law* 3 (1982). *See* Unger, "The Critical Legal Studies Movement," 96 *Harv. L. Rev.* 563 (1983); Gordon, "Historicism in Legal Scholarship," 90 *Yale L. J.* 1017 (1981); Tushnet, "Legal Scholarship: Its Causes and Cure," 90 *Yale L. J.* 1205 (1981); Note, "'Round and 'Round the Bramble Bush: From Legal Realism to Critical Legal Scholarship," 95 *Harv. L. Rev.* 1669 (1982); Symposium, 62 *Texas L. Rev* (1984); Critical Legal Studies Symposium, 36 *Stan. L. Rev.* 1 (1984).

148. For other recent expressions of concern about the legitimacy of law, see P. Nonet and P. Selznick, *Law and Society in Transition* (1978); E. Rostow, ed., *Is Law Dead?* (1971); R. Wolff, ed., *The Rule of Law* (1971); Mayor, "The Crisis of Liberal Legalism," 81 *Yale L.J.* 1032 (1972).

3. *"Principles Are What Principles Do": Lawyering in the New Deal*

1. *See* Frankfurter, "Democracy and the Expert," *Atlantic Monthly,* Nov. 1930, 649, 652; F. Frankfurter, *Felix Frankfurter Reminisces: Recorded Talks with Dr. Harlan B. Phillips* 190–93 (1960). However, exceptionally talented attorneys occasionally

served as government lawyers. Consider Elihu Root, Felix Frankfurter, and Henry L. Stimson. *See* H. Stimson and McG. Bundy, *On Active Service in Peace and War* (1948); E. Morison, *Turmoil and Tradition* (1960); *From the Diaries of Felix Frankfurter* (J. Lash, ed., 1975); P. Jessup, *Elihu Root,* 2 vols. (1938). Interview with Thomas Emerson, Madison, Wis., Nov. 11, 1978.

2. *See* Auerbach and Bardach, "'Born to an Era of Insecurity': Career Patterns of Law Review Editors, 1918–1941," 17 *Am. J. Leg. Hist.* 3 (1973); J. Auerbach, *Unequal Justice* 173 (1976); Solomon, "Practice of Law in the Federal Government— Career or Training Ground," 38 *Geo. Wash. L. Rev.* 753 (1970).

3. *E.g.,* Robert H. Jackson, William O. Douglas, Thomas I. Emerson, Dean Acheson, Alger Hiss, and Francis Biddle.

4. *See* Auerbach and Bardach, *supra* n. 2; Auerbach, *supra* n. 2, at 158–90; R. Swaine, *The Cravath Firm and Its Predecessors, 1819–1948,* II, 461–62 (1948) (New Deal legislation and Depression-induced bankruptcies produced an expansion of the Cravath firm); Gordon, "The Lawyer and the Civil Service," 1 *Nat'l Law. Guild Q.* 294, 295 (1938).

5. *See* Schudson, "Public, Private, and Professional Lives: The Correspondence of David Dudley Field and Samuel Bowles," 21 *Am. J. Leg. Hist.* 191 (1977); R. Hofstadter, *The Age of Reform* 156–64 (1955); L. Brandeis, *Business—A Profession* 313–27 (1914); J. Hurst, *The Growth of American Law* 328–33 (1950): Katz, "The Legal Profession, 1890–1915," Columbia University M.A. thesis, 1954.

On the rise of professionalism, see B. Bledstein, *The Culture of Professionalism* (1976); W. Johnson, *Schooled Lawyers* (1978); M. Larson, *The Rise of Professionalism* (1977); D. Calhoun, *Professional Lives in America* (1965); M. Keller, *Affairs of State* 349–53 (1977); Chase, "Harvard Law School and the Structure of Modern Professionalism," Harvard Law School LL.M. paper, 1979; Schlegel, "Between the Harvard Founders and the American Legal Realists: The Professionalization of the American Law Professor" (unpublished).

6. *See Frankfurter Reminisces, supra* n. 1, at 193; Frankfurter, "The Young Men Go to Washington," *Fortune,* Jan. 1936, reprinted in *Law and Politics: Occasional Papers of Felix Frankfurter, 1913–1938* (MacLeish and Prichard, eds., 1939); Root, "Public Service by the Bar," Presidential Address of American Bar Ass'n, Aug. 30, 1916; Jackson, "Government Counsel and Their Opportunity," 26 *A.B.A.J.* 411 (1940); Auerbach and Bardach, *supra* n. 2, at 21. This trend was also recalled in the following: interview with Thomas Emerson, Madison, Wis., Nov. 11, 1978 ("opportunity to engage in work with social significance"); interview with Alger Hiss, New York City, Sept. 11, 1978 ("Roosevelt captured our allegiance as a *true* noble knight in shining armor"; "We regarded ourselves as a civilian militia . . . enlisted for the duration"); interview with John Abt, New York City, May 7, 1979 ("We all came down there convinced, rather naively, that we could turn this country around"); interview with Nathan Witt, New York City, May 7, 1979 ("save the world").

7. *See* McAdoo, "The Government Lawyer," 3 *Fed. B.A.J.* 139 (1938); P. Ford, D. Reich, and C. Palmer, *The Government Lawyer* 5–6 (1952).

8. *See* E. Brown, *Lawyers, Law Schools, and the Public Service* (1948); D. Horwitz, *The Jurocracy* (1977); L. Huston, A. Miller, S. Krislov, and R. Dixon, *Roles of the Attorney General of the United States* (1968); American Bar Association, *Federal Government Legal Career Opportunities* (1970); American Bar Foundation, *The Legal Profession in the United States* (2d ed. 1970); V. Countryman and T. Finman, *The Lawyer in Modern Society* 3 (1966) (from 1951 to 1963 the percentage of lawyers in private

practice dropped from 86.8 to 74.7); American Bar Foundation, *The 1971 Lawyers Statistical Report* 10 (1972) (72.7 percent of attorneys engaged in private practice); A. Blaustein and C. Porter, *The American Lawyer* 8–11 (1954) (78.9 percent). The staff of the Department of Justice grew from approximately 250 in 1905 to 32,000 in 1968. *See* Fairlie, "The United States Department of Justice," 3 *Mich. L. Rev.* 352, 356 (1905); *Selected Papers from Homer Cummings* 3, 8–9, 15 (C. Swisher, ed., 1939); L. Huston, *The Department of Justice* (1967); Huston, "History of the Office of the Attorney General," in L. Huston, A. Miller, S. Krislov, and R. Dixon, *Roles of the Attorney General of the United States* 2, 5–6, 8 (1968); Clark, "The Office of the Attorney General," 19 *Tenn. L. Rev.* 150, 152 (1946); Buckley, "The Department of Justice—Its Origins, Development, and Present-Day Organization," 5 *B.U.L. Rev.* 177, 182 (1925); H. Cummings and C. McFarland, *Federal Justice* (1937). The Agricultural Adjustment Administration, a creation of the New Deal, quickly developed a legal staff of 130 lawyers. *See* Frank, "Memoir, Columbia Oral History Collection," at 77 (hereinafter cited as COHC). On the history of the legal profession generally, see Hurst, *supra* n. 5, at 249–375; R. Pound, *The Lawyer from Antiquity to Modern Times* (1953); A. Chroust, *The Rise of the Legal Profession in America*, 2 vols. (1965); M. Bloomfield, *American Lawyers in a Changing Society, 1776–1876* (1976); G. Gawalt, *The Promise of Power* (1979); D. Nolan, *Readings in the History of the American Legal Profession* (1980).

9. *See* Bernstein, "The New Deal: The Conservative Achievements of Liberal Reform," in *Towards a New Past* 263 (B. Bernstein, ed., 1968); Zinn, "The Limits of the New Deal," in H. Zinn, *The Politics of History* 118 (1970); Radosh, "The Myth of the New Deal," in *A New History of Leviathan* 146 (R. Radosh and M. Rothbard, eds., 1972); P. Conkin, *The New Deal* (1967); P. Conkin, *FDR and the Origins of the Welfare State* (1967); M. Rothbard, *America's Great Depression* (1963); W. Williams, *The Contours of American History* 343–89 (1961); Zieger, "Herbert Hoover: A Reinterpretation," 81 *Am. Hist. Rev.* 800 (1976).

10. *See* J. Shklar, *Legalism* (1964); Tushnet, "Perspectives on the Development of American Law: A Critical Review of Friedman's 'A History of American Law,'" 1977 *Wis. L. Rev.* 81, 87–94.

11. Frank, COHC at 12–13.

12. Frank, COHC at 13; T. Hiss, *Laughing Last* 62–82 (1977).

13. Although Frank's salary dropped significantly, the New Deal did not ask financial sacrifice of its neophyte young attorneys, as the starting salaries offered by private firms were very low (interview with Alger Hiss, New York City, Sept. 11, 1978; L. Pressman, COHC; interview with Telford Taylor, New York City, May 8, 1979).

Frankfurter played an instrumental role in placing numerous former students and acquaintances in important New Deal positions. *See* Murphy, "A Supreme Court Justice as Politician: Felix Frankfurter and Federal Court Appointments," 21 *Am. J. Leg. Hist.* 316, 317–18 (1977); H. Thomas, *Felix Frankfurter* 26–28 (1960); *From the Diaries of Felix Frankfurter* 52–54 (J. Lash, ed., 1975); L. Baker, *Felix Frankfurter* 162–64 (1969); *Roosevelt and Frankfurter: Their Correspondence*, 134, 156–57, 283, 307–10, 446, 457–58 (M. Freedman, ed., 1967); *Frankfurter Reminisces, supra* n. 1, at 247–50.

14. *See* V. Perkins, *Crisis in Agriculture* (1969); A. Schlesinger, Jr., *The Coming of the New Deal* 3, 28–39 (1959); J. Poppendieck, "Breadlines Knee Deep in Wheat" 48–56 (Ph.D. dissertation, Brandeis University, 1979). Arthur Schlesinger, Jr., has pithily described the human side of Depression:

The fog of despair hung over the land. One out of every four American workers lacked a job. Factories that had once darkened the skies with smoke stood ghostly and silent, like extinct volcanoes. Families slept in tarpaper shacks and tin-lined caves and scavenged like dogs for food in the city dump. In October the New York City Health Department had reported that over one-fifth of the pupils in public schools were suffering from malnutrition. Thousands of vagabond children were roaming the land, wild boys of the road. Hunger marchers, pinched and bitter, were parading cold streets in New York and Chicago. On the countryside unrest had already flared into violence. Farmers stopped milk trucks along Iowa roads and poured milk into the ditch. Mobs halted mortgage sales, ran the men from banks and insurance companies out of town, intimidated courts and judges, demanded a moratorium on debts. When a sales company in Nebraska invaded a farm and seized two trucks, the farmers in the Newman Grove district organized a posse, called it the "Red Army," and took the trucks back. In West Virginia, mining families, turned out of their homes, lived in tents along the road on pinto beans and black coffee. [*The Crisis of the Old Order* 3 (1975)]

15. *See* A. Schlesinger, Jr., *The Coming of the New Deal* 40–49 (1959); Poppendieck, *supra* n. 14, at 108–18.

16. *See* T. Arnold, *Fair Fights and Foul* 131–34 (1951).

17. Abe Fortas to Richard Rovere, Oct. 25, 1946.

18. *See* A. Weinstein, *Perjury* 133–57 (1978); W. Goodman, *The Committee* 71, 248–50, 387 (1968).

19. In the Progressive era, understaffed legal departments of questionable abilities hamstrung government effort to uphold Progressive legislation. *See* W. Letwin, *Law and Economic Policy in America* 103–6 (1965). In the 1920s, Attorney General Harlan Stone was unable to attract high-quality lawyers to the Department of Justice. *See* Auerbach and Bardach, *supra* n. 2, at 5; *see also* H. Pringle, *The Life and Times of William Howard Taft*, I, 108–17 (1939).

20. Interview with Alger Hiss, New York City, Sept. 11, 1978; interview with Telford Taylor, New York City, May 8, 1979.

21. *See* Hurst, *supra* n. 5, at 299–308 (1950); L. Friedman, *A History of American Law* 549–61 (1973); R. Hofstadter, *The Age of Reform* 158–64 (1955).

22. *See* R. Swaine, *The Cravath Firm and Its Predecessors, 1918–1948*, II, 1–12, 124–32, 461–66, 555–58, 748–79 (1948).

23. *E.g.*, Frank, Pressman, Hiss, Abt, Emerson, Wyzanski, and Tom Corcoran.

24. Interviews with Alger Hiss, New York City, Sept. 11, 1978; Thomas Emerson, Madison, Wis., Nov. 11, 1978 ("enormous responsibility, almost immediately"). This situation changed during the later years of the New Deal, when a movement began to bring legal positions within the ambit of the federal civil service. This movement, which was partially successful, tended to bureaucratize legal service and to control the kinds of power and responsibility that young attorneys might possess.

25. Fortas to Rovere, Oct. 25, 1946.

26. *See* Tugwell, сонс at 47, 51; Frank, сонс at 26–29, 37–44, 116–20; H. Wallace, сонс at 399.

27. Other notables with such careers include Thurman Arnold, Charles Wyzanski, Thomas Emerson, Telford Taylor, Abe Fortas, Lee Pressman, and Nathan Witt.

28. *See* Frank, COHC at 72, 81–82; R. Tugwell, *Roosevelt's Revolution* 46, 81, 106, 110, 151 (1977).

29. *See* Woodall, "Career Service for Federal Lawyers," 4 *Fed. B.A.J.* 235 (1941); Russell, "Employment of Federal Legal Personnel," 3 *Fed. B.A.J.* 187 (1938); "Committee on Professional Standards, 1937 Report," 3 *Fed. B.A.J.* 187 (1938); Editorial, "The Lawyer in Civil Service," 4 *Fed. B.A.J.* 100 (1934); Editorial, "Career Service," 1 *Nat'l Law. Guild Q.* 294 (1938); Reilly, "Founding a Career System for Government Lawyers," 1 *Law. Guild Rev.* 1 (1941).

30. *See generally* Schlesinger, *supra* n. 14.

31. *See* Frank, COHC at 124.

32. *See* R. Lord, *The Wallaces of Iowa* (1947).

33. *See* Schlesinger, *supra* n. 14, at 51. The story may be apocryphal, as Pressman insisted to Mrs. Frank (*see* Pressman to FKF, Mar. 9, 1959), or genuine, as Abe Fortas believed (*see* Fortas to Rovere, Oct. 25, 1946). In either case, nothing better expresses the bitterness farmers felt toward government lawyers.

34. Frank, COHC at 123; *see id.* at 150.

35. *See id.* at 131–39; A. Weinstein, *Perjury* 132–37 (1978); *Schlesinger, supra* n. 14, at 52–54; W. Goodman, *The Committee* 248n6, 250, 254, 289 (1968).

36. Frank, COHC at 157.

37. *See* Frank, "Experimental Jurisprudence and the New Deal," *Cong. Record,* vol. 78, pt. 2, 73d Cong., 2d sess., 12412–14 (1934).

38. *See* Frank, COHC at 134.

39. M. Parrish, *Securities Regulation and the New Deal* 180 (1970).

40. *Save America First* (1938) and *If Men Were Angels* (1942).

41. *See* J. Frank, *Fate and Freedom* (1945).

42. *See* Auerbach, *supra* n. 2, at 226–30. Auerbach argued that a philosophy of legalism set limits to the New Deal and concluded that if suffered from lawyers concerned only with how results were reached and not with what those results were. Preoccupation with process and with means prevented lawyers from bringing about substantial reform. However, Auerbach unfairly criticized New Deal lawyers who sought the substantive results desired by the administration: to control business, deal with massive depression and unemployment, and provide social services to redress human misery. Auerbach's "lawyer's deal" image is accurate but, as elaborated here, for reasons different from those he suggested.

43. Economists have largely rejected the New Deal's explanation of the causes of the Great Depression. For differing interpretations of the Depression, see J. Galbraith, *The Great Crash* (1955); M. Friedman, *The Great Contraction, 1929–1933* (1965); P. Temin, *Did Monetary Forces Cause the Great Depression?* (1976); C. Kindleberger, *The World in Depression, 1929–1939* (1973); E. Hawley, *The Great War and the Search for a Modern Order* (1979).

44. The achievements of the New Deal included enactment of social security, harmonizing of labor relations by guaranteeing the right to bargain collectively, establishment of rural electrification, management of public works and conservation projects, stabilization of the economic position of farmers, enhancement of the credibility of securities, and embracing of Keynesian economics. *See* A. Schlesinger, Jr., *supra* n. 14; A. Schlesinger, Jr., *The Politics of Upheaval* (1960); W. Leuchtenburg, *Franklin D. Roosevelt and the New Deal* (1963); J. Burns, *Roosevelt: The Lion and the Fox* (1956); E. Hawley, *The New Deal and the Problem of Monopoly* (1966); Klare, "Judicial Deradicalization of the Wagner Act and the Origins of Modern Legal Conscious-

ness, 1937–1941," 62 *Minn. L. Rev.* 265 (1978). One can acknowledge these reforms and yet recognize that the New Deal failed to resolve underlying problems of business cycle, money supply, inflation, and unemployment. *See* W. Williams, *The Contours of American History* (1960); C. Kindleberger, *The World in Depression, 1929–1939* (1973); M. Friedman and A. Schwartz, *Monetary History of the United States* (1963).

45. *See supra* n. 9. On saving capitalism, see Frank, COHC at 134–48.

46. *See generally* Auerbach, *supra* n. 2; Botein, book review, 21 *Am. J. Leg. Hist.* 60 (1977) (M. Bloomfield, *American Lawyers in a Changing Society, 1776–1876* [*1976*], and J. Auerbach, *Unequal Justice* [1976]).

47. *See, e.g.,* Leuchtenberg, *supra* n. 44, at 102, 182, 276–77 (1963).

48. *See Pacific Rural Press,* Aug. 4, 1934.

49. *See The Papers of Adlai E. Stevenson* (W. Johnson and C. Evans, eds., 1972), vol. 1, at 248–49.

50. Frank, COHC, at 73, 145.

51. *See* Schlesinger, *supra* 14, at 50–51.

52. *See* JNF to Frankfurter, April 18, 1933, and June 13, 1933. Frank's sensitivity to the composition of his staff is also evident in a letter to Steadman (Dec. 13, 1933) in which he referred to the "tabooed subject" and admitted having a secretary compile statistics on the number of Jews on his legal staff.

53. *See* Frank, COHC at 128.

54. *See* JNF to Hiss, Shea, and McConnaughey (memorandum), Dec. 28, 1934. Note that Jerome Frank, a Jew, was embarrassed by the recommendation of Jews made by three Gentiles.

55. *See* JNF to Henry Wallace (memorandum), May 18, 1933.

56. *See* JNF to General Westervelt, Dec. 12, 1933.

57. *See* JNF to Westervelt (memorandum), Dec. 1933; *see also* JNF to Westervelt, Dec. 12, 1933, where Frank regretted his angry comments about Westervelt's anti-Semitism.

58. *See* Frank, COHC at 145.

59. *See* JNF to Corcoran, Mar. 17, 1939.

60. JNF to Hopkins, Aug. 19, 1940.

61. *See* Hurst, *supra* n. 5, at 295–305; D. McCullouch, *The Path Between the Seas* 271–76 (1977) (on lobbying activities of William Nelson Cromwell with respect to the Panama Canal); A. Dean, *William Nelson Cromwell* (1957). For more recent accounts, see J. Goulden, *The Superlawyers* (1972); M. Green, *The Other Government* (1975). For an analysis of legal innovation surrounding the creation of giant trusts and holding companies in the late nineteenth century, see A. Chandler, *The Visible Hand* 145–87, 315–39 (1977).

62. *See* A. Mason, *Brandeis* (1956).

63. *See* Frank, COHC at 164. For an analysis of the tasks of government lawyers, see E. Brown, *Lawyers, Law Schools, and the Public Service* 17–90 (1948).

64. The term originated as the "Brains Trust" and referred to the academics who counseled FDR in the 1932 presidential campaign, principally Raymond Moley, Rexford Tugwell, and Adolf A. Berle, Jr. Gradually the term became singularized and broadened to include all presidential advisers. *See* E. Rosen, *Hoover, Roosevelt, and the Brains Trust* 4 (1977).

65. *See* Nat'l Ind. Rec. Act, §7, 48 Stat. 198–99 (1933).

66. Quoted in Poppendieck, *supra* n. 14, at 105.

67. JNF to Chester Davis (memorandum), May 4, 1934.

68. *See* Frank, COHC at 23, 89.

69. JNF to Victor Christgau (memorandum), Dec. 17, 1934.

70. One particular memorandum (JNF to Clay and Truith, July 3, 1935) explained the tactics underlying a draft brief:

> To my mind, the most powerful kind of argument that we can make against J. P. Morgan & Co. is . . .
>
> But, . . . I am fearful that, if such an argument is made, the court of its own motion, or because of a counter-suggestion made by Morgan when it comes to file a brief, may ask himself why . . .
>
> Accordingly, I do not recommend that the argument should be made with any degree of vigor.
>
> At the same time, I believe that, if that argument is not made, it will be difficult to offset the argument of Morgan which is . . .
>
> We could answer that contention if we could show . . . we could then argue that . . .
>
> Consequently, unless we are ready to ask for such a re-reference, I think we must recognize that Morgan and the master are in a very powerful position in justifying a classification of Morgan apart from us. The only way I can see, on the record, to knock out Morgan and the master is . . .

Frank was a brilliant lawyer with a remarkable ability to devise legal arguments. He would brainstorm strategy with associates, leaving no stone unturned. The intellectual bent of his mind relished exploring all facets of a problem (interviews with Telford Taylor, New York City, May 8, 1979; Nathan Witt, New York City, May 7, 1979; John Abt, New York City, May 7, 1979; Sigmund Timberg, Washington, D.C., May 21, 1979).

71. 297 U.S. 1 (1936); *see* JNF to Paul Appleby, Jan. 21, 1936.

72. *See* Schelsinger, *supra* no. 14, at 281–88.

73. *See* correspondence between JNF and Leon Green, Box 12, Folder 94, Jerome Frank Papers.

74. Frank, COT 242 (1949).

75. Pressman to JNF, Aug. 15, 1934.

76. *See* memorandum of JNF, In re: E. G. Nourse's Report on AAA, July 11, 1935; P. Irons, *The New Deal Lawyers* 142–55 (1982). Peter Irons has criticized Frank for the dismal litigation record compiled by the AAA because Frank delayed in establishing a litigation. section and recruited corporate lawyers rather than litigators. Frank did wish to avoid litigation, but that attitude made good sense in the face of an overwhelmingly Republican federal judiciary. Frank's corporate reorganization practice involved considerable litigation experience, as did the practice of some of his legal staff. From the outset, Frank anticipated the need for and inevitability of litigation. He thus recruited Abt from Frank's Chicago firm to handle litigation. Although there was not yet a separate litigation section, Abt specialized in litigation and assembled a litigation staff. Abt's first assignment, on joining the AAA legal staff in early autumn 1933, was to prepare a memorandum on the AAA's right to obtain injunctive relief, a remedy not explicitly granted by the statute (telephone interview with John J. Abt, Dec. 19, 1983).

The NLRB did compile a better litigation record; *see* Irons, *The New Deal Lawyers* 203–89. Several factors account for the difference. The NLRB legal staff was not so rushed and therefore selected better test cases; it learned from the NRA and AAA litigation experience; and the litigation occurred in a changed political/legal climate. *See* Rauh, book review, 96 *Harv. L. Rev.* 947 (1983) (P. Irons, *The New Deal Lawyers* [1982]).

77. *See* W. Rumble, *American Legal Realism* 76–79 (1968); W. Twining, *Karl Llewellyn and the Realist Movement* 57–58 (1973); Auerbach, *supra* n. 2, at 165–66, 177–79, 189.

78. Frank, *supra* n. 37, at 12413. In 1933 Frank considered writing a new preface to *Law and the Modern Mind* showing the relationship between its attitude and that of the New Deal. *See* JNF to Thomas R. Coward, June 24, 1933.

79. *See, e.g.,* A. Mason, *The Supreme Court from Taft to Burger* (1979).

80. *See L&MM* 50–52; *COT.*

81. Opinion of the General Counsel's Office, Oct. 3, 1934, at 2. In a similar vein, Frank commented on AAA milk licenses in a confidential memorandum, Nov. 16, 1934:

> It is very likely that our licenses in those intrastate markets will be held invalid on constitutional grounds, no matter how the Act is amended.
>
> To circumvent this constitutional objection . . . we have endeavored to work out 'butter theory'. . . . But although much time has been devoted to the 'butter theory' by the lawyers and the Dairy Section, neither the Department of Justice nor we believe that it has much chance of success in court on the basis of any economic data thus far presented to us by the Dairy Section.
>
> Consequently, *any milk program depending upon the use of federal licenses is very likely to fail in any except, at best, the limited number of interstate milk sheds above referred to.*

Contrast the economic data in Schechter Poultry Corp. v. United States, 295 U.S. 495 (1935), with NLRB v. Jones & Laughlin Steel Corp., 202 U.S. 1 (1937). *See* Stern, "The Commerce Clause and the National Economy, 1933–1946," 59 *Harv. L. Rev.* 645 (1946).

82. Frank, COHC at 87; *see* Irons, *supra* n. 76.

83. Frank, COHC at 87–88.

84. Quoted in Poppendieck, *supra* n. 14, at 110.

85. *See* memorandum of JNF, July 25, 1933.

86. Frank, COHC at 33–34.

87. Frankfurter to JNF, Nov. 27, 1935.

88. JNF to Frankfurter, Nov. 29, 1935.

89. Frankfurter to JNF, Dec. 2, 1935. The references are to Justices George Sutherland and James C. McReynolds of the U.S. Supreme Court.

90. *Id.*

91. JNF to Frankfurter, Dec. 4, 1935. At this time Frank worked for the Reconstruction Finance Corporation.

92. Frankfurter to JNF, Dec. 6, 1935.

93. JNF to Frankfurter, Dec. 9, 1935.

94. JNF to Frankfurter, Jan. 21, 1936.

95. *See* Frank, *supra* n. 37.

96. A notable example of similar legal resourcefulness occurred during the nineteenth century as private attorneys created corporations, trusts, pools, holding companies, stocks, bonds, and other instruments of finance. *See* J. Hurst, *Law and the Conditions of Freedom* (1955); Hurst, *supra* n. 5; Chandler, *supra* n. 61, at 119–31.

97. Quoted in Poppendieck, *supra* n. 14, at 129–30.

98. *Id.* at 131.

99. R. Tugwell, *Roosevelt's Revolution* 217 (1977).

100. Frank, COHC at 118.

101. *See* A. Walsh, *The Public's Business* (1978).

102. *See* Evans, "Federal Corporations: Their Purposes and Functions," 2 *Fed. B.A.J.* 319 (1936).

103. *See* Frank, COHC at 142–43.

104. *See* JNF to Federal Surplus Relief Corporation, Nov. 7, 1935. Frank later used the same independent corporate form to establish the Commodity Credit Corporation, which came under the auspices of the Reconstruction Finance Corporation. Stanley Reed, who was RFC counsel, approached Frank about forming the corporation, apparently because he knew of the Federal Surplus Relief Corporation. Frank assigned Lee Pressman to the task and ultimately Pressman became counsel to the RFC.

105. *See* Poppendieck, *supra* n. 14, at 131–39. For information on the FSRC, see Frank, COHC at 38–43, 116–27. For information on the Commodity Credit Corporation, see Frank, COHC at 38–43, 123–24, 126, 142–43. *See also* Tugwell to JNF (memorandum), Sept. 29, 1933; JNF to Tugwell (memorandum), Sept. 30, 1933; Pressman to FKF Mar. 9, 1959.

106. Frank, COHC at 95.

107. *Id.* at 83–84.

108. *Id.* at 82–86.

109. *See* R. Hale, *Freedom through Law* 461–500 (1952); A. Priest, *Principles of Public Utility Regulation*, 2 vols. (1969).

110. *See* JNF to Peek, Brand, Westervelt, and Howe (memorandum), July 7, 1933.

111. *But see* E. Brown, *Lawyers, Law Schools, and the Public Service* 78–90 (1948); V. Countryman and T. Finman, *The Lawyer in Modern Society* 44–46 (1966); S. Thurman, E. Phillips, and E. Cheatham, *Cases and Materials on the Legal Profession* 371–73 (1970). For a recent effort to direct legal education toward an awareness of planning and strategy, see L. Brown and E. Dauer, *Planning by Lawyers* 265–301 (1978).

112. J. Auerbach, *Unequal Justice* (1976).

113. Interview with Thomas Emerson, Madison, Wis., Nov. 11, 1978.

114. *See* B. Sternsher, *Rexford Tugwell and the New Deal* 198–207 (1964); Schlesinger, *supra* n. 14, at 55–84; Poppendieck, *supra* n. 14, at 108–18.

115. *See* Frank, COHC at 23, 89. NRA counsel operated in a quite different fashion, which in Frank's judgment produced the debacle that followed. *See* Frank, COHC at 31.

116. Frank, COHC at 164.

117. *See* JNF to Frankfurter, June 13, 1933; Wrigley, "Jerome Frank and the Reform Movement in the Agricultural Adjustment Administration, 1933–1935" at 48 (M.A. thesis, Trinity College, 1976).

118. JNF to Chester Davis (memorandum), Feb. 9, 1934.

119. *Id.;* JNF to Davis (memorandum), Oct. 26, 1934.

120. JNF to Davis (memorandum), June 27, 1934.

121. Frank suggested that any exemptions from the antitrust laws ought to be balanced by adequate benefits for farmers and consumers. The economic rubric of fair return for fair value he thought entirely meaningless, so he preferred his

creative notion of a "savings fund." He particularly urged the "books and records" clause as absolutely essential to effective implementation of the act. He also argued for benefits for both farmer and consumer, particularly at this early stage, when industries were most eager to be exempted from the antitrust laws. At this juncture, Frank thought industry would be willing to share some of the benefits with farmers and consumers. His concern with effective implementation prompted him to argue strongly against codes and licenses and in favor of marketing agreements. He thought that codes and licenses, binding everyone in the industry, had a dubious legal basis because of the lack of adequate notice and participation. A voluntary marketing agreement, in contrast, could accomplish the same thing without doubts about legality. Frank adhered to these fundamental principles throughout his tenure as general counsel. See JNF to Peck, Brand, Westervelt, and Howe (memorandum), July 7, 1933.

122. JNF to Davis (memorandum), June 27, 1934.

123. See JNF to Peek (memorandum), Nov. 6, 1933 (tentative, unsigned, not delivered, revised).

124. Frank, COHC at 90.

125. See Irons, supra n. 76, at 131, 170–71, 177, 179.

126. Frank, COHC at 91.

127. See JNF to Davis (memorandum), Oct. 26, 1934. He fought the same battle over the marketing agreements for the meat-packing industry.

128. See id. at 6.

129. See John P. Payne et al. to Henry Wallace (memorandum), Jan. 10, 1935.

130. See Frank, COHC at 175–80; Irons, supra n. 76, at 156–59, 176.

131. See W. C. Hutchins and E. A. Miller to Wallace (memorandum), Jan. 10, 1935; Margaret B. Bennett to Wallace (memorandum), Jan. 12, 1935; JNF to Wallace (memorandum), Jan. 12, 1935; Frank, COHC at 176.

132. The opinion was actually drafted by David Kreeger and reviewed by Telford Taylor and Francis Shea, the chief of the Opinion Section, before it went to Hiss and Frank (interview with Telford Taylor, New York City, May 8, 1979; Irons, supra n. 76, at 168–75; R. Lowe, "Fallen Warrior of Reform," Senior Essay, Yale University, 1979).

133. See N. C. Williamson to H. A. Wallace (telegram), Jan. 16, 1935; Mary Conner Myers to JNF (telegram), Jan. 18, 1935; e.g., Affidavit of Willie G. McConless, Jan. 18, 1935. On the plight of tenant farmers and sharecroppers, see D. Conrad, The Forgotten Farmers (1965); J. Agee and W. Evans, Let Us Now Praise Famous Men (1960).

134. See Irons, supra n. 76, at 179, 320; Lowe, supra n. 132. The Legal Division under Frank repeatedly took positions favoring marginal farmers and consumers. See D. Conrad, The Forgotten Farmers 56–59, 72–75, 110–11, 126–35 (1965).

135. Ironically, Frank ceased meeting weekly with Wallace because he did not want to upset Davis. See Frank, COHC at 115, 154–55.

136. See Frank, COHC at 179, 183; Pressman, COHC at 19; Tugwell, COHC at 67–68.

137. See Irons, supra n. 76; Pressman, COHC at 19.

138. Schlesinger, supra n. 14, at 79; Frank, COHC at 180. Wallace served as editor of The New Republic in 1946 and 1947.

139. See H. Wallace, COHC at 376. For accounts of the purge, see D. Conrad, The Forgotten Farmers 105–19, 136–53 (1965); Irons, supra n. 76, at 156–80; R. Lowe, supra n. 132; Wrigley, "Jerome Frank and the Reform Movement in the Agricultural

Adjustment Administration," 90–96 (M.A. thesis, Trinity College, 1976); Schlesinger, *supra* n. 14, at 77–81; B. Sternsher, *Rexford Tugwell and the New Deal* 194–207 (1964); A. Weinstein, *Perjury* 153–56 (1978). For other accounts of the struggle, see G. Fite, *George H. Peek and the Fight for Farm Parity* (1954); R. Lord, *The Wallaces of Iowa* (1947).

140. The lessons of this blend later gave rise to a major new theoretical model of law school education and of the law generally. In the 1940s Myres McDougal and Harold Lasswell articulated clearly the proposition that a lawyer is an indispensable adviser of every responsible policy maker in American society. "As such an adviser the lawyer, when informing his policy-maker of what he can or cannot *legally* do, is, as policy-makers often complain, in an unassailably strategic position to influence, if not create, policy" (Lasswell and McDougal, "Legal Profession and Public Policy: Professional Training in the Public Interest," 52 *Yale L.J.* 203, 208–11 [1943], at 209). Thus they argued for policy-oriented legal education.

141. Frank, *supra* n. 37, at 12413.

4. On Barking Up Trees: The Judge as an Activist

1. H. Abraham, *Freedom and the Court: Civil Rights and Liberties in the United States* (2d ed. 1967); R. Gordon, *Nine Men against America* (1958).

2. F. Dunne, *Mr. Dooley on the Choice of Law* 52 (E. Bander, ed., 1963). See R. Jackson, *The Struggle for Judicial Supremacy* (1941); P. Kurland, *Politics, the Constitution, and the Warren Court* (1970); F. Rodell, *Nine Men* (1955); C. Warren, *The Supreme Court in United States History* (1922).

3. *But see* Z. Chafee, *Free Speech in the United States* (1941); F. Frankfurter and J. Landis, *The Business of the Supreme Court* (1927); P. Freund, *The Supreme Court of the United States* 145–70; C. Jacobs, *Law Writers and the Courts* (1954); M. Schick, *Learned Hand's Court* 328–47 (1970); B. Twiss, *Lawyers and the Constitution* (1942).

4. *See* P. Bator, P. Mishkin, D. Shapiro, and H. Wechsler, *Hart & Wechsler's The Federal Courts and the Federal System* (2d ed. 1973). The authors focus extensive attention on the federal courts, but their perspective is entirely jurisdictional. They measure the jurisdiction of each court—the Supreme Court, the courts of appeals, and the district courts—but make little effort to relate one level to another. On another front, constitutional law casebooks seldom include opinions of lower-court judges. *But see* G. Gunther, *Cases and Materials on Constitutional Law* 1069 (9th ed. 1975) (reprinting Masses Publishing Co. v. Patten, 244 F. 535 [S.D.N.Y. 1917]).

5. *See, e.g.,* L. Levy, *The Law of the Commonwealth and Chief Justice Shaw* (1957); J. Reid, *Chief Justice: The Judicial World of Charles Doe* (1967); Vines, "Political Functions of a State Supreme Court," 8 *Tul. Stud. in Pol. Sci.* 51 (1962); *Judicial Decision-Making* (G. Schubert, ed., 1963).

6. *See* S. Presser, *Studies in the History of the United States Courts of the Third Circuit* (1982); R. Solomon, *Public Law Development in the United States Court of Appeals for the Seventh Circuit, 1891–1948* (forthcoming); H. Bourguignon, *The First Federal Court* (1977); M. Bonsteel Tachau, *Federal Courts in the Early Republic* (1978); J. Howard, Jr., *Courts of Appeals in the Federal Judicial System* (1981); J. Bass, *Unlikely Heroes* (1981); T. Yarbrough, *Judge Frank Johnson and Human Rights in Alabama* (1981); R. Carp and C. Rowland, *Policymaking and Politics in the Federal District Courts* (1983).

7. *But cf.* United States v. Rosenberg, 195 F. 2d 583 (2d Cir.), *cert. denied*, 344

U.S. 838 (1952); Harper and Etherington, "What the Supreme Court Did Not Do during the 1950 Term," 100 *U. Pa. L. Rev.* 354 (1951); Harper and Pratt, "What the Supreme Court Did Not Do during the 1951 Term," 191 *U. Pa. L. Rev.* 439 (1953); Harper and Rosenthal, "What the Supreme Court Did Not Do in the 1949 Term—An Appraisal of Certiorari," 99 *U. Pa. L. Rev.* 293 (1950).

8. *Compare* Brandenburg v. Ohio, 395 U.S. 444 (1969), *with* Masses Publishing Co. v. Patten, 244 F. 535 (S.D.N.Y. 1917). *Cf.* Gunther, "Learned Hand and the Origins of Modern First Amendment Doctrine: Some Fragments of History," 27 *Stan. L. Rev.* 719 (1975).

9. Gerald Gunther shows how a lower-court judge may write an opinion whose formulation is so incisive and wise that the influence proves enduring. *See* Gunther, *supra* n. 8. *Cf.* D. Fischer, *Historians' Fallacies* (1970).

10. *See* M. Schick, *Learned Hand's Court* 17, 305 (1970).

11. *See* John Frank, "The Top U.S. Commercial Court," *Fortune,* Jan. 1951, p. 108.

12. Hammond-Knowlton v. United States, 121 F. 2d 192, 204n35, 205n37 (1941); United States v. Rubenstein, 151 F. 2d 915, 919 (1945, dissenting); Perkins v. Endicott Johnson Corp., 128 F. 2d 208, 217n25 (1942); Standard Brands, Inc. v. Smidler, 151 F. 2d 34, 37 (1945, concurring); Skidmore v. Baltimore & Ohio R.R., 167 F. 2d 54, 68–69 (1948).

13. JNF to Frankfurter, Nov. 13, 1942.

14. Frankfurter to JNF, Nov. 14, 1942.

15. For a fine analysis of various problems with stare decisis that confront lower courts, see Kelman, "The Force of Precedent in the Lower Courts," 14 *Wayne L. Rev.* 3 (1967). *Cf.* Wise, "The Doctrine of Stare Decisis," 21 *Wayne L. Rev.* 1043 (1975).

16. *See* Tanenhaus, Schick, Muraskin, and Rosen, "The Supreme Court's Certiorari Jurisdiction: Cue Theory," in *Judicial Decision-Making* 111, 123–24 (G. Schubert, ed., 1963).

17. *See, e.g.,* United States v. On Lee, 193 F. 2d 306, 311 (1951).

18. *See Sup. Ct. R.* 19, 398 U.S. 1030 (1971).

19. *See* Johansen v. United States, 191 F. 2d 162, 163 (1951).

20. United States v. Costello, 221 F. 2d 668, 680 (1955). A former law clerk to Judge Frank has suggested that Frank's dissents were the effective equivalent of petitions for writs of certiorari (interview with Philip B. Kurland, Chicago, Oct. 10, 1975).

21. *See* B. Bittker, Preface to S. Smith, *Jerome N. Frank, 1889–1956: A Bibliography* 5–6 (1967).

22. *See* Schick, *supra* n. 3, at 114–22. However, the Second Circuit sporadically heard cases en banc as early as 1945. *See* JNF to Frankfurter, Sept. 6, 1945.

23. *See* Beiersdorf v. McGohey, 187 F. 2d 14 (1951). Initially Frank acquiesced in Second Circuit cases involving criminal law even though he disapproved the decisions. Later in his tenure he refused to follow precedents he deemed unjust. *See, e.g.,* United States v. On Lee, 201 F. 2d 722, 726 (1953, dissenting); United States v. Bennett, 152 F. 2d 342, 349 (1945, dissenting). *See also* JNF to Frankfurter, July 9, 1956.

24. *See* JNF to Frankfurter, Sept. 6, 1945.

25. *See* Beiersdorf v. McGohey, 187 F. 2d 14 (1951); Dickinson v. Mulligan, 173 F. 2d 738, 742 (1949); Schick, *supra* n. 3, at 116.

26. Field's Estate v. Commissioner, 144 F. 2d 62, 63 (1944).

27. *See* Beiersdorf v. McGohey, 187 F. 2d 14 (1951).

28. *See* Commissioner v. Hall's Estate, 153 F. 2d 172, 174 (1946, dissenting); United States v. Bennett, 152 F. 2d 342, 349 (1945, dissenting). In *Hall's Estate* Frank explained:

> Ordinarily, when a case has been decided by this court against my dissent, I do not again dissent when the same question again arises. But the fact that in the Fidelity-Philadelphia and Field cases, Mr. Justice Douglas, in concurring, indicated that the Supreme Court had not yet decided whether Heiner survived Hallock, persuades me that it is proper here once more to dissent for the reasons set forth in my dissenting opinion in Helvering v. Proctor [140 F. 2d 87 (2d Cir. 1944)]. [153 F. 2d at 175 (footnote omitted)]

29. The opinion is marked by such phrases as "Were this a case of first impression . . ." and "were we free. . . , we would hold . . ." (157 F. 2d 951 at 953 [1946]).

30. *Id.* at 955 (footnote omitted).

31. *See* Maggio v. Zeitz, 333 U.S. 56, 59 (1948).

32. Choate v. Commissioner, 129 F. 2d 684, 686 (1942).

33. *Cf.* JNF to Frankfurter, Mar. 13, 1945.

34. JNF Conference Memorandum, Jan. 15, 1945, in Duquesne Warehouse Co. v. Railroad Retirement Bd., 148 F. 2d 473 (1945). *See id.* 485 (Frank, J., dissenting); Wallace v. United States, 142 F. 2d 240, 243 (1944); Hammond-Knowlton v. United States, 121 F. 2d 192 (1941).

35. *See* Murphy, "Lower Court Checks on Supreme Court Power," 53 *Am. Pol. Sci. Rev.* 1017 (1959). *See also* K. Llewellyn, *The Common Law Tradition* 77–91 (1960) (identifying at least 64 techniques courts use in approaching precedent).

36. Professor Boris I. Bittker, a former law clerk to Judge Frank, has described how sincerely Frank took his obligation to be faithful to earlier decisions. *See* Bittker, *supra* n. 21, at 5–6. My reading of Frank's opinions confirms Bittker's observations. I found no case in which Frank, through discreditable methods, avoided Supreme Court precedent to reach a desired end. The most my research unveiled was a fairly debatable claim that a Frank opinion silently challenged a Supreme Court decision. *Compare* Maggio v. Zeitz, 333 U.S. 56, 81, 85–89 (1948), *with* In re Luma Camera Service, Inc., 157 F. 2d 951 (1946).

37. *See* United States v. Roth, 237 F. 2d 796, 801 (1956); Republic of China v. National City Bank, 208 F. 2d 627 (1953); United States v. Rosenberg, 195 F. 2d 583 (1952); Roth v. Goldman, 172 F. 2d 788 (1944); Wallace v. United States, 142 F. 2d 240 (1944); Picard v. United Aircraft Corp. 128 F. 2d 623 (1942); Hammond-Knowlton v. United States, 121 F. 2d 192 (1941).

38. On occasion Learned Hand also pointed to certiorari as the route to reverse law that he felt bound to follow. *See, e.g.,* Dickinson v. Mulligan, 173 F. 2d 738, 742 (1949).

39. 121 F. 2d 192, *cert. denied,* 314 U.S. 694 (1941).

40. Wallace v. United States, 142 F. 2d 240, 243 (1944) (footnotes omitted); *see* United States v. Nunnally Inv. Co., 316 U.S. 258, 264 (1942).

41. This approach has been discussed by judges and scholars. *See, e.g.,* Wyzanski, "A Trial Judge's Freedom and Responsibility," 65 *Harv. L. Rev.* 1281, 1298 (1952); Kelman, *supra* n. 15, at 11.

42. JNF to Learned Hand, April 5, 1944.

43. 237 F. 2d 796, 801 (1956). Frank had previously tried to persuade the Supreme Court to grapple with the constitutional issues arising from the obscenity prosecutions (*see* Roth v. Goldman, 172 F. 2d 788, 801 [1949, concurring]), but seven years had elapsed and the Court still had not dealt with these problems.

44. This insight anticipated a distinction between inciting conduct and abstract teaching or advocacy, made in later Supreme Court decisions. *See* Brandenburg v. Ohio, 395 U.S. 444, 447–48 (1969); Scales v. United States, 367 U.S. 203, 228–30 (1961); and Yates v. United States, 354 U.S. 298, 318 (1957).

45. The Commission on Obscenity and Pornography later confirmed this conclusion (*Comm'n on Obscenity and Pornography Rep.* 23–27 [1970]). An intervening Supreme Court opinion cited Frank's lower-court concurrence. That opinion focused on the lack of factual support for the position that obscenity produced antisocial conduct. *See* Memoirs v. Massachusetts, 383 U.S. 413, 431 (1966).

46. This perception anticipated the Court's decision in Ginsberg v. New York, 390 U.S. 629, 634–43 (1968).

47. Previously, obscenity was assumed to lie beyond the pale of First Amendment protection. *See* Beauharnais v. Illinois, 343 U.S. 250 (1952). For general statements on the void-for-vagueness doctrine, see Baggett v. Bullitt, 377 U.S. 360 (1964); Note, "The Void-for-Vagueness Doctrine in the Supreme Court," 109 *U. Pa. L. Rev.* 67 (1960).

48. Charles E. Clark to JNF (memorandum), Aug. 8, 1956.

49. Frankfurter to JNF, July 17, 1956.

50. JNF to Frankfurter, July 19, 1956.

51. JNF to Frankfurter, July 26, 1956.

52. Frankfurter to JNF, undated.

53. For a sampling of different attitudes, see Russell v. United States, 408 F. 2d 1280, 1283 (D.C. Cir. 1969) (Bazelon, C.J.); Ashe v. Swenson, 399 F. 2d 40, 46 (8th Cir. 1968) (Blackmun, J.); Blalock v. United States, 247 F. 2d 615, 621 (4th Cir. 1957) (Soboleff, J.); Spector Motor Serv., Inc. v. O'Connor, 181 F. 2d 150, 153–54 (2d Cir. 1950) (Clark, J.); United States v. Girouard, 149 F. 2d 760, 767 (1st Cir. 1945) (Mahoney, J.); Spector Motor Serv. v. Walsh, 139 F. 2d 809, 813–18, 822–23 (2d Cir. 1944) (Clark, J., majority opinion; L. Hand, J., dissenting opinion); Ashe v. Swenson, 289 F. Supp. 871, 873 (W.D. Mo. 1967) (Oliver, J.); Abendschein v. Farrell, 11 Mich. App. 662, 680–85, 162 N.W. 2d 165, 173–76 (1968) (Levin, J.); Predham v. Holfester, 32 N.J. Super. 419, 426–28, 107 A. 2d 458, 462–63 (1954) (Jayne, J.); Kelman, *supra* n. 15; Magruder, "The Trials and Tribulations of an Intermediate Appellate Court," 44 *Cornell L.Q.* 1 (1958); Wyzanski, "A Trial Judge's Freedom and Responsibility," 65 *Harv. L. Rev.* 1281 (1952); Note, "The Attitude of Lower Courts to Changing Precedent," 50 *Yale L.J.* 1448 (1941). *Cf.* Hopkins, "The Role of an Intermediate Appellate Court," 41 *Brooklyn L. Rev.* 459 (1975).

54. *See* United States v. Gold, 115 F. 2d 236, 238 (2d Cir. 1940) (L. Hand, J.); Rothensies v. Cassell, 103 F. 2d 834, 837 (3d Cir. 1939) (Clark, J.); Bullard v. Commissioner, 90 F. 2d 144, 150 (7th Cir. 1937) (Lindley, J.); Ostrom v. Edison, 244 F. 228, 236 (D.N.J. 1917) (Rellstab, J.); Louisville & N.R.R. v. Western Union Tel. Co., 218 F. 91, 93 (E.D. Ky. 1914) (Cochran, J.).

55. *See* Blaustein and Field, " 'Overruling' Opinions in the Supreme Court," 57 *Mich. L. Rev.* 151, 184–94 (1958); *The Constitution of the United States of America: Analysis and Interpretation*, S. Doc. No. 82, 92d Cong., 2d sess., 1789–97 (1973) (lists Supreme Court cases that have been overruled). *Cf.* Israel, "*Gideon v. Wainwright: The 'Art' of Overruling*, 1963 *Sup. Ct. Rev.* 211.

56. "I don't regard the Supreme Court as set over me to direct my trend or tendency. It only binds me in the very act of decision, and when it is going in the wrong direction, I am not going to beat it to the wrong decision by trying to

anticipate their next wrong turn" (Conference Memorandum of Judge Hutcheson, Jan. 15, 1945, in Duquesne Warehouse v. Railroad Retirement Bd., 148 F. 2d 473).

57. *See* Spector v. Walsh, 139 F. 2d 809, 814–18 (2d Cir. 1944) (Clark, J.); Barnette v. West Virginia State Bd. of Educ., 47 F. Supp. 251, 253 (S.D.W.Va. 1942) (Parker, J.); Kelman, *supra* n. 15, at 15–19; Wyzanski, *supra* n. 41, at 1298–99; Note, *supra* n. 53, at 1450–55.

58. Perkins v. Endicott Johnson, 128 F. 2d 208, 217–18 (1942) (footnotes omitted).

59. Learned Hand quoted with approval the language in the text of *Perkins. See* Picard v. United Aircraft, 128 F. 2d 632, 636 (1942). Judge Clark also relied on Frank's *Perkins* opinion in Spector v. Walsh, 139 F. 2d 809, 814 (1944).

60. Spector v. Walsh, 139 F. 2d 809, 823 (1944).

61. *See, e.g.,* Gardella v. Chandler, 172 F. 2d 402, 407, 408 (1949, L. Hand and Frank, JJ.) (separate opinions); Helvering v. Proctor, 140 F. 2d 87, 88, 89 (1944, L. Hand, J., majority opinion; Frank, J., dissenting opinion). *See also* Spector v. Walsh, 139 F. 2d 809, 823 (1944) (contrasting Clark and Frank perspectives).

62. *See generally* K. Griffith, *Judge Learned Hand and the Role of the Federal Judiciary* 83–181 (1973); L. Hand, *The Bill of Rights* (1958); Schick, *supra* n. 3, at 154–91; Hand, "Chief Justice Stone's Concept of the Judicial Function," in *The Spirit of Liberty* 201 (J. Dilliard ed., 3d ed. 1963).

63. *See* Duquesne Warehouse v. Railroad Retirement Bd., 148 F. 2d 473, 479 (1945, dissenting).

64. For an analysis of methods by which the Supreme Court may discredit its own rulings, see Kelman, *supra* n. 15, at 15–28.

65. *See* Gardella v. Chandler, 172 F. 2d 402, 412–15 (1949); Helvering v. Proctor, 140 F. 2d 87, 89–91 (1944, dissenting); Perkins v. Endicott Johnson, 128 F. 2d 208, 216–19 (1942). *Cf.* United States v. Grunewald, 233 F. 2d 556, 574–75 (1956, dissenting); Duquesne Warehouse v. Railroad Retirement Bd., 148 F. 2d 473, 486–87 (1945, dissenting).

66. *See* United States v. Roth, 237 F. 2d 796, 801 (1956, concurring); United States v. Scully, 225 F. 2d 113–19 (1955, concurring); Republic of China v. National City Bank, 208 F. 2d 627, 630 (1953); United States v. Rosenberg, 195 F. 2d 583, 604–9 (1952); Triangle Publications, Inc. v. Rohrlick, 167 F. 2d 969, 980–81 (1948, dissenting); Kelman, *supra* n. 15, at 7–10.

67. 195 F. 2d at 609n41. Frank's role in the *Rosenberg* case is analyzed further in chap. 5. *See also* Parrish, "Cold War Justice: The Supreme Court and the Rosenbergs," 82 *Am. Hist. Rev.* 805, 817 (1977), quoting Felix Frankfurter: "We ought to be moved by the fact that . . . [Judge] Frank . . . had given expression to a hope that we would take the case."

68. Frank's original draft opinion disclaimed the power to modify a sentence "merely because to [the] court, the sentence seems unduly harsh." The published version deleted this sentence at the urging of the other two panel judges, who considered it a criticism of the trial judge. *See* Harrie B. Chase to Thomas B. Swan, Feb. 16, 1952; Conference Memorandum of Judge Swan, Feb. 15, 1952. In the published opinion Frank repeatedly implied that the sentence was harsh. For criticism, *see, e.g.,* Hall, "Reduction of Criminal Sentences on Appeal," 37 *Colum. L. Rev.* 521–56, 762–83 (1937).

69. Brown v. Walker, 161 U.S. 591 (1896).

70. *See* United States v. Ullmann, 221 F. 2d 760 (1955). This approach retains

contemporary relevance. *See* Seidenburg v. McSorley's Old Ale House, 317 F. Supp. 593 (S.D.N.Y. 1970), where the district court refused to follow Goesaert v. Cleary, 335 U.S. 464 (1948). *Goesaert* upheld a prohibition of female barmaids. McSorley's motto had been "Good Food, Raw Onions, No Women," and McSorley's had tried to argue that the presence of women gave rise to "moral and social problems" (335 U.S. at 466). The district court rejected this analysis and reasoned that "[s]ocial mores have not stood still since that argument was used in 1948 to convince a 6–3 majority of the Supreme Court" (393 F. Supp. at 606).

71. 47 F. Supp. 251 (S.D.W.Va. 1942). *See* Minersville School Dist. v. Gobitis, 310 U.S. 586 (1940).

72.

The developments, with respect to the Gobitis case, however, are such that we do not feel that it is incumbent upon us to accept it as binding authority. Of the seven justices now members of the Supreme Court who participated in that decision, four have given public expression to the view that it is unsound, the present Chief Justice in his dissenting opinion rendered therein and three other justices in a special dissenting opinion in Jones v. City of Opelika, moreover, thought it worthwhile to distinguish the decision in the Gobitis case, instead of relying upon it as supporting authority. Under such circumstances and believing, as we do, that the flag salute here required is violative of religious liberty when required of persons holding the religious views of plaintiffs, we feel that we would be recreant to our duty as judges, if through a blind following of a decision which the Supreme Court itself has thus impaired as an authority, we should deny protection to rights which we regard as among the most sacred of those protected by constitutional guaranties. [47 F. Supp. at 253]

Parker's opinion, relying in part on the importance of the constitutional guarantee at stake, raises the question whether intermediate-court judges should be more willing to find a "new doctrinal trend" if "preferred freedoms" are in jeopardy. *Cf.* Chief Justice Stone's famous footnote 4 in United States v. Carolene Prods., 304 U.S. 144, 152–53n4 (1938).

73. *See* Magruder, *supra* n. 53, at 4.

74. The true objection to Parker's opinion may be that he stated that the emperor wore no clothes. By focusing on particular justices he stressed the human element in constitutional adjudication, much to the distress of those who believed the "cult of the robe" should be invincible. *See also* COT 254–61 (1949).

75. Parker's effort to count noses was unusual only because he published his tabulation. *See also* Liles v. Oregon, 425 U.S. 963 (1976) (Stevens, J., concurring in denial of certiorari); Gautreaux v. Chicago Housing Auth., 503 F. 2d 930, 935–36 (7th Cir. 1974) (T. Clark, J., sitting by designation), *aff'd sub nom.* Hills v. Gautreaux, 425 U.S. 284 (1976). Other judges, including Frank, have privately used nose counts to predict the result when an appeal is taken. *See* conference memoranda of Judges Clark and Frank, Mar. 13, 1950, in Spector v. O'Connor, 181 F. 2d 150 (1950); Schick, *supra* n. 3, at 150.

76. 259 U.S. 200 (1922).

77. *Compare* Carter v. Carter Coal Co., 298 U.S. 238 (1936), *limited by* United States v. Darby, 312 U.S. 100, 123 (1941); Federal Baseball Club v. National League, 259 U.S. 200 (1922); *and* Hammer v. Dagenhart, 247 U.S. 251 (1918), *overruled,* 312 U.S. 100 (1941), *with* Mandeville Island Farms, Inc. v. American Crystal Sugar Co.,

334 U.S. 219 (1948); United States v. South-Eastern Underwriters Ass'n, 322 U.S. 533 (1944); Wickard v. Filburn, 317 U.S. 111 (1942); *and* United States v. Darby.

78. Gardella v. Chandler, 172 F. 2d 402, 409 (1949).

79. *See* Flood v. Kuhn, 407 U.S. 258 (1972); Toolson v. New York Yankees, Inc., 346 U.S. 356 (1953).

80. *See* Frankfurter to JNF, July 17, 1956. *See also* JNF to Frankfurter, Mar. 17, 1945, and July 19, 1956.

81. *See* Maryland v. Baltimore Radio Show, 338 U.S. 912, 917 (1950) (opinion of Frankfurter, J., respecting Supreme Court's denial of certiorari); United States v. Carver, 160 U.S. 482, 490 (1923).

82. In Spector v. Walsh, 139 F. 2d 809 (1944), Judge Clark, joined by Judge Frank, refused to follow older Supreme Court cases dealing with state taxation of interstate commerce. Subsequently, the Court granted certiorari (322 U.S. 720 [1944]) but ducked the constitutional issue and remanded (Spector v. McLaughlin, 323 U.S. 101 [1944]). On remand, Judges Clark and Frank adhered to their initial position, and again prompted Supreme Court review (Spector v. O'Connor, 181 F. 2d 140 [1950]). Facing the constitutional issue, the Court rejected the position of Clark and Frank (Spector v. O'Connor, 340 U.S. 602 [1951]). Judge Frank's reasoning in Helvering v. Proctor, 140 F. 2d 87, 89 (1944, dissenting), that an earlier Supreme Court decision had been silently overruled by a later case, was adopted in Commissioner v. Church, 335 U.S. 632 (1949), *rev'g* 161 F. 2d 11 (3d Cir. 1947), where the Court embraced Frank's reasoning and overruled its earlier decision. The overruling came on a petition for a writ of certiorari to a different circuit because, for unknown reasons, the commissioner did not seek Supreme Court review in *Proctor.*

83. Another obvious route—certification of a question by the court of appeals to the Supreme Court—would immediately bring a case before the high bench. Yet Frank never urged this procedure. One letter to Frankfurter, however, did raise this possibility. *See* JNF to Frankfurter, undated, Box 53, Folder 321. On occasion Learned Hand used a different technique to draw the attention of the Supreme Court. When confronted by a High Court opinion he thought unsound, Hand might give it an extreme interpretation, making almost a caricature of the rule. This method of ridicule normally prompted Supreme Court review, although in one case the Court apparently did not realize Hand's tongue-in-cheek spoof. *See* Schick, *supra* n. 3, at 146–47. *See also* Clark to JNF, Jan. 26, 1951, referring to Hand's practices. There is no evidence that Frank ever resorted to this technique.

Subtle pressures may interfere with the smooth functioning of the Court. The dynamics of small-group decision making preclude those not privy to the conferences from knowing when and why the Court will take a case. *See, e.g.,* Brennan, "Chief Justice Warren," 88 *Harv. L. Rev.* 1 (1974); Brennan, "Justice Brennan Calls National Court of Appeals Proposal 'Fundamentally Unnecessary and Ill Advised,'" 59 *A.B.A.J.* 835 (1973); Warren, "Retired Chief Justice Attacks, Chief Justice Burger Defends Freund Study Group's Composition and Proposal," 59 *A.B.A.J.* 721, 724 (1973); Warren, "Let's Not Weaken the Supreme Court," 60 *A.B.A.J.* 677 (1974). They argue that the High Court must retain unfettered discretion and complete control over its own docket. Although broad political considerations occasionally determine whether the Court will plunge into a controversy, through experience it has developed tools to avoid untimely disputes. *See* Naim v. Naim, 350 U.S. 891 (1955); A. Bickel, *The Least Dangerous Branch* 111–98 (1962); Gunther, "The Subtle

Vices of the 'Passive Virtues'—A Comment on Principle and Expediency in Judicial Review," 64 *Colum. L. Rev.* 1 (1964).

84. 318 U.S. 332 (1943).

85. *See* United States v. Leviton, 193 F. 2d 848, 857 (1951, dissenting); United States v. On Lee, 193 F. 2d 306, 311 (1951, dissenting); In re Fried, 161 F. 2d 453 (1947). *Cf.* United States ex rel. Caminito v. Murphy, 222 F. 2d 698 (1955).

86. 351 U.S. 12 (1956).

87. 238 F. 2d 565, 572 (1956, dissenting) (footnote omitted). *See* United States v. Branch, 238 F. 2d 577 (1956, dissenting); United States v. Farley, 238 F. 2d 575 (1956, dissenting in part).

88. *But cf.* Frankfurter to JNF, July 17, 1956.

89. Since some of the interaction derives from friendship rather than from Frank's position as circuit judge, others in the legal profession—perhaps notable law professors—may relate to Supreme Court justices in similar ways.

Frank's relations with Supreme Court justices include meetings, dinners, and a host of social engagements that facilitated ongoing friendships. The following portrait of their interactions rests largely on letters—a colder, more formal, and less spontaneous type of communication. One senses that Frank and the justices were more candid when they met in person. *See* Frankfurter to JNF, Aug. 25, 1944.

90. *See* W. Douglas, *Go East, Young Man* 267, 374–76, 423–24 (1974); Douglas, "Jerome N. Frank," 10 *J. Legal Ed.* 1 (1957); Douglas, "Jerome N. Frank," 24 *U. Chi. L. Rev.* 626 (1957). Frank's *If Men Were Angels* (1942) is dedicated "To Mr. Justice William O. Douglas."

91. *See* Box 3, Folder 66; Box 12, Folder 84; Box 27, Folder 228; Box 53, Folders 320 and 321, Jerome Frank Papers.

92. Frank had friendships with other justices as well. He was on a first-name basis with Justice Stanley Reed, and also knew Justice Harlan, who had served with Frank on the Second Circuit before his elevation to the Supreme Court.

93. *See* JNF to Frankfurter, June 10, 1947.

94. *See* Hugo L. Black to JNF, Mar. 9, 1949. This dialogue had a public dimension: Frank had written an opinion on special verdicts. *See* Skidmore v. Baltimore & Ohio R.R., 167 F. 2d 54 (1948). *See also* Amendments to Fed. R. Civ. Pro. (strengthening ability of judges to control verdicts) (Mr. Justice Black's statement opposing submission to Congress), 274 U.S. 865, 867–68 (1963).

95. *See, e.g.,* JNF to Black, May 27, 1943; Reed to JNF, Dec. 30, 1946. Frank often took lunch in the courthouse cafeteria with his law clerks and with clerks for other judges who cared to join them. Because of his accessibility, he became acquainted with many of those who clerked for colleagues on the Second Circuit.

96. *See* "Developments in the Law—Federal Habeas Corpus," 83 *Harv. L. Rev.* 1038, 1055 (1970).

97. *See* JNF to Black, Sept. 11, 1956; JNF to Douglas, May 22 and Sept. 11, 1956; JNF to Frankfurter, Sept. 11, 1956; Frankfurter to JNF, Sept. 14, 1956.

On the topic of extrajudicial roles of justices, see Gunther, *supra* n. 4, at 61; B. Murphy, *The Brandeis/Frankfurter Connection* (1982); A. Mason, *Harlan Fiske Stone* 262–89, 698–720 (1956); *Roosevelt and Frankfurter: Their Correspondence* (M. Freedman, ed., 1967); *The Diaries of Felix Frankfurter* (J. Lash, ed., 1975); Landever, "Chief Justice Burger and Extra-Case Activism," 20 *J. Pub. L.* 523 (1971); Murphy, "In His Own Image: Mr. Chief Justice Taft and Supreme Court Appointments," 1961 *Sup.*

Ct. Rev. 159; Swindler, "The Chief Justice and Law Reform, 1921–1971," 1971 *Sup. Ct. Rev.* 241; Note, "Extrajudicial Activity of Supreme Court Justices," 22 *Stan. L. Rev.* 587 (1970).

98. *See* Frank's dissenting opinions in United States v. Antonelli Fireworks Co., 155 F. 2d 631, 642 (1946); United States v. Bennett, 152 F. 2d 342, 346 (1945); United States v. Mitchell, 137 F. 2d 1006, 1011 (1943); United States v. Liss, 137 F. 2d 995, 1001 (1943); Keller v. Brooklyn Bus Corp., 128 F. 2d 510, 513 (1942). *See also* Schick, *supra* n. 3, at 267–76.

99. Clark to Hand, Nov. 21, 1945, in Schick, *supra* n. 3 at 272.

100. JNF to Clark, May 15, 1946.

101. *See* Herbert Prashker to JNF, undated, Box 65, Folder 741, Jerome Frank Papers; Eugene Nickerson to JNF, May 14, 1956.

102. Clark to JNF, May 14, 1946.

103. JNF to Clark, May 16, 1946 (referring to United States v. Antonelli Fireworks, 155 F. 2d 631, 642).

104. JNF to Douglas, Mar. 29 and May 26, 1940; JNF to Reed, Feb. 4, 1939; JNF to Frankfurter, Feb. 3, 1939.

105. JNF to Frankfurter, July 25, 1956 (referring to United States v. Masiello, 235 F. 2d 279, 285 (1956).

106. JNF to Douglas, Nov. 16, 1945.

107. 152 F. 2d 342 (1945).

108. Bihn v. United States, 328 U.S. 633, 637 (1946).

109. JNF to Douglas, Nov. 22, 1943.

110. JNF to Douglas, Mar. 29, 1944.

111. JNF to Douglas, Jan. 8, 1945; JNF to Frankfurter, May 13, 1952.

112. Frankfurter to JNF, May 14, 1952.

113. JNF to Frankfurter, May 19, 1952.

114. Frankfurter to JNF, undated, Box 53, Folder 321, Jerome Frank Papers.

115. Judge Learned Hand once quoted a Frank opinion for the seminal idea that the court of appeals should "recognize 'a pronounced new doctrinal trend' which it is our 'duty, cautiously to be sure, to follow not to resist' " (Picard v. United Aircraft, 128 F. 2d 632, 635 (1942), *quoting* Perkins v. Endicott Johnson, 128 F. 2d 208, 218 (1942). Frank then attributed the idea to Hand rather than to himself (Gardella v. Chandler, 172 F. 2d 402, 409 n1) (1949, concurring).

116. To Justice Jackson, Frank wrote on March 10, 1942: "Just a line to thank you for your brilliantly conceived and splendidly worded opinion in *D'Oench v. F.D.I.C.*" To Hugo Black on June 17, 1954: "Your splendid opinion in *Leyra* raises hopes that a majority of your Court will more frequently follow you, especially in civil liberty cases." To Frankfurter on March 10, 1942: "Your *Bethlehem* opinion is surely one of the best ever delivered. The Magi and the star must have guided you." *See also* JNF to Harlan, Feb. 9, 1955; JNF to Douglas, Nov. 27, 1941. On occasion Frank would prepare a detailed critique of a Supreme Court opinion; *see* JNF to Jackson, Mar. 30, 1949.

117. Jackson to JNF, Mar. 13, 1942.

118. Frankfurter to JNF, Feb. 5, 1946.

119. Frankfurter, however, once commented on the form of a Frank opinion (Nov. 19, 1947):

I hope I may regard your opinion in *United States v. Monroe*, decided November 14th, as a good augury—an augury of your abandonment of dividing an opinion into two parts, the facts and then the legal discussion. I do not have to tell you that that was an old way of reporting Supreme Court opinions. And while I am not one of those who thinks wisdom was born with us and all that was old is bad, I, for the life of me, saw no benefit from your reversion to that old style. Quite the contrary. To my way of thinking an opinion is an organic whole and not an appropriate subject for dichotomy. So, please do not weary of the well-doing in the *Monroe* case.

120. Frankfurter to JNF, Jan. 11, 1944; Aug. 25, 1944; May 4, 1946; Aug. 11, 1955; Feb. 24, 1945; May 8, 1944; Aug. 11, 1955.

121. JNF to Jackson, Mar. 30, 1949.

122. Jackson to JNF, April 6, 1949.

123 *See,* e.g., JNF to Douglas, Jan. 8, 1945; JNF to Frankfurter, May 10, 1944; Frankfurter to JNF, May 8, 1944.

124. In addition to those on the Second Circuit, such judges included David Bazelon, Stanley Fuld, and Calvert Magruder. *See* Schick, *supra* n. 3, at 103.

125. *See* list, Box 179, Folder 13, Jerome Frank Papers.

126. Douglas to JNF, April 29, 1942 (referring to Valentine v. Chrestensen, 316 U.S. 52 [1942], and Prudence Realization Corp. v. Giest, 316 U.S. 89 [1942]). In *Valentine,* Frank distinguished commercial and noncommercial speech. On appeal, the Supreme Court accepted Frank's reasoning and embraced the distinction for the first time. Douglas's note is all the more interesting because he later repudiated the very doctrine that his note to Jerry had applauded. *See* Commarano v. United States, 358 U.S. 498, 514 (1959); Bigelow v. Virginia, 421 U.S. 809 (1975) (Justice Douglas joined the Court's opinion, further undermining the commercial/noncommercial distinction).

127. *See* Kurland, "Jerome N. Frank: Some Reflections and Recollections of a Law Clerk," 24 *U. Chi. L. Rev.* 661, 663 (1957).

128. *See* JNF to Douglas, Jan. 8, 1945.

129. *See* JNF to Frankfurter, Mar. 13, 1945.

130. Gerald Gunther has recently published letters between Justice Holmes and Judge Learned Hand focusing on First Amendment doctrine. Gunther argues forcefully that Holmes refined his theories under constant prodding from Hand. While both Holmes and Hand had authored judicial opinions on the subject, their correspondence did not concern specific pending decisions. *See* Gunther, *supra* n. 8. *See also* A. Mason, *Harlan Fiske Stone: Pillar of the Law* (1956).

131. *See* B. Murphy, *supra* n. 97; J. Lash, *From the Diaries of Felix Frankfurter* 49n (1975).

132. Frank's papers on file at Yale contain many letters commenting on his opinions. Often such letters came from counsel in the case or other interested observers.

133. *See* A. Bickel, *The Unpublished Opinions of Mr. Justice Brandeis* (1957); Totenberg, "Behind the Marble, Beneath the Robes," *New York Times Magazine,* Mar. 16, 1975, at 15; Freund, "An Analysis of Judicial Reasoning," in *Law and Philosophy: A Symposium* 288 (S. Hook, ed., 1964); Heineman, book review, 88 *Harv. L. Rev.* 678 (1975). *Cf.* "Judicial Secrecy: A Symposium," 22 *Buffalo L. Rev.* 797 (1973); Powell, "Myths and Misconceptions about the Supreme Court," 61 *A.B.A.J.* 1344 (1975).

134. These issues have recently been explored in B. Woodward and S. Armstrong, *The Brethren* (1979).

135. Frankfurter to JNF, Feb. 5, 1946.

5. *Legal Realism on the Bench*

1. *L&MM* 179.

2. *See id.* at xx, xxvii; *COT* 16, 33, 51, 182, 285–86. In correspondence with Felix Cohen (July 11, 1950), Frank insisted that his work as a judge did not reflect any change in his attitude on legal certainty.

3. Hamilton Watch Co. v. Benrus Watch Co., 206 F. 2d 738 (1953).

4. *See* Federal Baseball Club v. National League, 259 U.S. 200 (1922).

5. The reserve clause "possesses characteristics shockingly repugnant to moral principles that, at least since the War Between the States, have been basic in America as shown by the Thirteenth Amendment to the Constitution, condemning 'involuntary servitude'" (Gardella v. Chandler, 172 F. 2d 402, 409 [1949]).

6. 143 F. 2d 916, 922 (1944).

7. *See* Franke v. Wiltschek, 209 F. 2d 497, 500 (1953, dissenting).

8. Guttman v. Illinois Central R.R. Co., 189 F. 2d 927, 930 (1951).

9. Eastern Wine Corp. v. Winslow-Warren, 137 F. 2d 955, 958 (1943).

10. 128 F. 2d 632 (1942, concurring).

11. Cuno Engineering Corp. v. Automatic Devices Corp., 314 U.S. 84 (1941).

12. *See* Picard v. United Aircraft, 128 F. 2d 632, 641–45.

13. *See* Eastern Wine Corp. v. Winslow-Warren, 137 F. 2d 955, 958 (1943). Frank refused to grant an injunction to a wine seller who used the name "Chateau Martin" against another seller who used the name "Chateau Montay."

14. 167 F. 2d 969, 976, 978 (1948) (footnote omitted). For another example of Frank's insistence on consumer protection as the touchtone of trademark law, see Chas. D. Briddell, Inc. v. Alglobe Trading Corp., 194 F. 2d 416 (1952).

15. 151 F. 2d 34 (1945).

16. Frank's trademark opinions have been criticized for not recognizing that trade names and trademarks are necessary for effective competition. *See* Pattishall, "Trademarks and the Monopoly Phobia," 50 *Mich. L. Rev.* 967 (1952).

17. 125 F. 2d 949, 955, 967 (1942).

18. 121 F. 2d 336, 342 (1941).

19. For other Frank opinions broadly upholding damage judgments and other recoveries for seamen, see The C. W. Crane, 155 F. 2d 940 (1946); Kelsey v. Tankers Co., 217 F. 2d 541 (1954); Ahlgren v. Redstar Towing & Transportation Co., 214 F. 2d 618 (1954); Palazzolo v. Pan-Atlantic S.S. Corp., 211 F. 2d 277 (1954); Poignant v. United States, 225 F. 2d 595 (1955); Troupe v. Chicago, Duluth & Georgian Bay Transit Co., 234 F. 2d 253 (1956).

20. 221 F. 2d 189, 206 (1955).

21. *See, e.g.,* Uniform Commerical Code §§2-302, 2-312–2-318.

22. 189 F. 2d 939 (1951).

23. 202 F. 2d 866 (1953).

24. *See* Nimmer, "The Right of Publicity," 1949 *Law & Contemp. Probs.* 203; Note, "An Assessment of the Commercial Exploitation Requirement as a Limit on the Right of Publicity," 96 *Harv. L. Rev.* 1703 (1983).

25. *See* Cort v. Ash, 422 U.S. 66 (1975); P. Bator, P. Mishkin, D. Shapiro, and H. Wechsler, *Hart and Wechsler's The Federal Courts and the Federal System* 188–96 (Supp. 1981).

26. 229 F. 2d 499 (1956).

27. 49 U.S.C. §§484(b), 622(a), 642(c) (repealed 1958).

28. *See* 229 F. 2d at 501.

29. *See* Brown v. Board of Educ., 349 U.S. 294 (1954); Mayor of Baltimore v. Dawson, 350 U.S. 877 (1955); Holmes v. Atlanta, 350 U.S. 879 (1955); Gayle v. Browder, 352 U.S. 903 (1956).

30. *See* Reade v. Ewing, 205 F. 2d 630 (1953).

31. FCC v. Sanders Radio Station, 309 U.S. 470 (1940); Scripps-Howard Radio v. FCC, 316 U.S. 4 (1942).

32. 134 F. 2d 694, 704 (1943).

33. *Id.* at 705. For an additional opinion articulating the "private attorney general" theory, see Reade v. Ewing, 205 F. 2d 630 (1953).

34. 188 F. 2d 783 (1951).

35. *See* 15 U.S.C. §77k (1981) (originally enacted as Securities Act of 1933, §11, ch. 38, tit. 1, §11, 48 Stat. 82); 15 U.S.C. §78j(b) (1981) (originally enacted as Securities Exchange Act of 1934, §10[b], ch. 404, tit. 1, §10[b], 48 Stat. 891); 17 C.F.R. §240.10b-5 (1976).

36. *See* Ernst & Ernst v. Hochfelder, 425 U.S. 185 (1976); Herman & MacLean v. Huddleston, 103 S.Ct. 683 (1983). For an analysis of the securities law implications of *Fischman*, see L. Loss, *Securities Regulation*, III, 1781–92 (2d ed. 1961).

37. 198 F. 2d 883, 884 (1952).

38. 17 C.F.R. §240.10b-5 (1976).

39. *See, e.g.,* Shapiro v. Merrill Lynch, Pierce, Fenner & Smith, Inc., 495 F. 2d 228 (2d Cir. 1974).

40. 224 F. 2d 753, 767 (1955).

41. 377 U.S. 426 (1964).

42. 15 U.S.C. §78p (1981).

43. 232 F. 2d 299 (1956). The Supreme Court finally addressed this issue in Foremost-McKesson, Inc. v. Provident Sec. Co., 423 U.S. 232 (1976). It refused to follow Frank's lead, relying on legislative history and the intervening development of a cause of action under Rule 10b-5.

44. *See* E. Hawley, *The New Deal and the Problem of Monopoly* (1966).

45. The "expertise" theory of administrative law has since been abandoned. *See* Stewart, "The Reformation of American Administrative Law," 88 *Harv. L. Rev.* 1669 (1975).

46. *See, e.g.,* Callus v. Ten East Fortieth St. Bldg., 146 F. 2d 438 (1945).

47. Homework was limited to persons who because of age or other disabilities were unable to leave the home. *See* 144 F. 2d 608, 609 (1944).

48. *Id.* at 612, 620, 623.

49. 137 F. 2d 969, 974, 980 (1943). *See also* Perkins v. Endicott Johnson, 128 F. 2d 208 (1942).

50. *See* Sperry Gyroscope Co. v. NLRB, 129 F. 2d 922 (1942); Duquesne Warehouse Co. v. Railroad Retirement Bd., 148 F. 2d 473 (1945).

51. *See* Old Colony Bondholders v. N.Y., N.H. & H. R.R. Co., 161 F. 2d 413, 449, 450 (1947).

52. United States v. Rubenstein, 151 F. 2d 915, 923 (1945, dissenting).

53. 165 F. 2d 152 (1947).

54. 166 F. 2d 897 (1948).

55. 206 F. 2d 897, 903 (1953).

56. 234 F. 2d 715, 718 (1955).

57. 237 F. 2d 307 (1956).

58. In Bolling v. Sharpe, 347 U.S. 497 (1954), the Supreme Court had recognized an equal protection component to the Fifth Amendment due process clause. In Yick Wo v. Hopkins, 118 U.S. 356 (1886), the Court first acknowledged that an otherwise valid statute could be unconstitutionally administered.

59. 212 F. 2d 919, 926 (1954).

60. 238 F. 2d 565, 572 (1956).

61. 193 F. 2d 848, 865 (1951).

62. In re Fried, 161 F. 2d 453, 462 (1947).

63. *Id.*

64. 137 F. 2d 995, 1005 (1943). *See also COT* 80–103.

65. 222 F. 2d 698, 704, 706 (1955).

66. In re Fried, 161 F. 2d 453 (1947).

67. *See* United States v. Calandra, 414 U.S. 338 (1974); Fed. R. Cr. P. 5.1(a).

68. 125 F. 2d 928, 937 (1942).

69. 153 F. 2d 757, 764 (1946).

70. United States v. Antonelli Fireworks, 155 F. 2d 631, 662 (1946).

71. United States v. Rubenstein, 151 F. 2d 915, 923 (1945). Frank insisted that rhetoric not obscure the function of a legal doctrine because "[a] concept is what it does," and he encouraged judges to "peer behind the mere verbal articulation of a legal rule or concept to observe the policy it embodies, whenever a logical application of that rule or concept as previously articulated, will yield socially disvaluable results" (Triangle Publications, Inc. v. Rohrlich, 167 F. 2d 969, 982 [1948, dissenting]).

72. *See* United States v. Castro, 228 F. 2d 807, 810 (1956).

73. In re Barnett, 124 F. 2d 1005, 1011 (1942).

74. 195 F. 2d 692, 696–97 (1952).

75. 204 F. 2d 88 (1953).

76. Tennessee Coal Co. v. Muscoda Local, 321 U.S. 590 (1944); Jewell Ridge Corp. v. Local No. 6167, 325 U.S. 161 (1945); Anderson v. Mt. Clemens Pottery Co., 328 U.S. 680 (1946).

77. Battaglia v. General Motors Corp. 169 F. 2d 254 (2d Cir.), *cert. denied,* 335 U.S. 887 (1948); Darr v. Mutual Life Ins. Co., 169 F. 2d 262 (1948).

78. 334 U.S. 446 (1948).

79. 204 F. 2d 88, 98 (1953).

80. Frank's *Addison* dissent favored a theory that would prevent any significant redistribution of property by the legislature. The facts in *Addison,* however, did not involve such a redistribution. On the contrary, the *Addison* majority denied workers a wage arguably mandated by the FLSA and approved by the Supreme Court in *Bay Bridge.*

81. *See* Hammond-Knowlton v. United States, 121 F. 2d 192 (1941); Wallace v. United States, 142 F. 2d 240 (1944).

82. Frank, "Why Not a Clinical Lawyer-School?" 81 *U. Pa. L. Rev.* 907, 911 (1933).

83. 124 F. 2d 1005 (1942).

84. 165 F. 2d 152, 154 (1947 dissenting).

85. Triangle Publications v. Rohrlich, 167 F. 2d 969, 982 (1948 dissenting).

86. Interview with Honorable Patricia Wald, U.S. circuit judge, Detroit, June 19, 1982.

87. *See* Hoffman v. Palmer, 129 F. 2d 976, 987 (1942).

88. *See* United States v. St. Pierre, 132 F. 2d 837, 847–48 (1942, dissenting).

89. *See* Old Colony Bondholders v. N.Y., N.H. & H., 161 F. 2d 413, 449 (1947, dissenting).

90. Fed. R. Civ. P. 56(c).

91. *See* Doehler Metal Furniture Co. v. United States, 149 F. 2d 130 (1945); Weisser v. Mursam Shoe Corp., 127 F. 2d 344 (1942); Colby v. Klune, 178 F. 2d 872 (1949).

92. 154 F. 2d 464, 475 (1946).

93. 180 F. 2d 537, 540n7 (1950).

94. 167 F. 2d 54 (1948).

95. Keller v. Brooklyn Bus Corp., 128 F. 2d 510, 515 (1942).

96. 201 F. 2d 165 (1952).

97. United States v. Liss, 137 F. 2d 995 (1943, dissenting).

98. *See, e.g.,* United States v. Delli Paoli, 229 F. 2d 319 (1956).

99. *See* United States v. Kelinson, 205 F. 2d 600 (1953).

100. 221 F. 2d 944 (1955).

101. *See* R. Meeropol and M. Meeropol, *We Are Your Sons* (1975); W. Schneir and M. Schneir, *Invitation to an Inquest* (rev. ed. 1983); R. Radosh and J. Milton, *The Rosenberg File* (1983); L. Nizer, *The Implosion Conspiracy* (1973); Anders, "The Rosenberg Case Revisited: The Greenglass Testimony and the Protection of Atomic Secrets," 83 *Am. Hist. Rev.* 388 (1978); Radosh and Milton, "Were the Rosenbergs Framed?" *New York Review of Books,* July 21, 1983, p. 17; W. Schneir, M. Schneir, R. Radosh, and J. Milton, "'Invitation to an Inquest': An Exchange," *New York Review of Books,* Sept. 29, 1983, at 55.

102. *See* Parrish, "Cold War Justice: The Supreme Court and the Rosenbergs," 82 *Am. Hist. Rev.* 805, 811 (1977).

103. *See* Conference Memorandum of Judge Swan, Feb. 15, 1952.

104. *But see* Quint, "Toward First Amendment Limitations on the Introduction of Evidence: The Problem of *United States v. Rosenburg,*" 86 *Yale L.J.* 1622 (1977) (criticizing aspects of Frank's opinion).

105. *See* United States v. Rosenberg, 195 F. 2d 583, 588–608 (1952).

106. Interview with FKF, Aug. 12, 1974; Parrish, *supra* n. 102, at 816n34.

107. United States v. Rosenberg, 344 U.S. 838 (1952). Only three justices, Black, Burton, and Frankfurter, voted to review the case. Justice Douglas cast the decisive negative vote. *See* Parrish, *supra* n. 102, at 816–20.

108. The petition was brought under 28 U.S.C. §2255 (1948).

109. *See* United States v. Rosenberg, 108 F. Supp. 798 (S.D.N.Y.), *aff'd,* 200 F. 2d 666 (2d Cir. 1952); Rosenberg v. United States, 345 U.S. 965 (1953). There is some indication that Frank helped shape Swan's opinion. *See* Conference Memorandum of JNF, Dec. 27, 1952; Parrish, *supra* n. 102, at 821.

110. *See* United States v. Rosenberg, 109 F. Supp. 108 (S.D.N.Y.), *aff'd,* 204 F. 2d 688 (2d Cir.), *cert. denied,* 345 U.S. 989 (1953); Parrish, *supra* n. 102, at 827–32.

111. *See* Rosenberg v. United States, 346 U.S. 273 (1953); Parrish, *supra* n. 102, at 832–39. Douglas based his stay on an issue that had not previously been raised: whether the Espionage Act had been superseded by the Atomic Energy Act of 1946. If so, the death sentence could be imposed only (1) on a jury's recommendation and (2) with evidence of an intent to injure the interests of the United States.

112. A. Kinoy, *Rights on Trial* 123 (1983).

113. *See* Parrish, *supra* n. 102, at 820.

114. *See* M. Schick, *Learned Hand's Court* 200–201 (1970).

115. *See COT* 80–102.

116. *See* W. Douglas, *The Court Years, 1939–1975* 79 (1980).

117. *See* Kinoy, *supra* n. 112, at 125.

118. *See* United States v. Antonelli Fireworks, 155 F. 2d 631, 642 (1946, dissenting); United States v. Austmeier, 152 F. 2d 349 (2d Cir. 1945).

119. The convictions were upheld by the Second Circuit, with Learned Hand writing for the court, and affirmed by the Supreme Court. *See* United States v. Dennis, 181 F. 2d 201 (2d Cir. 1950), *aff'd,* 341 U.S. 494 (1951).

120. *See* United States v. Sacher, 182 F. 2d 416 (1950).

121. For criticism, see Schick, *supra* n. 114, at 290–99.

122. *See* Conference Memorandum of JNF, Feb. 8, 1950.

123. *See* United States v. Sacher, 343 U.S. 1, 3 (1952).

124. *See, e.g.,* Codispoti v. Pennsylvania, 418 U.S. 506 (1974); Taylor v. Hayes, 418 U.S. 488 (1974). *Compare* United States v. Field, 193 F. 2d 92 (2d Cir. 1951), *cert. denied,* 342 U.S. 894 (1952), *with* Spevack v. Klein, 385 U.S. 511 (1967). *Compare* United States v. Davis, 151 F. 2d 140 (2d Cir. 1945), *aff'd,* 328 U.S. 582 (1946), *with* Chimel v. California, 395 U.S. 752 (1969).

6. *The Influence of a Circuit Judge in Shaping Constitutional Law*

1. *See* J. Hurst, *The Growth of American Law* (1950); *Law and the Conditions of Freedom* (1956); "Legal Elements in United States History," in *Law in American History* 3 (D. Fleming and B. Bailyn, eds., 1971). *Cf.* Gordon, "J. Willard Hurst and the Common Law Tradition in American Legal Historiography," 10 *L. & Soc'y Rev.* 11 (1975); Tushnet, "Lumber and Legal Process," 1972 *Wis. L. Rev.* 114 (1972).

2. *See, e.g.,* L. Friedman, *A History of American Law* (1973); M. Horwitz, *The Transformation of American Law, 1780–1860* (1977); R. Kluger, *Simple Justice* (1975); J. Auerbach, *Unequal Justice (1976); D. Fleming and B. Bailyn, eds., Law in American History* (1971); L. Levy, *Law of the Commonwealth and Chief Justice Shaw* (1956); J. Noonan, *Persons and Masks of the Law* (1976).

3. *See, e.g.,* A. Bickel, *The Supreme Court and the Idea of Progress* (1970); A. Cox, *The Warren Court* (1968); F. Graham, *The Self-Inflicted Wound* (1970); F. Rodell, *Nine Men* (1955).

4. *But see* C. Jacobs, *Law Writers and the Courts* (1954); R. Kluger, *Simple Justice* (1975); J. Schmidhauser, *The Supreme Court* (1960) and *Judges and Justices* (1979); A. Paul, *Conservative Crisis and the Rule of Law* (1960); B. Twiss, *Lawyers and the Constitution* (1942).

5. *Compare* C. Pritchett, *The Roosevelt Court* (1948), *with* C. Pritchett, *Civil Liberties and the Vinson Court* (1954).

6. *But see* Dennis v. United States, 183 F. 2d 201 (2d Cir. 1950); Masses Publishing Co. v. Patten, 244 F. 535 (S.D.N.Y. 1917); Gunther, "Learned Hand and the Origins of Modern First Amendment Doctrine: Some Fragments of History, 27 *Stan. L. Rev.* 719 (1975); Murphy, "Lower Court Checks on the Supreme Court," 53 *Am. Pol. Sci. Rev.* 1018 (1959).

7. *See, e.g.,* MacPherson v. Buick Motor Co., 217 N.Y. 382, 111 N.E. 1050 (1916) (Cardozo, J.).

8. Psychological factors might extend this list indefinitely. *See COT;* Hopkirk, "The Influence of Legal Realism on William O. Douglas," in *Essays on the American Constitution* (G. Dietze, ed., 1964); J. Oakley and R. Thompson, *Law Clerks and the Judicial Process* (1980); J. Wilkinson, *Serving Justice* (1974); "Judicial Clerkships: A Symposium on the Institution," 26 *Vand. L. Rev.* 1125 (1973).

9. Other important factors contributed to the behavioral approach in political science. *See* Dahl, "The Behaviorial Approach in Political Science," 55 *Am. Pol. Sci. Rev.* 763 (1961).

10. *See, e.g.,* C. Pritchett, *The Roosevelt Court* (1948); M. Schick, *Learned Hand's Court* 304–47 (1970); G. Schubert, *The Judicial Mind* (1965) and *The Judicial Mind Revisited* (1974); D. Rohde and H. Spaeth, *Supreme Court Decision Making* 70–97, 134–71, 193–210 (1976). *Cf.* Howard, "Judicial Biography and the Behavioral Persuasion, 65 *Am. Pol. Sci. Rev.* 604 (1971); "A Symposium: Social Science Approaches to the Judicial Process," 79 *Harv. L. Rev.* 1551 (1966).

11. *See* G. Schubert, *The Judicial Mind Revisited* (1974).

12. During this period the Second Circuit enjoyed a glowing reputation. In addition to Jerome Frank, its members included Learned Hand, Augustus Hand, Charles Clark, Thomas Swan, Harrie Chase, and John Marshall Harlan.

13. *See* Schick, *supra* n. 10, at 344–47.

14. Tabulations based on S. Smith, "Jerome N. Frank, 1889–1957: A Bibliography," (1967) (unpublished paper in Yale Law Library).

15. *See* Schick, *supra* n. 10, at 330, Table 24. Since the Second Circuit tabulation includes Frank, the discrepancy in percentages actually should be somewhat higher.

16. Frank was second only to Clark in number of dissents. *See id.* at 339, Table 29. Frank's concurrences often urged very different results and rationales from those of the majority. *See* United States v. Roth, 237 F. 2d 796, 801 (1956). *See also* Frankfurter to JNF, Nov. 14, 1942.

17. *See, e.g.,* United States v. Roth, 237 F. 2d 796, 801 (1956, concurring).

18. *See* Schick, *supra* n. 10, at 330, Table 24. Once again, the difference in percentages between Frank and his colleagues should be higher since the Second Circuit figure includes Frank himself. Frankfurter once noted that the quality of lower-court opinions substantially affected the Supreme Court's decision in granting review. *See* Frankfurter, "Calvert Magruder," 72 *Harv. L. Rev.* 1201, 1202 (1959), reprinted in Frankfurter, *Of Law and Life* 141 (P. Kurland, ed., 1967).

19. *See* Tannehaus, Schick, Muraskin, and Rosen, "The Supreme Court's Certiorari Jurisdiction: Cue Theory," in *Judicial Decision-Making* 111 (G. Schubert, ed., 1963).

20. The Court dismissed six cases as moot or on the stipulation of counsel. The percentage would increase if such cases as Field's Estate v. Commissioner, 144 F. 2d 62 (2d Cir. 1944), *rev'd,* 324 U.S. 113 (1945), were included. In *Field* the Supreme Court reversed Frank, but Frank had almost explicitly invited reversal. *See also* Republic of China v. National City Bank, 208 F. 2d 627 (2d Cir. 1953), *rev'd,* 348 U.S. 356 (1955).

21. *See* Schick, *supra* n. 10, at 338–45.

22. *See, e.g.,* In re Luma Camera, Inc., 157 F. 2d 951 (2d Cir. 1946), *rev'd,* 333 U.S. 56 (1948).

23. *See* G. Schubert, *The Judicial Mind Revisited* (1974).

24. 183 F. 2d 201 (1950); 237 F. 2d 796, 801 (1956).

25. 328 U.S. 750 (1946). *See* Frank's dissents in United States v. Antonelli

Fireworks Co., 155 F. 2d 631, 642 (1946); United States v. Bennett, 152 F. 2d 342, 346 (1945); United States v. Mitchell, 137 F. 2d 1006, 1011 (1943); United States v. Liss, 137 F. 2d 995, 1001 (1943); Keller v. Brooklyn Bus Corp., 128 F. 2d 510, 513 (1942).

26. *Cf.* A. Mason, *The Supreme Court from Taft to Warren* (rev. ed. 1968).

27. *See, e.g.,* L&MM 137–38 (1930):

All judges exercise discretion, individualize abstract rules, make law. Shall the process be concealed or disclosed? The fact is, and every lawyer knows it, that *those judges who are most lawless, or most swayed by the "perverting influences of their emotional natures," or most dishonest, are often the very judges who use most meticulously the language of compelling mechanical logic, who elaborately wrap about themselves the pretence of merely discovering and carrying out existing rules, who sedulously avoid any indications that they individualize cases.* If every judicial opinion contained a clear exposition of the actual grounds of the decision, the tyrants, the bigots and the dishonest men on the bench would lose their disguises and become known for what they are.

28. Frankfurter, for one, read regularly the slip opinions of the Second Circuit. *See* Schick, *supra* n. 10, at 113, 329; Frankfurter to JNF, Nov. 19, 1947.

29. For a sampling of these cases, see the references in *Shephard's Citations* for Arnstein v. Porter, 154 F. 2d 464 (1946); Fischman v. Raytheon, 188 F. 2d 783 (1951); and Bell & Co. v. Catalda Fine Arts, 191 F. 2d 99 (1951).

30. 191 F. 2d 162 (1951).

31. *See* United States v. Nugent, 346 U.S. 1, 10 (1953) (Frankfurter, J., dissenting): "That so strong a court and one so strong in literary endowment—Swan, C.J., Learned Hand and Frank, J.J.—should rely, as did the Court of Appeals in this case [in a Frank opinion, reported at 200 F. 2d 46, 49–50], on the opinion of a District Judge, impressively attests the persuasiveness of that opinion."

32. *See* Tanenhaus, Schick, Maraskin, and Rosen, "The Supreme Court's Certiorari Jurisdiction: Cue Theory," in *Judicial Decision-Making* 111 (G. Schubert, ed., 1963).

33. *See, e.g.,* United States v. Neustadt, 366 U.S. 696, 702 (1961), *citing* Jones v. United States, 207 F. 2d 563 (1953); Smith v. Shaughnessy, 318 U.S. 176, 181 (1943), *citing* Commissioner v. Beck's Estate, 129 F. 2d 243 (1942); Jersey Cent. Power & Light Co. v. Federal Power Comm'n, 319 F. 2d 61, 70 (1943), *citing* Hartford Elec. Light Co. v. Federal Power Comm'n, 131 F. 2d 953 (1942); Altvater v. Freeman, 319 U.S. 359, 363 (1943), *citing* Cover v. Schwartz, 133 F. 2d 541 (1942).

34. *See, e.g.,* Kotteakos v. United States, 328 U.S. 750, 762, 765 (1946), *citing* United States v. Mitchell, 137 F. 2d 1006 (1943) and United States v. Antonelli Fireworks, 155 F. 2d 631 (1946); United States v. Midland-Ross Corp., 381 U.S. 54, 65 (1965), *citing* Williams v. McGowan, 152 F. 2d 570 (1945).

35. *See, e.g.,* FTC v. Simplicity Pattern Co., 360 U.S. 55, 67 (1959), *citing* Elizabeth Arden, Inc. v. FTC, 156 F. 2d 132 (1946); Smith v. Shaughnessy, 318 U.S. 176 (1943), *citing* Commissioner v. Marshall, 125 F. 2d 943 (1942).

36. *See* Linzer, "The Meaning of Certiorari Denials," 79 *Colum. L. Rev.* 1227 (1979). Some per curiam affirmances may occur for procedural reasons, such as mootness, which reflect a changed posture of the case. In these instances one may not assume that affirmance bespeaks influence.

37. *See* Maryland v. Baltimore Radio Show, 338 U.S. 912, 917 (1950) (Frank-

furter, J.); United States v. Carver, 260 U.S. 472, 490 (1923) (Holmes, J.); Dickinson v. Mulligan, 173 F. 2d 738, 738–40 (2d Cir. 1949) (L. Hand, J.).

38. *Quoted in* Schick, *supra* n. 10, at 331n72.

39. Black to Edmond Cahn, Jan. 18, 1957, *quoted in* Cahn, "Fact-Skepticism and Fundamental Law," 33 *N.Y.U.L. Rev.* 1, 11 (1958). A former law clerk to both Jerome Frank and Hugo Black has confirmed the high esteem Black had for Frank (telephone conversation with Sidney Davis, New York City, July 1975).

40. *See* Reed to JNF, Dec. 30, 1946, and Jan. 19, 1954.

41. Frankfurter, "Jerome N. Frank," 24 *U. Chi. L. Rev.* 625 (1957); 208 F. 2d 605, 611 (2d Cir. 1953) (Frank, J., dissenting), *rev'd,* 347 U.S. 556 (1954). *See* Douglas to JNF, Jan. 30, 1956. Justice Black echoes this view; *see* Black to JNF, June 29, 1954. For another recognition of Frank's influence, see Douglas, "Jerome N. Frank," 10 *J. Legal Ed.* 1, 8 (1957): "His dissent in *United States v. Johnson* called for a liberal construction of the *in forma pauperis* statute so that an indigent defendant with a meritorious case would not suffer a penalty 'because he is guilty of the crime of being poor'—a plea that did not go unnoticed" by the Supreme Court, which reversed the Second Circuit and followed Frank's line of argument; *see* Johnson v. United States, 357 U.S. 565 (1957).

42. *See* Wyzanski, "Augustus Noble Hand," 61 *Harv. L. Rev.* 573, 585 (1948); Frankfurter, "Calvert Magruder," 72 *Harv. L. Rev.* 1201, 1202 (1959), *reprinted in* Frankfurter, *Of Law and Life* 141 (P. Kurland, ed., 1967).

43. Other renowned judges who were cited by name by the Supreme Court include Circuit Judge Henry J. Friendly in United States v. Ash, 413 U.S. 300, 316–17 (1973) and Circuit Judge Learned Hand in Dennis v. United States, 341 U.S. 494, 510 (1951).

44. *See also* Schick, *supra* n. 10, at 338–47. Unlike Schick, I have examined the merits of each case to determine whether in fact Frank desired the Supreme Court to affirm or reverse. My analysis thus includes those cases in which Frank sought reversal and the Court did reverse him as supporting Frank's position. *See* In re Luma Camera Service, Inc., 157 F. 2d 951 (2d Cir. 1946), *rev'd sub nom.* Maggio v. Zeitz, 333 U.S. 56 (1948); Field's Estate v. Commissioner, 144 F. 2d 62 (2d Cir. 1944), *rev'd,* 324 U.S. 113 (1945).

45. *See, e.g.,* Maggio v. Zeitz, 333 U.S. 56, 81 (1948). *Cf.* Schick, *supra* n. 10, at 343, 345, Tables 35 and 36.

46. Frankfurter, "Jerome N. Frank," 24 *U. Chi. L. Rev.* 625 (1957).

47. Douglas, "Jerome N. Frank," 10 *J. Legal Ed.* 1, 6 (1957).

48. *See* United States v. Costello, 221 F. 2d 668, 679 (2d Cir. 1955), *aff'd,* 350 U.S. 359 (1956); United States v. Michelson, 165 F. 2d 732 (2d Cir. 1948), *aff'd,* 335 U.S. 469 (1948).

49. *See* Commissioner v. Rogers' Estate, 135 F. 2d 35 (2d Cir.), *aff'd,* 320 U.S. 410 (1943); Perkins v. Endicott Johnson, 128 F. 2d 208 (2d Cir. 1942), *aff'd,* 317 U.S. 501 (1943).

50. *See* United States ex. rel. Leyra v. Denno, 208 F. 2d 605, 611 (1943, dissenting), *rev'd,* 347 U.S. 556 (1954); Brown v. United States, 209 F. 2d 463, *aff'd,* 348 U.S. 110 (1954); in re N.Y., N.H. & H. R.R. Co., 197 F. 2d 428 (1952, dissenting), *rev'd,* 344 U.S. 293 (1953); Orvis v. McGrath, 198 F. 2d 708 (1952), *aff'd,* 345 U.S. 183 (1953); United States ex rel. Hinshberg v. Malanaphy, 168 F. 2d 503, 507 (1948, dissenting), *rev'd,* 336 U.S. 210 (1949); Aaron v. Bay Bridge Operating Co., 162 F. 2d

665 (1947), aff'd, 334 U.S. 446 (1948); Duquesne Warehouse Co. v. Railroad Retirement Bd., 148 F. 2d 473, 479 (1945, dissenting), rev'd, 326 U.S. 446 (1946); Williams v. Green Bay & Western R. Co., 147 F. 2d 777, 779 (1945, dissenting), rev'd, 326 U.S. 549 (1946); Hoffman v. Palmer, 129 F. 2d 976 (1942), aff'd, 318 U.S. 109 (1943); In re Marine Harbor Properties, Inc., 125 F. 2d 296, 299 (1942, dissenting), rev'd, 317 U.S. 78 (1942); Geist v. Prudence Realization Corp., 122 F. 2d 503, 507 (1942, dissenting), rev'd, 316 U.S. 89 (1942).

51. See United States v. Shaughnessy, 206 F. 2d 897, 901 (1953, dissenting), rev'd sub nom. Accardi v. Shaughnessy, 347 U.S. 261 (1954); Republic of China v. National City Bank, 208 F. 2d 627 (1953), rev'd, 348 U.S. 356 (1954); United States v. Jerome, 130 F. 2d 514, 519 (1942), rev'd, 318 U.S. 101 (1943).

52. See United States v. Grunewald, 233 F. 2d 557, 571 (1956, dissenting), rev'd, 353 U.S. 391 (1957); United States v. Sacher, 182 F. 2d 416, 453 (1950, concurring), aff'd, 343 U.S. 1 (1952); In re Luma Camera Service, 157 F. 2d 951 (1946), rev'd sub nom. Maggio v. Zeitz, 333 U.S. 56 (1948); United States v. Bennett, 152 F. 2d 342, 346 (1945, dissenting), rev'd sub nom. Bihn v. United States, 328 U.S. 633 (1946).

53. See Acme Fast Freight, Inc. v. Chicago, M. St. P. & P. R.R. Co., 166 F. 2d 778 (1948), rev'd, 336 U.S. 465, 489 (1949); Ricketts v. Pa. R.R. Co., 153 F. 2d 757, 760 (1946), aff'd sub nom. Callen v. Pa. R.R. Co., 332 U.S. 625, 631 (1948); M. Witmark & Sons v. Fred Fisher Music Co., 125 F. 2d 949, 954 (1942), aff'd, 318 U.S. 643, 659–60 (1943).

54. Acme Fast Freight, Inc. v. Chicago, M. St. P. & P. R.R. Co., 336 U.S. 465, 489 (1949).

55. Mr. Justice Douglas once asserted the contrary opinion. See Warth v. Seldin, 422 U.S. 490, 559 (1975) (Douglas, J., dissenting); see also Glennon, "'Do Not Go Gentle': More Than an Epitaph," 22 Wayne L. Rev. 1305 (1976).

56. See Parker, "Improving Appellate Methods," 25 N.Y.U.L. Rev. 1, 13 (1950); Schick, supra n. 10, at 339–40; Tanenhaus, Schick, Muraskin, and Rosen, "The Supreme Court's Certiorari Jurisdiction: Cue Theory," in Judicial Decision-Making (Schubert, ed., 1963) at 129–30, 334, Tables 24 and 27.

57. See Schick, supra n. 10, at 330, 334, Tables 24 and 27.

58. Frank dissented in 128 cases, and the Supreme Court granted certiorari and reversed in 19.

59. See cases cited in n. 25 supra.

60. See United States v. Roth, 237 F. 2d 796, 801 (1956), aff'd, 354 U.S. 476 (1957).

61. See United States v. Carolene Prod. Co., 304 U.S. 144, 152–53n4 (1938); L. Hand, The Bill of Rights (1958); Hand, "Chief Justice Stone's Concept of the Judicial Function," in Hand, The Spirit of Liberty 201 (J. Dilliard, ed., 1952).

62. Compare C. Pritchett, The Roosevelt Court (1948), with C. Pritchett, Civil Liberties and the Vinson Court (1954). See A. Mason, The Supreme Court from Taft to Warren (rev. ed. 1968); P. Murphy, The Constitution in Crisis Times, 1918–1969 (1972).

63. Compare United States ex rel. Leyra v. Denno, 208 F. 2d 605, 611 (1953, dissenting), rev'd, 347 U.S. 556 (1954), with Chrestensen v. Valentine, 122 F. 2d 511, 517 (1941, dissenting), rev'd, 316 U.S. 52 (1942).

64. Cf. United States v. Sacher, 182 F. 2d 416, 453 (1950), aff'd, 343 U.S. 1 (1952).

65. See J. Frank, Fate and Freedom (1945).

66. See Z. Chafee, Free Speech in the United States 196–218 (1941).

67. United States v. Parrino, 212 F. 2d 919, 924 (1954). *See, e.g.,* United States ex rel. Hintopoulos v. Shaughnessy, 233 F. 2d 705, 709 (1956); United States v. Shaughnessy, 306 F. 2d 897, 901 (1953).

68. 237 F. 2d 796, 801.

69. *See* Pinkus v. United States, 436 U.S. 293 (1978); Hamling v. United States, 418 U.S. 87 (1974); Jenkins v. Georgia, 418 U.S. 153 (1974); Miller v. California, 413 U.S. 15 (1973); Mishkin v. New York, 383 U.S. 502 (1966); Memoirs v. Massachusetts, 383 U.S. 413 (1966).

70. 390 U.S. 629 (1968).

71. *See* Jenkins v. Georgia, 418 U.S. 153 (1974); Paris Adult Theatre I v. Slaton, 413 U.S. 49, 73 (1973) (Brennan, J., dissenting). Frank also raised an issue the Supreme Court has yet to consider: why may the government prohibit obscenity, even assuming a particular work is obscene as defined by the Court? Before Yates v. United States, 354 U.S. 298 (1957), Frank urged that illegality of obscenity be linked to the conduct of the person exposed to obscene material. Absent conduct caused by exposure to obscenity, Frank argued, no permissible governmental objective was served by regulation of obscenity. Since the social sciences failed to document a link between exposure to obscenity and conduct, Frank's argument was effectively against such regulation. Upon review, the Supreme Court's response, that obscenity simply is not protected by the First Amendment, seems wholly inadequate.

72. *See* Stanley v. Georgia, 394 U.S. 557, 566n9 (1969); Memoirs v. Massachusetts, 383 U.S. 413, 431n10. Frank also influenced two dissenting justices: Brennan in Paris Adult Theatre I v. Slaton, 413 U.S. 49, 110, and Douglas in Ginsburg v. United States, 383 U.S. 463, 486 (1966).

73. 122 F. 2d 511, 517 (1941).

74. *See* Douglas to JNF, April 29, 1942.

75. 376 U.S. 254 (1964). *See* Dun & Bradstreet, Inc. v. Grove, 404 U.S. 808, 905 (1971) (Douglas, J., dissenting). *See also* Ohralik v. Ohio State Bar Ass'n, 436 U.S. 447 (1978); In re Primus, 436 U.S. 412 (1978); Bates v. State Bar of Ariz., 433 U.S. 350 (1977); Linmark Assoc. v. Willingboro, 431 U.S. 85 (1977); Virginia State Bd. of Pharmacy v. Virginia Citizens Consumer Council, 425 U.S. 376 (1976); Pittsburgh Press Co. v. Human Relations Comm'n, 425 U.S. 376 (1973). The Supreme Court's recent decisions distinguish commercial from noncommercial speech, but grant First Amendment protection to commercial speech. *See* Central Hudson Gas & Elec. Corp. v. Public Serv. Comm'n of N.Y., 447 U.S. 557 (1980); Bolger v. Youngs Drug Prod. Corp., 103 S.Ct. 2875 (1983).

76. *See* conference memoranda of Judge Swan, June 17, 1941, and Judge Clark, June 19, 1941.

77. 341 U.S. 494 (1951). *See* M. Belknap, *Cold War Political Justice* (1977); United States v. Sacher, 182 F. 2d 416 (1950), *aff'd* 343 U.S. 1 (1952).

78. *See* Codispoti v. Pennsylvania, 418 U.S. 506 (1974); Taylor v. Hayes, 418 U.S. 488 (1974) (distinguishing summary contempt from posttrial proceedings).

79. Conference Memorandum of Charles E. Clark, Feb. 15, 1950. *See also* United States v. Sacher, 182 F. 2d 416, 463 (2d Cir. 1950) (Clark, J., dissenting).

80. *See, e.g.,* United States v. Roth, 237 F. 2d 796, 801 (1956, concurring).

81. 193 F. 2d 305 (1951).

82. 277 U.S. 438 (1928); 316 U.S. 129 (1942).

83. 277 U.S. 438, 478–79 (1928).

84. 365 U.S. 505 (1961).

85. *Id.* at 512.

86. 373 U.S. 427 (1963).

87. 389 U.S. 347 (1967).

88. Frank was fond of citing E. Borchard, *Convicting the Innocent* (1932).

89. *See, e.g.*, United States v. Leviton, 193 F. 2d 848, 857 (1951, dissenting), *cert. denied*, 343 U.S. 946 (despite three dissenting votes and a memorandum by Justice Frankfurter quoting Frank).

90. *See, e.g.*, United States v. Farley, 238 F. 2d 575, 577 (1956); United States v. Johnson, 238 F. 2d 565, 567 (1956, dissenting); United States v. Delli Paoli, 229 F. 2d 319, 322 (1956, dissenting); United States v. Rosenberg, 195 F. 2d 583 (1952).

91. *See* Miranda v. Arizona, 384 U.S. 436 (1966); Powell v. Alabama, 287 U.S. 45 (1932).

92. 208 F. 2d 605 (1953).

93. 314 U.S. 219 (1941).

94. *See* 208 F. 2d at 612 and n. 3.

95. JNF to Black, June 17, 1954; Black to JNF, June 29, 1954. *See also* Douglas to JNF, Jan. 30, 1956.

96. *See* JNF to Frankfurter, May 22, Sept. 11, and Sept. 18, 1956; JNF to Black, Sept. 11, 1956; Douglas to JNF, Jan. 30 and Sept. 27, 1956; JNF to Douglas, Sept. 11, 1956; 28 U.S.C. §2254 (Supp. 1977).

97. Douglas to JNF, Jan. 30, 1956.

98. *See* JNF to Douglas, May 22, 1956.

99. 222 F. 2d 698, 701 (2d Cir. 1955).

100. *See* Miranda v. Arizona, 384 U.S. 436 (1966). The *Miranda* Court also relied on a book Frank wrote with his daughter on cases in which innocent persons had been convicted. *See* 384 U.S. at 455n24; J. Frank and B. Frank, *Not Guilty* (1957).

101. 229 F. 2d 319 (1956).

102. *See* 352 U.S. 232, 248 (1957).

103. 391 U.S. 123 (1968).

104. 352 U.S. at 248.

105. 391 U.S. at 129. *See* 336 U.S. 440, 453 (1949).

106. *See* 391 U.S. 123, 132n8, 134n10; 233 F. 2d 556 (2d Cir. 1956).

107. For Frank's assessments of the intervening doctrinal developments, see 233 F. 2d at 572–78.

108. 378 U.S. 52, 55 (1963).

109. *See* Tehan v. Shott, 328 U.S. 406, 414n12 (1965). The Court also referred to Frank by name and quoted from his *Grunewald* opinion in Miranda v. Arizona, 384 U.S. 436, 460, (1966), and Bruton v. United States, 391 U.S. 123 (1967).

110. 351 U.S. 12 (1955).

111. 238 F. 2d 565, 569 (1956).

112. *See also* United States v. Farley, 238 F. 2d 575 (1956).

113. Justice Douglas acknowledged Frank's impact in *Johnson*. *See* Douglas, "Jerome N. Frank," 10 *J. Legal Ed.* 1, 8 (1957).

114. 146 F. 2d 154, 157 (1944, dissenting).

115. 353 U.S. 657 (1957).

116. *See* 28 U.S.C. §391 (1976); *Fed. R. Crim. P.* 52(a).

117. *See* United States v. Antonelli Fireworks, 155 F. 2d 631, 642 (1946); United

States v. Bennett, 152 F. 2d 342, 346 (1945); United States v. Mitchell, 137 F. 2d 1006, 1011 (1943); United States v. Liss, 137 F. 2d 995, 1001 (1943); Keller v. Brooklyn Bus Corp., 128 F. 2d 510, 513 (1942).

118. *See* United States v. Rubenstein, 151 F. 2d 915, 924 (1945, dissenting):

We should reverse where error has been committed, regardless of our belief as to guilt or innocence, unless we conclude that in all probability the error had no effect on the jury; or, to phrase it differently, that the record is such that, if there had been no error, no reasonably sane jury could have acquitted, or that there is no reasonable ground for thinking that the jury was misled by the error.

119. *See* United States v. Bennett, 152 F. 2d 342, 349 (1945, dissenting): "[A]lthough I usually concur in the established precedents of this court, even when I think them erroneous, I deem it not improper to continue to dissent in cases of this kind until the Supreme Court tells me that I am wrong."

120. *See e.g.,* United States v. Liss, 137 F. 2d 995, 1001, *cert. denied,* 320 U.S. 773 (1943).

121.

As stated by Judge Frank in his dissenting opinion below: "Literally interpreted, the judge's charge told them that this was not sufficient to justify acquittal, for it was their "duty" (a) to decide that appellant committed the theft unless (b) they decided that some other specific person did. So interpreted, this charge erred by putting on appellant the burden of proving her innocence by proving the identity of some other person as the thief. [Bihn v. United States, 328 U.S. 633, 637 (1946)]

122. *See* Kotteakos v. United States, 328 U.S. 740 (1946); Bollenbach v. United States, 326 U.S. 607 (1946).

123. 134 F. 2d 694, 704 (1943). Frank's idea stemmed originally from the public/private dichotomy developed by Wesley Hohfeld. *See* W. Hohfeld, *Fundamental Legal Conceptions as Applied to Judicial Reasoning* (1923).

124. *See* Flast v. Cohen, 392 U.S. 83, 119 (1968) (Harlan, J., dissenting); FCC v. National Broadcasting Co., 319 U.S. 239, 265 (1942) (Douglas, J., dissenting).

125. 405 U.S. 727, 741, 755 (1972) (Douglas and Blackmun, JJ., dissenting).

126. 392 U.S. 83, 119 (1968) (Harlan, J., dissenting).

127. 140 F. 2d 87 (1944).

128. For an explanation of the government's action, see Commissioner v. Hall's Estate, 153 F. 2d 172, 175 (1946).

129. *See id.*

130. *See* Commissioner v. Church, 335 U.S. 632, 685 (1949) (Frankfurter, J., dissenting).

131. *See, e.g., L&MM* 183–99; *If Men Were Angels* 82–84; *COT* 108–45; "Words and Music: Some Remarks on Statutory Interpretation," 47 *Colum. L. Rev.* 1259 (1947).

132. 167 F. 2d 54, 64.

133. Krulewitch v. United States, 336 U.S. 440, 453 (1949) (Jackson, J., concurring).

134. *See* Leviton v. United States, 343 U.S. 946, 948 (1952) (Frankfurter, J.); Jackson v. Denno, 378 U.S. 368, 388n15 (1964) (White, J.); Biancone v. United States, 405 U.S. 936, 937 (1972) (Douglas, J., dissenting).

135. 157 F. 2d 951, 955 (1946).

136. 333 U.S. at 67.
137. *Id.* at 59.
138. 278 U.S. 368 (1929).
139. *See* 333 U.S. at 78.
140. *See id.* at 81–90.

There is nothing else in the record, except Judge Frank's statement below that the bankrupt was ordered to perform although the court knew that it was impossible for him to perform. But this assertion of "impossibility" was not derived from the record in these contempt proceedings. It derives from Judge Frank's familiar hostility to what he deems the unfairness of his Court's rule of presumption in ordering turnover. Judge Frank here merely repeats his conviction that a turnover order like that rendered against Maggio is an order to turn over goods which could not be turned over. But that was water over the dam in the contempt proceeding. To give it legal significance when enforcement of the turnover order is in issue is to utter contradictory things from two corners of the mouth. It is saying that the turnover order cannot be relitigated—that we cannot go back on the adjudication that the bankrupt had the goods at the time he was ordered to turn them over—but we know he did not have the goods, so we contradict the turnover order and do not respect it as *res judicata*. [*Id.* at 85–86 (citations omitted)]

INDEX

Library of Congress Cataloging in Publication Data

Glennon, Robert Jerome, 1944–
  The iconoclast as reformer.

  Includes index.
    1. Frank, Jerome, 1889–1957.   2. Law—United
States.   3. Law—Philosophy.   4. Judges—United
States—Biography.   I. Title.
KF373.F7G55   1985   347.73'2034 [B]   84-17504
ISBN 0-8014-1565-9 (alk. paper)   347.307234 [B]